# TOP
# 10
of everything
# RUGBY

# TOP
## 10
### of everything
# RUGBY

# GREGOR PAUL

EXISLE
PUBLISHING

To Doug,
who left long ago but whose voice is still clearly heard,
and to Fiona,
who has no idea how much she means.

First published 2012

Exisle Publishing Limited,
P.O. Box 60-490, Titirangi, Auckland 0642, New Zealand.
'Moonrising', Narone Creek Road, Wollombi, NSW 2325, Australia.
www.exislepublishing.com

National Library of New Zealand Cataloguing-in-Publication Data

Paul, Gregor, 1972–
Top 10 of everything rugby / Gregor Paul.
ISBN 978-1-927147-52-8
1. Rugby football—History. 2. Rugby football players—History.
I. Title.
796.3330993—dc 23

10 9 8 7 6 5 4 3 2 1

Text design and production by IslandBridge
Cover design by Dexter Fry
Printed in Singapore by KHL Printing Co Pte Ltd
This book uses paper sourced under ISO 14001 guidelines from well-managed
forests and other controlled sources.

# CONTENTS

# INTRODUCTION

At some stage, probably shortly after reading Nick Hornby's *High Fidelity*, I became a regular list-maker, spending more and more time scribbling down the five best of this and the ten worst of that. It always seemed such a good way to fill in twenty minutes, and then there was the fun of coming back to a list after a while. Lists can't be left to stagnate – the maintenance required is significant and it could often feel as if entire days at a time were lost to list-making. But it was, still is, addictive. When I began working at the *Herald on Sunday*, my list-making took on a new dimension – it became interactive. My sports-writing colleague Dylan Cleaver was an equally avid list-maker and we would hurriedly scribble down our five best Olympic champions, or our five luckiest FA Cup winners, then compare lists.

We didn't get a lot of work done – but that didn't really matter. The pure joy of list-making was impossible to resist, and increasingly we focused on making lists about rugby. Rugby seemed to lend itself to lists – there was always more variation in our views when we listed rugby topics; always more room for debate and deliberation.

So one day the penny finally dropped. Instead of endless bits of random paper with endless random lists – why not a book? Why not one handy volume of lists that everyone could read? Hence ... this book.

Unquestionably there will be heroes, villains, psychos and random acts of madness that others will feel should have been included. No apology will be offered for that; the list-maker's code prevents it. The beauty of a list is the scope it provides for disagreement. If you read the book and feel outraged at an omission or an inclusion, so much the better. That's the intention, as well as to provide a bit of insight and, most importantly, a bit of a chuckle.

# The Best

---

## 10 best captains

---

**10** **Brian O'Driscoll** (Ireland and British & Irish Lions)

It is only the elderly who can remember a time when Brian O'Driscoll wasn't captain of Ireland. His tenure has been extraordinarily long, and to have survived in the job for nine years, as he has, is truly remarkable.

With O'Driscoll at the helm, the Irish transformed from nearly men to a team of substance and achievers. Shortly after he took over from Keith Wood, Ireland won the Triple Crown – their first since 1985. Another two would follow in 2006 and 2007, with a coveted Grand Slam secured in 2009.

It was a mark of the Irishman's standing that he was asked to captain the 2005 Lions tour to New Zealand, and his greatest regret that he was injured in the opening exchanges of the first test.

Approachable, articulate and not afraid to poke fun at himself,

O'Driscoll was one of the boys yet also set that little bit apart. The respect he commanded was enormous, and was founded on his ability as a world-class centre. For most of the first decade of the new millennium, O'Driscoll was rated the best in the world.

He was also brave – playing through numerous injuries – and he has been an inspiration to thousands of young Irishmen. As speculation mounted that he would retire after the 2011 World Cup, he provided yet more evidence of how driven and focused he is, saying in an interview with *New Zealand Rugby World* that he wanted to try to hang on until the 2013 Lions tour.

'For me, the inspiration is about trying to be the best that you can be, trying to show those who doubt me, the people who think I'm over the hill, that I still have it … I don't want to be someone who just petered off towards the end of his career, I want to go out on a high.'

## 9　Dave Gallaher (New Zealand)

It is almost 100 years since Gallaher was killed in combat and yet his name looms large over New Zealand rugby. As the captain of the first All Black side to tour Britain in 1905, he was always going to hold a special place in the heart of a nation obsessed with the game and their beloved team. The team Gallaher captained became known as 'The Originals' and were the men who established the reputation of the All Blacks. This great team – the best the world has ever known and one with a record few of any code can match – set the standards on Gallaher's watch.

Irish by birth, Gallaher was a big man for the period and played with aggression and stunning insight. He was obviously light-years ahead of his time in the way he picked up in 1905 that there would likely be more conflict to arise as a consequence of the British teams' propensity to kill second-phase ball. The British media in turn hammered him personally for what they saw as dubious play from a wing forward.

He compiled a book following the tour called the *Complete Rugby Footballer* where he wrote: 'I must confess that the unfair criticism to which I have been subjected, while in Wales especially, has annoyed me.'

Gallaher shifted into coaching and selecting before he faked his age and joined the troops on the frontline. He was killed at Passchendaele in 1917.

## 8 Francois Pienaar (South Africa)

Francois Pienaar thought he'd made an indelible footprint in rugby history when he captained the Springboks to World Cup glory in 1995. He had, but he made an even bigger one – without actually doing anything – when he was played in the movie *Invictus* by Oscar winner Matt Damon.

The fact Pienaar has been immortalised in film says it all – this was a man who could lead. Pienaar, as became apparent in *Invictus*, was a genial, quietly spoken but fiercely loyal and determined captain. He'd arrived in the job as the shock choice but left it with everyone unanimous that the right one had been made.

South Africa was on the brink of a new political beginning when Pienaar took over the captaincy in 1994. Pienaar's open mind and force of will were a huge part in carrying his team to the tape. In a 2011 feature for America's *Sports Illustrated*, entitled the 'Best Team I Ever Covered' journalist Ian Thomsen wrote about the 1995 Springboks: '[Matt] Damon's understated performance was just right: Pienaar's muted dignity was crucial to the team's success, because a more boisterous leader would have inflamed the social and political tensions and distracted the Springboks from their mission on the field.'

## 7 Richie McCaw (New Zealand)

There was never any question about Richie McCaw's status as a player. He made his debut for the All Blacks as a 20-year-old and was man of the match, and he's been IRB Player of the Year three times when no one else has even won it twice.

His captaincy, which he assumed full-time in 2006, was not of such quality at first. But the thing about McCaw is that he never lets anything get the better of him. He was hurt by the All Black failure at the 2007 World Cup and privately vowed to make amends in 2011 and to begin the process of becoming an iconic and hugely influential leader.

He did that by driving cultural change within the team he captained. He demanded individuals take more responsibility both on and off the field; he learned the art of manipulating referees and gaining their respect, and he was erudite and open in all his media and stakeholder dealings. He pulled this off while managing somehow to add new dimensions to his game that saw him collect back-to-back IRB awards in 2009 and 2010.

His crowning moment was the 2011 World Cup when he led the All Blacks to the title with a broken foot. After the tournament coach Graham Henry said: 'Richie's leadership stands out to me. He shouldn't have been playing the game. He didn't play all week in the hope he could get through the 80 minutes.

'He walked behind the team in training and his attention to detail was amazing. He walked around behind Aaron Cruden and talked to him a lot. Although he couldn't train, he was right on the job mentally. He had every detail covered. His leadership was phenomenal. He was an inspiration. He could be prime minister, governor general, coach of the All Blacks all put together.'

## 6 Hugo Porta (Argentina)

Argentina may never have made it to the lofty heights they now occupy had it not been for Hugo Porta. An elegant fly-half with all the classic skills, Porta dragged Argentina up the world pecking order in the 1980s.

Under Porta the Pumas beat Australia twice (once in Brisbane), they beat France and they drew with the All Blacks.

It was on Porta's watch that the Argentineans learned the art of forming a clever game-plan and sticking to it.

Three things mark Porta as a great captain: he was dragged out of retirement to lead the team to the World Cup in 1987; he was made

Minister of Sport, a huge call in a soccer-mad nation; and the third was that when his car was stolen in 2000, the thieves returned it after news media revealed whose vehicle it actually was.

Just to remind everyone how sage he is, he spoke eloquently and passionately about his fears for modern rugby a few days after the 2011 World Cup. 'I think those that forget the past don't have a future. We can't stop the evolution of the game, but we should at least try to preserve the essence of rugby. Nowadays it's a war of muscles. I saw more blood and injured players during the World Cup than ever before.'

## 5 John Smit (South Africa)

Few jobs carry as much pressure as being captain of the Springboks. The fact John Smit was at the helm from 2004 to 2011 is irrefutable proof he was at the very least a politically savvy operator.

Knives are constantly out in the Republic and even the best captains don't normally last long. Smit was different – he was able to galvinise his peers and somehow avoid polarising the country. He retained the support and respect of the people who mattered throughout his career and delivered results.

He led the Boks to victory at the 2007 World Cup and then against the British & Irish Lions in 2009. The fact he played the latter series at prop was further proof of his value as a leader. He'd been surpassed at hooker by the younger and more dynamic Bismarck du Plessis. But coach Peter de Villiers didn't want to be without his captain, so he persuaded Smit to revert to his original position as tight-head. De Villiers refused to lose faith in Smit, appointing him captain through to 2011 despite Smit struggling to hold his form at either prop or hooker.

What de Villiers knew was that under pressure, Smit was the man to whom the rest of the team would turn for sage advice and calming words, as happened in 2007 when the quarter-final was in danger of slipping away. Fiji were rampant and had clawed their way back to 20-all in the second half. Smit gathered the troops and gave the speech of his life. It saved the game.

Coach at the time, Jake White, revealed after: 'John told the players that he could see in their eyes what he had seen in those of the Australian and New Zealand players at the same stage in their games the previous day. He told them to snap out of it and it was a magnificent example of leadership under the most intense pressure.'

## 4　John Eales (Australia)

What set John Eales apart was his range of skills. He was the world's best aerial forward throughout the 1990s. He was rugged yet mobile, brutal yet subtle, and he could kick goals.

That was the freaky part: Eales would famously back himself to kick pressure goals, as he did to secure the Bledisloe Cup in the last minute against the All Blacks in 2000. It was because of this phenomenal range of abilities that he earned the nickname 'Nobody' – as in 'nobody is perfect'.

Recognised as one of the most talented players ever produced by Australia, Eales had the immediate respect of his team-mates when he took over the captaincy in 1998. It was an easy transition for him to make, as among his range of freakish abilities was his capacity to read any game's strategic flow. It was that calm authority and ability to stay task-focused and unemotional that helped Eales captain the Wallabies to a World Cup title in 1999. He followed that up with back-to-back titles in the Tri Nations and then a series defeat of the Lions before he retired in 2001.

Former Wallaby legend Mark Ella was happy to write this for *The Australian* on the day Eales retired: 'I thought his personality wasn't strong enough [when he first got the job]. He's not become aggressive or overbearing, he's become a lot smarter. He'd be the number one in my book, there'd be very few players who'd come close to him in ability and with what they've done in rugby.'

## 3　Sean Fitzpatrick (New Zealand)

The aura of Fitzpatrick has grown since he retired in 1997. He has become a sought-after motivational speaker and analyst for media outlets. For the better part of 10 years Fitzpatrick was New Zealand's most capped player and most capped captain. He led the All Blacks in 51 tests and his roll of honour includes a series win over the Lions in 1993, two Tri Nations titles, and a series win in South Africa.

He also led the side to the 1995 World Cup final, but it was events off the field at that tournament which showed Fitzpatrick's strength of personality. Australian mogul Kerry Packer was trying to hijack the game with his World Rugby Corporation. It was a difficult period for all the leading players – being wooed by both the WRC and their national union administrators. Fitzpatrick took the opportunity to ensure he and his troops would be particularly well paid for staying loyal.

He was a tough negotiator and willing to hold out for what he believed was fair and reasonable. To survive in the All Blacks for 11 years as he did took talent, determination and a little cunning. When 'Fitzy', as he was universally known, finally retired, All Black coach John Hart said, 'I would say Sean is arguably, alongside Colin Meads, one of the greatest players we have seen in our time. He leaves a huge hole in New Zealand rugby, a hole we will never fill because there is only one Sean.'

## 2  Martin Johnson (England and the British & Irish Lions)

Martin Johnson is the only man to captain the Lions on two separate tours, and he also led England to World Cup glory. Almost everyone in world rugby was intimidated by Johnson, a huge, physical beast of a man. He was a scowling, brooding 2.02-metre mass of muscle, who demanded the highest standards from himself and those around him.

His finest moment came in the 2003 World Cup final when he took charge in the last minute of extra time to set up the drive that led to Jonny Wilkinson dropping the winning goal. Johnson was colossal in those final minutes – he gathered the team, told them what was required and set about doing it. Classic Johnson.

Fran Cotton, the Lions manager in 1997, said when Johnson retired in 2004, 'He has been an absolutely outstanding captain and player and as far as England are concerned, he has been an all-time great. His leadership comes down to his total and utter focus on winning and this incredible desire to be successful. To replace Martin Johnson in the short term will be impossible – he is a once in a generation player.'

## 1 Willie John McBride (British & Irish Lions)

There are significant numbers of terrifying men – resilient, brave resourceful types who captained their own countries – who will swear to the day they die that there has never been a better leader than Willie John McBride.

The Irish lock led the British Lions to a series win in South Africa and had been a key figure in the only successful tour of New Zealand three years earlier.

Extraordinary – the two toughest places in the world to tour, places where the Lions had never won before and only once since, and McBride nailed them both: bang-bang.

But as impressive as his credentials are, McBride's legend is way more than results. Stories of him are many and probably apocryphal. The most famous is from the 1974 Lions tour when his team-mates were running wild in a hotel. The manager had heard furniture being smashed and fire extinguishers being set off, and water was trickling into the lobby.

He hammered on the captain's door and found McBride cross-legged on his bed, wearing only his pants and smoking a pipe. 'Your players are wrecking my hotel,' screamed the manager.

To which the skipper responded with no great interest: 'Are there many dead?'

'I've called the police,' replied the manager.

'And tell me, these police of yours,' McBride said, 'will there be many of them?'

A character for the ages with a strength of personality rarely found, McBride's former team-mates remain in awe of him even today (and perhaps a little scared, too). He was fearless, intelligent, fair and a brilliant motivator and tactical instigator.

# 10 best selections

## 10 Wales' Second XV 2003 RWC

The Welsh had secured their place in the quarter-final of the 2003 World Cup but were desperately short of confidence ahead of their last pool encounter against the All Blacks. A hammering would have seen them in poor spirits to play England in the knockout round.

So coach Steve Hansen decided to pick his second team. And the players largely decided to ignore Hansen's tactical input and chose to play brave, ambitious, expansive football.

It was absorbing, and after 45 minutes there was a real chance Wales were going to win. They led 37–33 and had rattled the All Blacks by scoring three tries in 15 minutes. It was all on. The Welsh suddenly believed in themselves and played magnificent rugby. The All Blacks eased out in the end, but Wales had discovered their swagger and rattled England just as hard the following week.

## 9 Stephen Larkham

Stephen Larkham was pretty much minding his own business playing at halfback in reserve grade club rugby one day in 1995 when he was spotted by a member of the Brumbies coaching team.

They saw something in him and he was signed to the Brumbies as a utility back. It took him just 18 months to make the Wallabies, winning his first cap as a replacement on the wing before settling at fullback on the 1997 tour of the UK.

Obviously talented and blessed with a different set of skills to most, the problem was finding the right position for Larkham. Wallaby coach Rod Macqueen reckoned Larkham had the capacity to be the tactical general of the highly sequenced football he was going to employ. Defence coach John Muggleton thought Larkham had the robust defensive qualities to lead the line in a new era of league-style structures and patterns.

It was agreed then: the utility back would be used at fly-half – and Larkham became one of the greats. He was instrumental in Australia's World Cup win in 1999 as well as their era of Bledisloe dominance between 1999 and 2002.

No one else had seen the possibility of Larkham being a No 10, and a major risk reaped a major reward.

## 8 Jason White, Scotland 2000

Scotland were in a dreadful state in 2000. They lost their opening game to Italy in a shambolic performance. They were no better when they were ripped apart by Ireland and then swept aside by France and Wales.

It was desperate times for a nation in desperate straits. England came north on the final weekend in imperious form. They were enormous favourites to win and secure the Grand Slam they had been denied the year before. There was a little payback coming, too, for Scotland's victory in 1990 that had also denied England their Grand Slam.

No one gave Scotland a chance, and the fact they had drafted in 21-year-old blindside flanker Jason White to make his debut hardly changed the equation. What no one other than the coaches knew, however, was that White was one of the biggest tacklers in the global game.

White smashed everything, and by half-time England were shaken. By the final quarter they were running scared, every ball carrier fearful of where White was lurking. It was one of the best aggressive/defensive performances ever delivered and helped Scotland to a famous 19–13 win.

White said after the game: 'I remember a couple of rucks where the punches came raining in, and thinking, "This is a little different." There was a desperation about the way England attempted to smash us backwards and get the try that would have turned the game. But I remember clearly the moment it was all over. Their hooker Phil

Greening took the ball up one final time and when I threw myself at him he spilled the ball and it was all over.'

## 7 Lions Pack 1997

The expectation was that the British Lions of 1997 would play the biggest pack they could to match the set-piece power of the Springboks. That would see the likes of Jason Leonard, Graham Rowntree and Simon Shaw selected in the tight five.

But Lions coaches Ian McGeechan and Jim Telfer had different ideas. Yes, they wanted to match the Boks in the scrums and line-outs, but they also wanted to run them around, too. Their test XV included the small, but enormously mobile, Tom Smith at loose-head, the similarly built Paul Wallace at tight-head and the rangy and athletic Jeremy Davidson at lock – none of whom were well known or greatly experienced. These were selections no one had predicted, but they were the men who won the series for the Lions.

The Boks couldn't dominate these men physically and nor could they out-run them. It was brave, tactically smart selecting, backed with heroic performances.

## 6 Kevin Skinner, All Blacks 1956

The 1956 series between the All Blacks and Springboks was an epic. The All Blacks won the first test, and the South Africans the second in a match that was marked as one of the most brutal ever played.

New Zealand's prop Tiny White was singled out for some savage treatment, and the All Black selectors responded by bringing Kevin Skinner out of retirement for the third test. The former boxer had retired in 1954, citing his need to concentrate on work, but he had continued to turn out for local clubs in the interim. An intimidating figure, the selectors asked him to 'sort out' the South African props.

Skinner held the All Black scrum rock-steady in the critical third test and there was no nonsense from the South Africans. He did indeed 'sort them out'. The All Blacks took out the series 3–1 and Skinner returned to retirement.

## 5 Jeremy Guscott, British Lions 1989

Jeremy Guscott was not in the original British Lions tour party selected for the 1989 tour of Australia. He was called up after he proved his readiness by scoring a hat-trick for England against Romania.

Young and inexperienced, he wasn't wanted for the first test. But after the Lions were shredded by a more physical, hungrier Wallaby side 30–12 in the first test, Guscott was thrust into the No 12 jersey.

Guscott was a player who would take risks, back himself to find space or create it for others. He was a make-or-break choice and there were many who felt his selection was the last roll of the dice, and one likely to be doomed.

But Guscott tackled everything that moved that day, and later in the game nudged the perfect grubber into a gap in the Wallaby midfield no one else saw. And it was Guscott who chased after it, caught it after it sat up beautifully, and then touched it down for the winning try. An inspired selection.

## 4 Raphaël Ibanez, France 2007

When Raphaël Ibanez retired after the 2003 World Cup, French coach Bernard Laporte never accepted that would be a permanent state of affairs. Even when Ibanez headed to England and began a new life for himself, Laporte never gave up hope. And so it was that in early 2007, Ibanez was persuaded out of retirement and resumed his international career.

When regular captain Fabien Pelous was ruled out of the Six Nations, Ibanez took over and stayed there through to the World Cup. His decision to come out of retirement was vindicated in the quarter-final where he gave one of the best hooking displays in memory and also extolled his side to one of the great shocks.

The French made more than 300 tackles to beat the All Blacks in Cardiff and pull off the greatest upset since ... Ibanez had led the French to an unexpected semi-final triumph against the All Blacks in 1999.

### 3 Dan Carter to fly-half

As hard as it may seem now, following the Tri Nations in 2004 the All Black coaches were considering shifting Dan Carter to outside centre from inside centre.

There was a view that the All Blacks were weak there, especially as incumbent Tana Umaga was in his mid-30s and talking of retiring in 2005. But shortly before naming the squad to travel to Europe in November, the selectors changed their minds and shifted Carter the other way, to fly-half. They weren't sure he had the force of personality or tactical understanding for the role.

They made a bold decision to take him as their only fly-half. Not only was Carter immediately brilliant on that tour, he went on to become, probably, the best fly-half to ever play the game. His crowning moment came in July, 2005 when he scored a spectacular 33 points in the 48–18 defeat of the Lions.

'Have I ever seen a better display from a No 10? Probably not,' proffered All Black coach Graham Henry, who is notoriously curmudgeonly with praise.

'For a 23-year-old he was quite outstanding. He kicked his goals, he ran the line, his defence was outstanding, he scored tries, he navigated the ship. Phenomenal.'

### 2 David Young, Wales 1987

When the Welsh picked their squad for the 1987 World Cup, David Young was nowhere near selection. The 19-year-old Swansea prop was just making his way in the world of senior rugby so had no expectations of playing for his country.

He decided to head to Australia in the northern hemisphere summer of that year to play for the Sydney club, Northern Suburbs. It was after one game for Suburbs, when he was relaxing with a few beers, that word reached Young that he needed to head to Brisbane immediately. He was being called up to the Welsh squad ahead of their quarter-final clash with England.

Stuart Evans had broken his foot in the game against Tonga, and on account of already being in Australia, Young was the man the selectors turned to.

'I'll always remember the moment I got that phone call, though it was hard to believe at the time,' recalled Young as he neared retirement. 'I had to check the message twice to make sure it was genuine. I don't know if it was luck or judgment that I happened to be in Australia, but to pick up a cap at such a young age was never the plan.

'I never thought I'd actually play, even in training. I barely slept after I was named in the team.'

It was a massive step up for the youngster, but he was sensational in the 16–3 victory. Young was the right man in the right place and went on to win 51 test caps as well as become a British Lion.

## 1  Jonah Lomu, RWC 1995

There was a real danger that Jonah Lomu was going to miss selection for the 1995 World Cup. The 20-year-old had made his debut in 1994 but the world hadn't sussed there was something special in Lomu.

He was asked to play on the wing on his debut despite all his schoolboy rugby having been played at No 8. Out of his depth and part of a weak All Black side – the last to lose a series on home soil – Lomu's confidence was shattered. His weight ballooned and when the All Blacks were fitness-tested in February 1995, Lomu was overweight and badly out of shape.

Coach Laurie Mains was reluctant to pick him. He didn't like the fact Lomu had let himself go and wasn't convinced he'd get it back either. The All Blacks had to be super-fit to play the type of rugby Mains had in mind. But Lomu's mates, men such as Eric Rush, Frank Bunce and Glen Osborne, gave Mains assurances they would mentor the youngster and keep him in shape.

It was a knife-edge call, but Mains decided in the end to take Lomu although he had his doubts. It took about 20 minutes of the opening game for Mains' faith to be repaid and to look like the smartest piece of selection ever seen.

Lomu stole the tournament. He scored a record eight tries – four coming in the semi-final against England. No one had ever seen anything like it and, according to legend, Australian media tycoon Rupert Murdoch saw Lomu destroying England and ordered his stooges to buy the broadcast rights to Super Rugby.

'He is a big bastard' was the Scotland captain's less than charming analysis of Lomu, while England's captain Will Carling famously said of the wing: 'He's a freak.'

# 10 best individual performances

**⑩ Greg Cornelsen,** Australia v New Zealand, September 1985

The Bledisloe Cup was safely back in New Zealand's trophy cabinet when they came to play the Wallabies at Eden Park in the third test of the series. The first test had been a scrap, the second had been won at a canter, and the third was expected to be a rout by the All Blacks.

What actually happened was that the Wallabies dug deep and played extraordinarily good rugby to win 30–16. No one played better than bruising No 8 Greg Cornelsen, who scored a staggering four tries. There are teams who would be lucky to score that many in four tests against the All Blacks. For one man to score four against the All Blacks was unheard of, and the efforts of Cornelsen that day had a profound effect on future Wallaby captain John Eales.

'The first game of rugby I ever remember the Wallabies playing was 1985 and I will never forget it because I was at home, I watched it on the ABC and the Wallabies won,' Eales recalled in an interview. 'It was the day the Wallabies scored five tries against the All Blacks and Greg Cornelsen scored four of those five tries.

'I walked outside and met my neighbour. He said, "Did you watch the test against the All Blacks?" I said, "Yeah, we flogged them easy, it was just New Zealand," and he pulled me aside and said, "You don't realise what you've just seen, because what you have just seen has never happened before in the history of Australia–New Zealand test matches. When it comes to rugby there is no team better than the All Blacks. What you have seen is something very, very rare." '

## 9  Chris Oti, England v Ireland, March 1988

England had been, to put it nicely, in a bit of a flat patch throughout the mid-1980s. They had been hammered by the Scots in 1986 and were woeful at the inaugural World Cup a year later.

Things were bumbling along in much the same vein in 1988 until they burst into life against Ireland. Well, they actually didn't burst into life until the second half when left wing Chris Oti hit a new gear.

Strong and elusive, Oti, playing in just his second test, was finally given the ball. England decided to dash it all and have a bit of fun, and it turned out Oti was electric and maybe should have been given the ball a bit more. When Oti touched down for a try, it was the first time an England wing had scored a Five Nations try for three years, and equalled the number of tries they had scored in total at Twickenham in the previous two years.

Oti ended up scoring a highly memorable hat-trick to seal a 35–3 victory. As he cantered in for that third try, a group from the Benedictine Douai School began to sing their own First XV anthem, 'Swing Low, Sweet Chariot'. For some reason it struck a chord and has become the unofficial English fans' anthem ever since.

## 8  Brian O'Driscoll, Ireland v France, March 2000

Those who had followed the fledgling career of Brian O'Driscoll could see that the young Irish midfielder was going to be something special. After helping the Irish Under-19s to a world title, O'Driscoll forced his way into the full Ireland side and played against France in Paris in 2000.

The Irish hadn't won in Paris for 28 years, and when the French came at them hard in the first 20 minutes there were fears things could turn ugly – the French could be on track to post a big win. No chance.

The Irish held on, found a second wind – and also a new hero in the 21-year-old O'Driscoll. This was the day he came of age: he tackled everything and cut huge holes in the French midfield.

He also scored three well-taken tries that showed his awareness, his pace, his instincts and his determination were all there. It was a magical performance by a young man who would go on to become arguably the best player ever produced by Ireland.

Almost 10 years later, new Irish hope Keith Earls, who had been 12 the day O'Driscoll steered the men in green to their famous 27–25 victory, revealed how inspired he'd been. He said: 'I remember watching the game at home on the weekend and then going into school on the Monday. I remember drawing a picture of Brian scoring a try and having three French fellas crying behind him.'

## 7 Jonathan Davies, Wales v Scotland, February 1988

Jonathan Davies was in his prime as a rugby union player in 1988. He was the touch of class Wales had been desperately seeking in their fly-half – a player they had been looking for since Phil Bennett had retired almost 10 years previously.

Davies was a sprite of a thing – much like Bennett – in that he could shimmy and sway and then suddenly be heading forward at an advanced rate. Wales' clash with Scotland in the 1988 Five Nations had brewed into a classic encounter, a shining light in a competition that had been memorable for its dismal lack of rugby that season. Davies was the man who had set it alight with his poise and vision, and his ability to probe the fringes and play others into space.

The highlight was an incredible try where a Welsh scrum on the Scots' 22 was in trouble. Scrum-half Robert Jones fired a brilliant reverse pass and Davies, going backwards, stepped the rushing defence, came back to the traffic and then kicked the ball ahead into a huge hole where he beat the cover and scored.

Such was its impact that six years later Scotland's newly installed 20-year-old fly-half Gregor Townsend was compared with the great Davies. 'I felt really flattered but I didn't deserve it,' said Townsend. 'But I often think about Jonathan Davies' try against Scotland in 1988 when he chipped and chased. I'm always dreaming of scoring a try like that.'

## 6  Gavin Hastings, Scotland v France, February 1995

The Scots hadn't beaten France in Paris for 26 years and were not greatly fancied to break that losing run in 1995. But there was something in the air and captain Gavin Hastings could sense it.

'Big Gav' had an appetite for the dramatic – he was a big-game player with the right temperament to deliver his best in the toughest games. Early in the game he split the French defence with a stunning break that set up a try for Gregor Townsend. Shortly after half-time he landed a penalty from just inside his own half that really put the pressure on the French.

The moment of Hastings magic to crown them all came with a few minutes remaining – he latched onto a magical back-handed pass from Townsend and stormed away to score and convert his own try to seal the win.

Scotland flanker Rob Wainwright would recall a few years later the significance of the win. 'A lot changed that day. Up until that point, I think subconsciously we all doubted whether we could beat the French in France.

'We'd had a series of outstanding games, but when we went over there somehow it just didn't happen. The sense of relief was amazing; that night we went out and the team manager's bill was enormous, the biggest I've ever seen; pushing up towards £10,000 for the night if I remember rightly.'

## 5  Jean Prat, France v England, February 1951

It took France an inordinately long time to find their feet after they were invited into the Five Nations early in the twentieth century. There were numerous defeats to be endured, particularly away from home and particularly against England.

The French went 44 years without winning in London – that was until 1951, when Jean Prat played as if he'd been blessed by the gods. Prat was years ahead of his time, a versatile, ball-playing flanker who could do everything including goal-kick. He scored a drop goal, a try and a conversion to become the first Frenchman to captain a winning team at Twickenham. Prat earned the nickname 'Monsieur Rugby' in the English press.

He was possibly helped by England deviating from their usual preparation. As the *Guardian* would later report, English lock Squire Wilkins confessed that the England team had broken with convention: 'At the lunch before the game, they [the French team] tried to get us drunk by pretending they were all glugging down wine. Of course their glasses were full of something else entirely.

'Usually we'd have a half of beer, but on this occasion someone suggested a glass of sherry, because it dried you out.'

### 4   Keith Jarrett, Wales v England, April 1967

Wales were in dire straits in 1967, staring down the barrel of their first-ever Five Nations whitewash. Such was the pressure, the selectors went a bit loopy and picked the uncapped 18-year-old Keith Jarrett at fullback. The national selectors had persuaded Newport to play Jarrett at fullback instead of his normal position of centre in a club game the week before. He'd only lasted a half before he was switched back to centre – he was just awful at fullback, yet there he was wearing the Welsh No 15 jersey to play England.

It was partly for his goal-kicking that he was selected, and when he landed his first shot via a goal-post, there was a feeling it was going to be his day.

'This laddie can do no wrong,' said an excited Bill McLaren when commentating for the BBC. Jarrett then scored a spectacular solo try when he collected a deep kick and left defenders clutching at nothing. He added five more successful kicks to complete a 19-point haul. He was the youngest man to ever play for Wales and equalled the national points record on debut.

### 3   Richie McCaw, New Zealand v Australia, July 2006

There might have been a few blades of grass at Suncorp Stadium that All Black captain Richie McCaw didn't stand on the night the All Blacks clinched the Bledisloe Cup with a 13–9 win.

The skipper was colossal in everything he did. An epic game was in progress and McCaw was at the core. He stole turnover ball, he made crucial passes and support plays and, most significantly, he made a 70-metre run to claw down an escaping Mark Gerrard with his fingertips.

That try-saving tackle epitomised the effort and ability of this once-in-a-lifetime player. Delighted to have won such a tense and thrilling encounter, All Black coach Graham Henry paid the ultimate tribute to his captain: 'I don't think anyone could play any better than he did tonight.'

## ② Richie McCaw, New Zealand v South Africa, August 2008

When Graham Henry said in 2006 that he didn't think anyone could play better than Richie McCaw had in Brisbane, he was prepared to admit two years later he'd been wrong.

Someone did play better – that someone being McCaw, whose performance against the Springboks in Cape Town was scarcely believable. He rampaged all over Newlands winning the ball at his leisure and hunting down Boks like they were prey.

His ball carrying was an improved feature on the Brisbane effort, and there was even a deft grubber kick to set up Conrad Smith for a try. The All Blacks won 19–0, but Dan Carter uncharacteristically missed seven kicks at goal that would have taken it close to 40.

This was the only time South Africa have been held scoreless at home, and McCaw's defensive contribution was a huge factor in that. 'He's been colossal, in a word,' said Henry. 'He came in with no rugby for a month against the Australians in Auckland and I thought he was pretty special. Then he upped that performance in Cape Town where he probably played his best game as an All Black. He might debate that, but I thought he was outstanding and his leadership was equal to his playing ability. His influence on this group is colossal.'

## 1 Daniel Carter, All Blacks v British Lions, July 2005

The filthy weather in the first test between the All Blacks and British & Irish Lions in 2005 prevented the hosts from being able to inflict all the damage they wanted. The All Blacks had decided the Lions were an ordinary team, and when they encountered a balmy evening in Wellington the following week, it was men against boys. It was a proper demolition job by the All Blacks – they won 48–18 – and the chief architect of this extraordinary performance was fly-half Daniel Carter.

In only his fifth test in the No 10 jersey, Carter scored 33 points in a performance that featured two breathtaking solo tries as part of an all-round game of sublime genius.

As well as his second try where he beat three men and then collected his own kick ahead, the other iconic moment came when Carter retrieved a high ball, danced past two defenders, then side-stepped Jonny Wilkinson, leaving the Englishman prone on the turf. It was a poignant moment, confirming that the man once deemed the king of fly-halves had lost his crown to the new pretender.

'Dan is our leader,' said All Black captain Tana Umaga that night. 'His nous, his kicking game, his awareness ... on the field, he's the bloke who makes it happen for us.'

# 10 best rivalries

### 10 Schalk Burger (South Africa) v Jerry Collins (New Zealand)

It was a point of honour between these two whenever they played to see who could inflict the most damage. Fiercely proud of the respective No 6 on their backs, they took the idea of being enforcers rather seriously.

Burger must have the biggest head in world rugby – literally, not figuratively– and is a giant of a man. Collins wasn't naturally as big, but his work in the gym enabled him to build his biceps to a diameter of 56 cm. Being hit by Big Jerry was similar to being hit by a car.

Their 2005 clash in Cape Town was unforgettable, one of those games where they were exclusively interested in maiming each other.

'He's a different breed, is Schalk,' Collins once remarked.

Burger repaid the compliment in 2008, when Collins had unexpectedly terminated his contract a year early, just weeks before the All Blacks faced the Boks. 'It was always fun playing against Jerry,' he quipped with maximum sarcasm.

The beauty of this rivalry, however, was the mutual respect both men felt and their insistence they share a beer after every game they played. Old school, to the end.

### 9 Will Carling (England) v Gavin Hastings (Scotland)

These two were never destined to be the best of friends, but nor did they seem obviously likely to become sworn enemies.

That was until Scotland fullback Gavin Hastings was elected captain of the 1993 British Lions and pushed to have Will Carling dropped after the first test. The skipper wanted the young Welsh tyro Scott Gibbs in the midfield, and Carling, who many felt was going to be the tour captain, never forgave Hastings.

The rivalry became fierce, exemplified when Hastings cried on national TV the following year when England stole a late victory at Murrayfield. Carling's gloating was an arrow through his heart. As it was in 1995 when the Scots were outmuscled at Twickenham when the Grand Slam was on the line for both teams.

These days Hastings, a popular after-dinner speaker, occasionally starts a speech thus: 'People say I don't like Will Carling ... Well, it's not true. I hate the bastard.'

## 8 Phil Kearns (Australia) v Sean Fitzpatrick (New Zealand)

All Black captain Sean Fitzpatrick knew the value of psychological warfare, and understood that a few choice words in the ear of a young rival could be massively disruptive. In 1989, he mercilessly sledged Wallaby debutant Phil Kearns, suggesting, kind of, that the Australian hooker should have stayed at home with mum.

A year later, and with a great All Black team on the decline, Kearns pounced on a wayward lineout tap and barrelled over for a critical try. He gave the prostrate Fitzpatrick the fingers as well as some choice abuse, although he insisted he'd only said, 'Two sausages at tonight's barbecue please.'

For the next six years these two went at each other and loved it – two hard men, two great players, two great captains and two men who knew that once the final whistle blew they could laugh it all off. That point was proven when they made a TV ad together – filmed holding hands – nearly 20 years after they first clashed.

## 7 David Sole (Scotland) v Jeff Probyn (England)

In Tom English's excellent book, *The Grudge*, Scotland captain David Sole makes it clear how he felt about Jeff Probyn: 'I didn't particularly like him [Probyn]. He was all yap, yap, yap.'

The feeling was mutual. Probyn, the immensely strong English tight-head, didn't respect Sole, a dynamic loose-head who could carry the ball, pass, tackle and play like a back, but who wasn't a great scrummager.

So when these two clashed, they would go for each other. Sole used to cut his sleeve off to play against Probyn, claiming the Englishman only managed to go so low by clinging illegally to his opponent's jersey.

In the 1990 Grand Slam decider, Probyn wanted to humiliate Sole, crush him in the scrum. The most famous phase of that game came early in the first half when the English continually won penalties from the pressure they exerted in the set-piece, and then chose to scrum again. Somehow the Scots survived, but two years later, Sole took his revenge for being targeted like that when Scotland scored a pushover try.

They continued to bicker about each other in the press long after they retired.

## 6 Luke Watson (South Africa) v Springbok Rugby

The son of a white activist, Chalky, Luke Watson had been fighting the South African system from birth. His father had played club rugby for black teams – angering the Establishment. Luke inherited his father's desire to defy the regime and was permanently in conflict with the Springboks, the most poignant symbol of the 'old South Africa' and apartheid.

After he was named South Africa's Super 14 player of the year in 2006, there were calls for Watson to be elevated to the Springboks. National coach Jake White disagreed and even went so far as to publicly criticise Watson. Watson responded by claiming in a magazine interview that White wasn't honest and lacked integrity.

The following year SARU officials forced White to include Watson in an extended World Cup squad. On greeting that squad, White said: 'Welcome to the team and welcome to Luke. I didn't select you Luke, but you are here anyway.'

Shortly afterwards, video footage was leaked of Watson giving a speech to university students where he claimed he 'had to keep himself from vomiting on his Springbok jersey'.

Mind you, Watson might have had good cause. In explaining why he had nearly vomited on his jersey, Watson said that in 2008 team captain John Smit had addressed the squad before one game. In one of his 'let's unify and be as one' moments, Smit urged his team to bond even as he asserted that Watson had destroyed morale.

It might have been better had Watson not actually been part of the squad Smit was addressing, and listening in abject horror as he was singled out.

## 5  George Gregan (Australia) v Byron Kelleher (New Zealand)

Gregan felt he was rugby royalty, so he took enormous exception to the way a young Byron Kelleher hounded him all game in 2000 when the Brumbies played the Highlanders. The Wallaby halfback didn't much appreciate the close personal attention and was just as irate later that year when Kelleher got into him in the Bledisloe Cup encounter.

So in 2003, when the All Blacks had just blown their last chance of salvaging the World Cup semi-final in Sydney, Gregan stood over a distraught Kelleher and yelled in his face: 'Four more years. Four more years.'

It was a low, but beautifully timed, sledge that ate away at Kelleher for ... four more years. 'There is a bit of rivalry there which has built up over the years between George and myself,' said Kelleher in 2006 with ridiculous understatement. Before going on to confuse everyone by saying the 2003 taunt was 'water off a duck's back, but I do keep it in the back of my mind'.

## 4  Richard Cockerill (England) v Norm Hewett (New Zealand)

In 1997, Richard Cockerill was desperate to establish himself as England's starting hooker under new coach Clive Woodward.

He won his second cap against the All Blacks and thought he could make a name for himself by showing some kind of plucky bulldog spirit during the haka. He encroached on Norm Hewett until the two men were touching foreheads. The tension was electric and in that opening exchange, lifelong enemies were made.

The confrontation greatly bothered Hewett, who had spent years on the bench rarely starting. The game against England meant everything to him – usual hooker Sean Fitzpatrick was injured – and as a proud Maori, Hewett didn't appreciate having his performance of the haka physically impeded.

The following year England came to New Zealand and the battle continued when the two hookers clashed late at night. They brawled in the street and even ended up fighting in the back of a taxi until team-mates separated them.

## 3 Brendan Venter v RFU

The former Springbok is aptly named – he has often needed to get things off his chest. As coach of London club Saracens he had been openly critical of referees, fans and players, which saw him spend ample time in front of disciplinary committees.

In 2010 he was trying to overturn a 14-week touchline ban for allegedly making inappropriate and provocative gestures during a match against Leicester. At his appeal, he further incurred the wrath of the administrative body for ... eating a biscuit. Venter says that on being asked to leave the room to allow the committee to deliberate their findings, he grabbed a biscuit on his way out. He was still eating it when called back in and Judge Jeff Blackett took great offence.

Venter raged after the hearing: 'There was a plate of biscuits and I took one. As I took my first bite they called us back in. It was like "come in, come in, come in, they're calling you".

'I had nowhere to throw the biscuit. I couldn't drop it on the carpet. So I walked in with it and took my last bite inside the room. I didn't go in and deliberately eat the biscuit in front of them. If that is how it was seen, then honestly it was not my intention. Why provide a plate of biscuits if no one was meant to eat them? Perhaps it is time for English rugby to be run like a modern professional sport, and not a rural prep school.'

Venter later made a bizarre protest at copping a £22,000 fine for being critical of a referee after a Heineken Cup. Following Saracens' next game, Venter gave the weirdest live post-match TV interview where he refused to answer any questions.

## 2 Robbie Deans (New Zealand/Australia) v Steve Hansen (New Zealand)

It wasn't that long ago that Deans and Hansen were a tight coaching unit in charge of Canterbury, and they won the national title in 1997.

Then something happened between these two. Neither has spoken publicly about what caused the rift, but whatever it was, it left them holding each other in contempt.

That mutual loathing intensified in 2007 when Deans challenged for the All Black job. He lost, with seven of the eight-man board voting to retain Graham Henry and his assistants Wayne Smith and Hansen.

Deans was confirmed as Wallaby coach a week later and the rivalry went up another level – especially when Australia hammered New Zealand in their first encounter in 2008. But 10 consecutive All Black wins followed, which ripped Deans apart, and in 2010, when the Wallabies were invited to share a post-match drink in the All Black changing room, Deans prevented anyone from attending.

Later that year he accused the All Blacks of cheating in every facet of the game, but particularly scrums, leading Hansen to respond: 'Rob's obviously under a bit of pressure. He seems to always fall back and talk about New Zealand when he's actually involved with Australia. I just dismiss the comment. It's a man trying to divert attention from his own team and himself.'

## 1 Brian O'Driscoll (Ireland) v Tana Umaga (New Zealand)

Arguably the best two centres in world rugby when they faced each other as the respective captains of the British & Irish Lions and the All Blacks in 2005, Brian O'Driscoll and Tana Umaga had an obvious and easy rapport between them.

That was irreversibly broken just 41 seconds into the first test. O'Driscoll's shoulder was dislocated after an illegal cleanout by Umaga. When Umaga wasn't even cited for the challenge, bad blood boiled.

O'Driscoll was bitter. His tour was over and he attacked Umaga verbally, assassinating his character. And he just kept on and on.

When Umaga released his autobiography in 2007, he wrote: 'The sustained personal attack was hard to believe. You don't want to take it personally but it's almost impossible not to when another player, a guy you had some respect for, attacks your character.

'O'Driscoll kept going on about the fact that I hadn't rung him to say sorry. I finally obtained his number and got hold of him but it wasn't a warm exchange.

I said, "I'm sorry for what happened to you, but there was no intent in it." He said, "Yeah, but you could've helped it." "Okay, mate," I said, "all the best." And that was where we left it.'

# 10 best reinventions

## 10 Brian Moore as a commentator

Brian Moore was a pugnacious hooker with the England team of the late 1980s and early 1990s. He was notoriously combustible and driven to the point of obsession, and while it made him an effective player, it came with the downside of making him hard to like.

The thing about Moore was that you could rely on him to say something or do something inflammatory that would set the blood boiling. It seemed a rather strange choice, then, for the BBC to use a retired Moore as a comments man in their Six Nations TV coverage.

But he has been a revelation as a broadcaster. His analysis is astute and entertaining, and he provides a humorous honesty that is compelling and endearing.

His best moments came in 2008 when he once shouted live on air: 'They've kicked it away again, *for God's sake!*' when England once again refused to attack through the hands against Italy. Even better was when he yelled 'you halfwit!' after an English forward knocked-on from a kick-off.

'I call it as it is in my commentary. I think that's what people like,' Moore explained about his broadcast style. 'Whether or not it's the best way to go, it's my way, and actually it's quite simple. If people don't like it and the BBC don't like it, then they don't have to employ me.'

## 9 England as the All Blacks

Since the beginning of time England have played in white jerseys. Pretty simple really: they have a white flag with a red cross and their jerseys are white with a red rose. Even in the professional age of developing alternate shirts, they initially tried to stay true to their existing colours by having a red jersey with a white trim.

Then somewhere along the way they began to tinker. A navy blue alternate jersey was developed and then, shock of all shocks, England decided in 2011 to create what they called 'an anthracite' colour for their second shirt. It was effectively black, and no one was entirely sure why they had done it. Was it in the hope that by dressing up as the All Blacks they would play like the All Blacks?

'It has got the red rose on it and that is all that matters to us,' flanker Tom Wood said just before the World Cup kicked off. 'It is a bit of a marketing tactic and will raise a few eyebrows, I am sure. But I don't think ultimately it will concern the All Blacks themselves. Perhaps the media will make something of it, but we like it. It looks good and it is good to wear.'

England certainly looked exactly like the All Blacks when they ran out to play the Pumas in Dunedin in their opening World Cup game. The similarities ended there, however.

## 8 Graham Henry as a coach

Search the annals of New Zealand rugby history and there will be no mention of Graham Henry as one of the country's great players. He wasn't even a moderate player, managing only a handful of senior club games. Yet his footprint in the national game is enormous as he has proven unequivocally that you don't need to have been a good player to be a good coach.

Henry has laid claim to being considered one of New Zealand's, if not the world's, best coaches. Maybe even the best. What he lacked as a player, he has found at the helm of the various teams of which he has had charge.

He won four consecutive titles with Auckland, back-to-back Super 12 campaigns with the Blues, and led Wales to 11 consecutive victories after he arrived there in 1998. He's coached the Lions and the All Blacks to an 86 per cent win ratio in more than 100 tests. Staying ahead in the coaching game has been a continuous process of reinvention.

'The education system has changed from a pretty authoritarian system with set examinations to a consensus system where the students' ideas are put into play,' said Henry before the 2011 World Cup. 'I used to be an authoritarian coach when I came through the grades and even with Auckland and the Blues, but that wouldn't work now. You have to adapt to the clientele you are coaching.'

## 7 Pat Lam as Samoan

Growing up in Auckland with Samoan parents, Pat Lam always dreamed of being an All Black. He was a good No 8 with ample potential and leadership skills.

His dream finally came true when he was called up to play against Sydney in 1992. It was the break he thought would never come, as he was unfortunate to be playing at the same time as legendary loose forwards Zinzan Brooke and Michael Jones.

But the game was one of the worst in All Black history. The New Zealand team played as badly as they ever had in their near 100-year history and were beaten 40–17. That was enough to convince Lam that he should ditch his All Black ambitions and commit himself to playing for Manu Samoa.

It was an inspired move, as Lam would become the captain of the Samoan team and earn international fame and recognition. From being out of his depth as an All Black, he suddenly looked like a charismatic test captain born to play international football.

He helped Samoa to the quarter-finals of the 1995 World Cup and then captained them to a famous win against Wales in 1999.

He was named Allied Dunbar Premiership Player of the Year when he captained Newcastle to their one and only title, and when he joined Northampton a year later, incumbent Saints captain Tim Rodber voluntarily stepped down, saying this after Lam had skippered the side to Heineken Cup glory in 2000: 'I decided with [coach] Ian McGeechan last season that appointing Pat as captain would be the best course of action. Pat Lam is the best leader for this team and I didn't feel sore about it at all. He is a very uplifting guy and has the ability to say and do things which are exactly right.'

## 6 Michael Jones as a blindside flanker

Michael Niko Jones amazed the world in 1987 when he changed, forever, the expectations for openside flankers. He was this incredible mix of aggression, athleticism, brutality and silky, creative skills – a back in a forward's body, capable of a hybrid game that made him the star of the inaugural World Cup.

He is, to this day, rated as one of the best, if not the best openside to ever play – as confirmed by *Rugby World* magazine when they named him the third best player of all time.

But injury, and religious beliefs that prevented Jones from playing on Sundays, opened the All Black door for Josh Kronfeld, who established himself as a world-class No 7 at the 1995 World Cup. No problem – Jones switched to the blindside and between 1996 and 1998 amazed the world again. From being a whippet who covered every inch of the park, he reinvented himself as a bone-crushing No 6 who knocked bodies down and drove them back with the power of his ball carrying.

It was a remarkable conversion, and there are plenty of astute judges who consider Jones to be New Zealand's best-ever openside *and* best-ever blindside. When Jones retired in 1998, All Black coach John Hart spoke for the nation when he said: 'There is unlikely to ever be another athlete like him.'

## 5 Alain Rolland as a referee

Alain Rolland won three Irish caps at scrum-half and played 40 games for Leinster, and yet his footprint in history felt lighter than that. He may have been a good player but he has gone on to establish himself as a great referee – probably the best referee in the world between 2009 and 2011.

Rolland, who took up the whistle immediately after retiring in 1996, has not only technical expertise but also a genuine feel for the game, having been a top player himself. His standing in the world game was endorsed by no less an authority than former All Black coach Graham Henry, who said in 2010: 'I think Alain Rolland is the best referee in the world, personally. We had him in Marseille last year and we've had him a number of other times. I think he's a players' referee. In other words, they like playing under him because he has a feel for the game and he's very experienced.'

## 4 Paul Ackford as a sports writer

International locks are not renowned for their brain power. They spend most of their lives bashing their heads into things and few have ever given the impression they are Mensa material.

Paul Ackford seemed to be a run-of-the-mill lock when he played for England in the 1980s and 1990s. A huge man, he never suggested his intelligence was a great burden to carry. He played with his head down, bum up, and didn't worry too much about doing anything other than smashing into things.

He was famous mostly for being a British Lion and also for being knocked out cold by an 18-year-old Argentinean schoolboy at Twickenham.

These days he's most famous for being one of the leading writers on the game. He is the rugby correspondent for the UK's *Sunday Telegraph* and his flowing prose, insightful analysis, and colourful and elegant descriptions of the game place him as one the most authoritative and respected scribes on the world scene. Not bad for a bloke everyone thought was just a big donkey when he played.

## 3 Jonah Lomu as a wing

It is almost too difficult to comprehend that Jonah Lomu came virtually straight out of school, where he had starred as a loose forward, and into the All Blacks, where he made his debut on the wing.

Whether anyone else will ever make such a rapid and dramatic transformation is doubtful. What Lomu achieved was incredible.

He'd shown up on the radar of New Zealand's national age-grade selectors in 1993 and 1994, making both the Under-19 and Under-21 teams. His power and ability were obvious, and he gave the teams he played for enormous capacity to play off the back of the scrum.

But All Black coach Laurie Mains saw an athlete he thought would be best suited to playing on the wing. It was a massive call, but Mains had the bravery to award Lomu his first cap in June 1994.

Lomu, at 19 years and 45 days, became the youngest-ever All Black, and had not the first clue what he was supposed to be doing while in the No 11 jersey.

But by June the following year, he knew all right. Lomu became the first global superstar of rugby when he demolished Ireland, Wales, Scotland and England with his incredible power, balance and pace.

'The power of the man was amazing, but it was also his speed, his agility and balance,' said All Black team-mate Andrew Mehrtens. 'He had some beautiful skills, moves and offloads. I hope that is not forgotten about him.'

Had he stayed a loose forward, the legend of Lomu may never have been created.

## 2 Robbie Deans as an Australian

Born and schooled in Christchurch, Robbie Deans is a proud member of a Cantabrian family dynasty that can trace its heritage back to the first immigrant ships to drop anchor at Lyttelton.

Deans fulfilled his lifetime ambition of playing for the All Blacks, and then in 2001 he was appointed coaching coordinator, serving under head coach John Mitchell. When his time in that role ended abruptly, Deans returned to the Crusaders where he steered the side to four finals in five years, winning two titles.

At the end of 2007 the All Black coaching job was up for grabs and became a two-horse race between incumbent Graham Henry and Deans. The expectation was that Deans would get the job he so desperately coveted, as no coach had ever survived a doomed World Cup campaign.

But amazingly Henry was retained, and from being on the verge of coaching the All Blacks, Deans, two days later, signed a four-year contract to coach the Wallabies.

It took all of six months for Deans, effectively New Zealand aristocracy, to pick up the moniker 'Dingo' and become a fair dinkum Aussie. He settled effortlessly across the Tasman, winning hearts and minds, and in 2011 was offered a two-year contract extension.

It was a job he may never have envisaged taking until the day he actually signed, but it was one Australian Rugby Union chief executive John O'Neill wanted Deans to have from as early as 2004. O'Neill's efforts were blocked then by a policy that prevented foreigners from being appointed, but when that rule was amended, O'Neill began chasing Deans from the middle of 2007. 'He [Deans] has had a long, successful record, he has been there and done that. I think he has got the right make-up, personnel and man-management skills and culture we want to re-establish in Australia,' said O'Neill.

## 1 Andrew Sheridan as a prop

Andrew Sheridan was in danger of being a good player who blew the chance of being something more. He was 1.95 m and 122 kg at the age of 22 and only able to win the occasional game at lock for his club Bristol.

That was until former All Black selector Peter Thorburn turned up as coach at the club in 2001 and persuaded the gargantuan Sheridan to shift to prop. The rationale was that he wasn't tall enough for lock or light enough to be lifted. Sheridan was named in the British & Irish Lions squad to tour New Zealand four years after his conversion. It was from there that he paid tribute to his Kiwi mentor.

'I was interested in making the move and Thorbs [Thorburn] helped me out,' recalled Sheridan in 2005. 'It was pretty good of him. He persevered and gave me some chances in the second team at Bristol and then put me into the first team. I thought the move would suit my physique. I prefer scrums.'

Sheridan went on to become the world's best scrummaging loose-head, earning man of the match plaudits for his destruction of the Wallaby scrum in the 2007 World Cup quarter-final, and he made the Lions again in 2009.

# 10 best signings

## 10  David Hill to Western Force

The struggling Western Force were left without a fly-half on the eve of the 2010 Super 14 after star import Andre Pretorius was ruled out of action for six months with a serious knee injury. Coach John Mitchell was left to scour the world for a replacement.

His focus fell on David Hill, the former All Black who Mitchell knew from their days together at Waikato. Hill was contracted to Japanese club Toshiba and was effectively coming to Perth on a short-term loan. The 31-year-old made an instant name for himself when he landed the winning drop goal against the Stormers. The Force were desperate for a win as they were glued to the bottom of the table. The Stormers ended up making the final and looked to be the most dangerous side in the competition, which is why the Force were not fancied at all.

But they dug in and were 15–13 behind as the clock struck 80 minutes. Hill dropped into the pocket, and from 35 metres landed only the third drop goal of his career to win the game. 'I had just missed a kick, so as a kicker or playmaker you have to deal with the highs and lows, and try not to get too disappointed when you miss one because you'll have to try to get the next one,' Hill said.

With one beautifully struck kick, Hill had justified the decision to bring him to the Force.

## 9  Warren Gatland to Connacht

Warren Gatland had previously been most famous for not being Sean Fitzpatrick. The Waikato hooker had spent a lifetime on the bench for the All Blacks, never actually getting on the field due to the indestructible qualities of the legendary Fitzpatrick.

It was possibly the frustration of being in the shadows as a player that brewed a ferocious determination in Gatland to be more as a coach. He'd spent a few off-seasons playing and dabbling in coaching at the Irish club Galwegians – balancing that with a coaching role at the Thames Valley province in New Zealand.

He was still only 33, but when the game turned professional and the tiny and under-resourced Irish province Connacht needed a coach, they asked Gatland. They had no money and he had no experience – it seemed like a fair deal.

It seemed like an even better deal when Gatland turned Connacht into a deceptively good side who enjoyed unprecedented success on the big stage. They twice beat English giants Northampton and twice made the quarter-finals of the European Challenge Cup. Such was Gatland's reputation that he was elevated to coach of Ireland in 1998.

## 8　Jason Holland to Munster

There was confusion over why Jason Holland was never offered a contract with the Hurricanes. The Manawatu fly-half was a natural talent who appeared to be as good as any young challenger in the country. But the Hurricanes never saw it that way, so after six years of slogging his guts out Holland left for Ireland in 1999 with no real ambition but to enjoy himself.

He initially joined the strictly amateur side Midleton, who were toiling in the lower reaches of the All Ireland League. The standard was dire but Holland attracted the interest of Munster, who offered him a two-year deal worth a staggeringly low €25,000. It was peanuts – a brilliant deal for the club, especially when Holland became a first-team regular and scored a critical try in their shock semi-final win in 2000 on their way to winning the Heineken Cup for the first time. He was voted the unsung hero of the 2003 season at the Irish Players Awards.

In total Holland would play 102 games for the province and was so highly thought of he would be retained as backs coach after he retired.

## 7 Rua Tipoki to Bay of Plenty

Rua Tipoki was something of an *enfant terrible* when he reached the professional ranks in the late 1990s. He was involved in a number of incidents both on and off the field that tarred his reputation and led to him heading for a stint in Japan.

He returned in early 2004 hoping to make a fresh start – hoping that the rugby fraternity would be prepared to see he had matured. He had enrolled to study law and was playing club rugby in Hamilton. Waikato coach John Mitchell had said he'd be keen to have Tipoki in his squad but only if he could prove he was a reformed character. When Tipoki was sent off in a club match for two yellow-card offences, Mitchell dumped him, and it was only on the eve of the National Provincial Championship that the Bay of Plenty came in for the talented midfielder and took him on loan.

Tipoki was on the minimum contract despite being in his mid-20s and having Super Rugby experience. But he didn't care – he was there to prove he could still play. He was the catalyst for the Bay winning the Ranfurly Shield and then making the semi-finals for the first time. 'He was outstanding for us this year,' said Bay of Plenty coach Vern Cotter. 'Rua has matured a lot in the past couple of years. He's an intelligent man and while he might have been a little bit impulsive in his early years, he's got that well under control.'

## 6 Jarrad Hoeata to the Highlanders

Jarad Hoeata had been on the New Zealand scene for several years without ever giving the impression he was a test player in waiting. A rugged, abrasive character who played on the edge, he was mobile enough to play at blindside and big enough to be a lock. That was actually part of his problem – he was neither one nor the other, and as a result he struggled to gain a regular place in any Super Rugby squad.

When he joined the Chiefs in 2010 he hoped he was on the verge of a new beginning. But things actually got worse. He barely played, and when his big chance came, he was yellow-carded. Things got worse again when after a heavy night of drinking he jumped in his car and decided to drive to his home town in Taranaki. He veered across the centre line several times and had a brush with another car before motorists blocked him when he stopped for coffee. He was fined and banned for driving for six months, saying to the *Waikato Times* on the steps of the court: 'I was just gutted with what happened.'

The Highlanders decided they could save him and brought him to Dunedin. Hoeata was ready to be saved. He gave up drinking, took up studying and did voluntary work. He was impossible to leave out of the side – and did more than anyone to spark the Highlanders' revival. From being the easy-beats of the competition they ended the Bulls' three-year unbeaten run in Pretoria and were in the mix for a play-off spot before they faded.

It was an astonishing recovery by the Highlanders and Hoeata. His contribution was recognised when he was named in the All Blacks, winning three caps.

## 5   Sonny Parker to Pontypridd

There weren't many New Zealanders who had heard of Sonny Parker in the late 1990s. He was under the radar at that point. The 20-year-old Auckland midfielder was playing for the Marist club when the opportunity came up to play for Viadana in Italy. Parker had damaged a knee during the New Zealand season, so he was keen for the game time.

While he was in Italy the Pontypridd club in Wales were looking for a robust centre to take the ball up hard and make aggressive tackles. Wales coach Graham Henry recommended Parker, a player he knew from when he was coach of Auckland and the Blues in 1998. Pontypridd snapped him up for a salary that was believed to be in the region of £40,000 a year – crumbs by professional standards.

The style of rugby suited Parker. It was direct and physical, and he thrived. After he had been in Wales for three years he was called into the national side and made his debut in 2002. He won a total of 31 caps, played at two World Cups for his adopted country and even played against the All Blacks on several occasions.

## 4 Tony Marsh to Clermont

Clermont probably didn't realise what they were buying when they signed Tony Marsh in 1998. Marsh had been on the fringes of the New Zealand professional scene for a few years without ever establishing whether he was up to it.

He had been with the Blues in 1996 but seldom played, and the same was true when he was transferred to the Crusaders.

Clermont thought they were buying a solid midfielder who would be an excellent squad man to cover for injuries to frontline players. And because Marsh was only in his mid-20s and had been picked up cheaply, there was no real risk to the club if he turned out to be a total flop.

Marsh could hardly have played better, and after one season in France everyone in New Zealand was asking how he had been allowed to escape so easily. Hadn't anyone in New Zealand noticed how good he was? Clermont made the final of the Top 14 in 1999 and again in 2001 – with Marsh a big contributor to their success. They also won the European Challenge Cup twice.

It was in 2001 that Marsh became eligible for France, and coach Bernard Laporte didn't hesitate to pick the New Zealander. Marsh would win 21 caps, score seven tries and help them to a Grand Slam as well as to the semi-final of the 2003 World Cup. He played his last game for Clermont in 2007, recognised as one of the best players in the club's history.

## 3 Rocky Elsom to Leinster

Leinster had been the sleeping giant of European rugby for the better part of two decades. They were a constant source of disappointment in the Heineken Cup, where they were overshadowed by their fierce rivals and neighbours, Munster. There was quality and depth in the Irish side, but there was something missing – they lacked controlled aggression.

That was until they lured Wallaby flanker Rocky Elsom for the 2008–2009 season. Elsom was finally fulfilling his enormous potential as a bruising and athletic loose forward when he ran into financial difficulties. The Australian Rugby Union reluctantly granted him an early release on compassionate grounds – effectively so he could head to Dublin for a year to make some money to repay his debts. There was an obvious risk that Elsom's motivation could be suspect – that he was there for the wrong reasons.

But that wasn't the case. Elsom woke Leinster up. He gave them the edge they were missing. They were a different side and they made the breakthrough they were after when they won the Heineken Cup, hammering Munster in the semi-final then edging out Leicester in the final. Elsom was man of the match in the final.

'Rocky had quite a big impact on Irish rugby during the brief time he was playing in Ireland,' said Dennis Leamy, the Munster back-rower, at the 2011 World Cup. 'In his time at Leinster he was excellent, from what I could gather looking in. He brought on the guys around him. He's left a bit of a legacy there. Jamie [Heaslip] and Seán [O'Brien] were younger than him and he's definitely rubbed off on them. You can see the dynamism in their game, it's very similar to the way Rocky plays.'

## 2 Rupeni Caucaunibuca to Awanui

The Awanui club in Northland is not necessarily the place one would expect to find rugby gold. But it was this tiny club in the far north of New Zealand that brought Rupeni Caucaunibuca to the world's attention.

Club stalwart Glen Subritzky had a number of contacts in Fiji, and each year he would bring a few players over from the islands, give them a job in his forestry business and sign them up for Awanui. In 2001 he brought over Caucaunibuca, or Rupeni as he was better known.

It took the 21-year-old about four minutes to prove he was something special. Northland signed him, and the youngster continued to score tries and play magnificently on the wing. He helped them to a rare win over Auckland and by 2003 was picked by the Blues, who already had the likes of Doug Howlett, Rico Gear,

Joe Rokocoko and Mils Muliaina in their squad. But Rupeni was the pick of them all and he was on the wage bill at the minimum salary of $65,000.

Blues manager Ant Strachan would tell *New Zealand Rugby World* in 2011: 'I played with Jonah [Lomu] and all respect to the big man, but Rupes was better. He was incredible. I can remember one day the boys decided to have a sprint – Joe Rokocoko, Doug Howlett, Mils Muliaina and Rupeni. They were all lined up on the goal-line and Rupeni slipped. He got up and still beat them all.'

The 2003 Super 12 was all about Rupeni. He scored incredible tries to help the Blues to their first title in six years and then went to the World Cup later that year, where he scored a never-to-be-forgotten try against Scotland.

He was even better in 2004 when he scored a hat-trick against the Crusaders in a famous win in Christchurch, but the Blues couldn't keep him – they had the best wing in the world who they had found by good luck, and Rupeni left for France for almost 10 times his New Zealand wage.

## 1 Martin Johnson to Tihoi

John Albert was passionate about his Tihoi club. The King Country outfit had to perennially battle for players and Albert was always on the hunt. In 1989 he saw that an England youth side had won a tournament featuring New Zealand and Australia, so Albert wrote to the RFU to see if any of those young players fancied a stint in New Zealand.

'I still owe that lady at the RFU a bottle of wine. It wouldn't happen now, but she passed on my letter to all the players and I had something like 17 replies,' Albert told the *Daily Telegraph* in 2011. 'Five of the guys ended up in New Zealand, the first being Martin Johnson.' Tihoi had lured the man who would come back to New Zealand four years later as a British Lion, and the man who would lift the World Cup for England in 2003.

Johnson wasn't the glowering, frothing ball of aggression he would be in his later years, but he was still good enough to win selection for King Country. His skills and understanding of the game were obvious and he was a class act in the lineout.

Johnson really started to become something after the legendary Colin Meads, who was the chairman of King Country at the time, began mentoring him. 'Martin was a quiet, nice young fella. They gave him a bit of a King Country barracking. He changed from being a soft Pom, and then he developed. There's nothing surer than he would have been an All Black,' Meads told the *Telegraph*.

Tihoi enjoyed two of their best years when Johnson was around – and he was good enough to win selection for the New Zealand Colts before deciding to head home to England.

# 10 acts of defiance

### 10 Johnson and the red carpet

England came to Dublin for the last game of the 2003 Six Nations and, amazingly, both teams could still win a Grand Slam. Having blown last-day opportunities on three previous occasions, England were anxious not to stuff up again, while the Irish were in an emotional frenzy at still being undefeated.

England captain Martin Johnson led his team out and lined them to the right of the tunnel for the national anthems. Unbeknown to Johnson, protocol was the home team went to that side, and the Irish were agitated. An official was sent to ask Johnson to move his team.

'If Jonathan Kaplan, the referee, had said "shuffle up", we would have moved,' recalls Johnson. 'I wouldn't have thought anything about it. But a guy came out of nowhere to move us and it felt like it was just some random official, so I said, "Don't tell us to do anything, pal."

'And then, bang, it became such a huge stand-off and I was thinking, "Now what have we got ourselves into?" It was never pre-planned, never intended.'

The crowd jeered as Johnson refused to move, standing staunchly, and the Irish decided to take their stance to the right of the tunnel as they were supposed to, but much further down the field.

That meant that Irish President Mary McAleese was introduced to the Irish team on the mud of Lansdowne Road rather than the red carpet that had been put down.

'President McAleese walked on to the red carpet in front of us,' says Johnson. 'I never made President McAleese stand on the grass. If the Ireland boys had stayed where they were to the right, then she would have been on the red carpet for them, too.'

## 9　Feeling a bit twitchy

As protests go the Scots came up with a quirky show of solidarity for their suspended team-mate Martin Leslie. The New Zealand-born flanker had copped a 12-week ban in the second game of the 2003 World Cup for kneeing USA player Jason Keyter.

The punishment was unusually harsh and the Scots were angry they couldn't get it overruled or at least reduced on appeal. They decided, as a mark of respect for their team-mate, who suffered from a severe twitch, that they would conduct a 'team twitch' during the playing of the national anthem before their next clash against France. As the camera panned down the assembled Scots, one by one they would flick their heads in the most bizarre and violent motion.

Flanker Cameron Mather would reveal after the game: 'It wasn't a protest, it was a tribute. I thought it was a good, fitting tribute to Marty. I think the crowd enjoyed it. I think the most unimpressed person was Martin Leslie. I don't think it distracted the players at all.'

## 8　Using the head

The French nuclear testing programme in the Pacific was, unsurprisingly, not well received in New Zealand. It particularly troubled All Black flanker Josh Kronfeld, who decided to conduct his own protest at events by customising his distinctive scrum-cap.

Kronfeld wrote the words 'No Nukes' on his cap and 'Stop Testing'. All Black officials weren't terribly keen on players using their profile to promote moral and political campaigns, however worthy, or however much public support they had.

So he was banned from wearing his doctored cap when the All Blacks toured France later that year. He did manage one last protest by writing an open letter to President Chirac before the All Blacks headed to France. Kronfeld was also quoted on the tour as saying: 'We keep ruining this world at a pretty fast rate. I am keen to do everything I can to ensure that all children have the chance to get the same enjoyment out of life. We are heading in a downward spiral in this world and it's not wrong for someone to say: "Hey, this isn't quite right." '

## 7 The Murrayfield walk

Scotland versus England is always emotionally charged as it is. In 1990 it was supercharged as both countries came to the Murrayfield encounter undefeated. It was winner takes all, made even more intense by the fact many of the Scots players held their English counterparts in contempt. There was personal animosity as well as a wider political backdrop – protests had broken out all over Scotland at the London-based Government's introduction of the poll tax, initially to be trialled in Scotland alone.

The Scots were very much the underdogs and knew they would have to muster all their pent-up fury to have a chance. They knew their best weapon was to psychologically hammer England any way they could; to make Murrayfield a cauldron of hate and venom to unsettle their old foe.

'For more than a week everyone talked about how England were going to pick up their first Grand Slam for 10 years,' said Scotland captain David Sole. 'I was sitting in the bath wondering what we could do that would be a bit different. That was when the idea hit me about the slow walk.'

It was a genius idea. Instead of running out of the tunnel as was the custom, a steely-eyed Sole walked slowly and deliberately onto the field in the most defiant means imaginable.

'We were saying to England: "If you want the Grand Slam, you've got to get past 15 determined, bloody-minded blokes and we're going to do things on our terms, not yours." The longer we kept walking, the more the crowd lifted the roof off the stand.' The mood was set and the Scots – rank outsiders – won the game 13–7.

## 6 Mum's the word

In August 2006 All Black coach Graham Henry hatched a plan to rest 22 chosen players from the first seven weeks of the 2007

Super 14. Henry was paranoid about his players burning out in World Cup year, so he wanted them to have an extended period where they could train and condition without having to play. The 22 players he wanted to withdraw were the best in the country – the list included the likes of Richie McCaw, Dan Carter, Carl Hayman and Mils Muliaina.

The NZRU approved the plan, but did so before it had informed any of its key commercial partners. The union kept News International – the broadcast group that had pumped more than $400 million into the game – in the dark about its plans. It was a deliberate snub and damaged the relationship, but the NZRU wasn't going to be denied.

News International was incensed, and after crisis talks warned the New Zealanders that if there was a decrease in viewing figures they would seek compensation. But the NZRU was not going to be intimidated. 'Our advice is, from a legal perspective, obtained by SANZAR and by the NZRU independently, is that we're fully entitled to do what we've announced,' NZRU chief executive Chris Moller told the *New Zealand Herald*.

'The players can't go smashing their bodies in the game as we know it today, without some time away from it.' The 22 players were indeed withdrawn, a move that would backfire when the All Blacks bombed at the World Cup, and then fan interest in the game sharply declined in 2008.

## 5 Eyeing the haka

A rampant All Black team toured Wales and Ireland in 1989 and were in no mood to surrender an unbeaten record that stretched back to 1987. The Irish knew they were in for a battle of epic proportions when it came to the test at Lansdowne Road. Captain Willie Anderson knew that his side had to do what they could to gain an advantage, and he struck on the novel idea of facing down the haka in the most defiant way.

Back then there was no protocol on what teams had to do during the haka – there was no requirement to stay 10 metres back, as there is now. That was an opportunity reckoned Anderson. 'I sat down with [coach] Jimmy Davidson and we looked at how the haka would get applause for the away team rather than the home team,' he says. 'So we wanted to turn that psychology around.'

They did that by linking arms and then advancing towards the haka once it was under way. It was incredible theatre – the mad-eyed Anderson screaming like a dervish, urging his team to continue on their march. As the haka came to its conclusion, Anderson was almost nose to nose with All Black captain Buck Shelford.

'It wasn't meant to be in any way disrespectful,' said Anderson. 'Then we ended up very close, eyeball to eyeball, and obviously not everybody in the Irish team, depending on their personality, was totally in line with it. The feeling that I had on the day was that you could have cut chunks from the atmosphere. People have said to me down the years, "What a game, what an atmosphere; the hairs on the back of our neck were standing. It meant so much for us to be involved as an audience." '

## 4  The Hamilton sit-in

The 1981 Springbok tour of New Zealand divided the host country. There were those who were angry that it was allowed to take place while South Africa pursued its apartheid policy; and there were those who felt sport and politics should never mix. Households were divided, neighbours ended up being at war with neighbours, and the mood was volatile and occasionally violent.

Throughout the tour there were protests – march down the street with banners protests – and guerilla-style attempts to impact upon the ability of games to be played.

On 25 July several hundred protesters were able to storm the field in Hamilton ahead of the Boks' game against Waikato and take up residence in the middle of Rugby Park. There was a full house of about 30,000 who were angry at the invasion, and the atmosphere was nasty. The crowd had paid and wanted to see a game. The heavily outnumbered protesters stayed staunch and wouldn't be moved by the police.

On the 25th anniversary of the tour, 1981 Springbok captain Wynand Claasen would tell the *New Zealand Herald*: 'That whole debacle with the Waikato game, that really was quite frightening, very intense. We didn't know if the tour was going to carry on, then the [police] red squad came in – it was like war. The scary part was in the changing room standing on a bench looking out the back window.

'A whole bunch of demonstrators came out the back of the pavilion and overturned one of the those big trailers, we realised they wanted to come in and have a go at us. There were a few policemen that held them out.'

The protesters would eventually win – the game was called off.

### 3  Strike while the iron is hot

Unable to obtain the pay deal they were after, England's international squad shocked the world when they went on strike just 72 hours before they were due to play Argentina in November 2000.

The decision was made after weeks of negotiating had failed to deliver the outcome the players wanted. They were holding out for more money, and when it wouldn't come they went on strike – refusing to train or to play against Argentina if the matter wasn't resolved. They had made their threat on a Monday night and were warned that they had until 11am on the Wednesday to make themselves available or an alternate squad would be called in to take their place.

That didn't scare them. Leading coach Clive Woodward had this to say: 'This is the saddest day in the history of English rugby. I feel badly let down by players I have done so much for in the last couple of years.'

Captain Martin Johnson wasn't going to budge: 'It's not just an issue about money. It's the principle, the way the RFU have handled the situation. They are affecting the guys' livelihoods on a matter of principle.'

The situation was unresolved until one hour before the deadline, when Johnson and RFU chief executive Francis Baron emerged from Twickenham to announce a deal had been agreed and the strike was off. 'We're happy with our deal and we're now going off to train in preparation for Saturday,' said Johnson.

## 2  French boycott

In April 2007 the French professional clubs showed how powerful and defiant they could be when they announced they would be boycotting the 2008 Heineken Cup. Europe's premier cross-border competition was the jewel in the northern hemisphere crown, with enormous revenues attached. Pulling out would significantly damage the finances of the leading clubs, but the French were angry that the RFU was refusing to hand over a 50 per cent shareholding in the tournament to Premier Rugby, the umbrella body in charge of professional clubs in England.

The French and English clubs were the big players and they wanted control of the Heineken Cup, which couldn't happen if the RFU retained its shareholding and attached voting rights. The English clubs immediately made the same threat after the French had announced their plans, and the danger was that nearly every major club in Europe would be negatively impacted by the boycott.

Such was the outrage that even IRB chairman Syd Millar waded into the debate: 'The decision by the French and English clubs to withdraw from the European Rugby Cup has been described as regrettable, unfortunate and shameful. It is more than that. It is absolutely disgraceful and selfish to destroy a tournament which has developed into a hugely successful and special annual rugby event that is vital to the well-being of European Rugby.'

The threat brought a round of fierce negotiations that eventually led to a compromise deal where the French clubs were appeased by reassurances that the RFU would be conscious of any changes that would result in yet more congestion to the French domestic calendar.

# 1 Roundheads and cavaliers

The All Blacks had a long and treasured rivalry with the Springboks and the two sides had skirted controversy over the years to play each other. The New Zealanders had been prepared to leave Maori players at home to satisfy South Africa's apartheid laws, while the decision to host the Boks in 1981 was one that almost created a civil war.

When the New Zealand Rugby Union received an invitation for the All Blacks to tour South Africa in 1985 they rejected it on legal grounds. It was agreed that if they accepted they would be breaking their own mandate to foster and promote the game. But the South Africans, in sporting isolation during this period, then issued secret invitations to the players who would have toured with the All Blacks. Supposedly payments of $100,000 were used as enticement, and 28 of the 30 All Blacks agreed to play the following April as part of a team known as the Cavaliers.

They were warned by the NZRU that if they went they would face serious consequences, but only three men – David Kirk, Bruce Hemara and a young John Kirwan – decided not to go.

The headmaster of Auckland Grammar School, John Graham, himself a former All Black, wrote to the NZRU demanding the players be banned for life, and accused them of betrayal. The *New Zealand Herald* accused the players in an editorial of 'selfish irresponsibility', while Frank van der Horst, the president of the South African Council on Sport, an anti-apartheid body, called them: 'Sporting prostitutes ... they are not coming here to enhance sport, they are coming here to debase humanity.'

Kirk, a Rhodes Scholar who would captain the All Blacks to World Cup glory in 1987, would say more than 20 years later that it wasn't an easy decision to turn down the offer. 'Because the 1985 tour had been cancelled at the last minute, I think there was a sense of solidarity within the squad, a sense of "let's go to South Africa". But the reality was that sporting contacts with an apartheid regime weren't a good idea, particularly as it was a rebel tour. We wouldn't be representing anything or anyone, and there was the stench of money underneath the table.'

# 10 great individual comebacks

## 10 Matt Stevens (England)

South African-born Matt Stevens had everything in 2009. He was an England regular and still only 28. He loved playing for his club, Bath, had already won 32 test caps, and was also able to indulge in his other passion – singing.

Stevens was a finalist on the hit TV show *The X-Factor: The Battle of the Stars* in 2006 and had earned fame as a musician. But it was dabbling in this other life of entertainer/celebrity that Stevens developed a recreational drug habit. He became addicted to cocaine, a substance for which he tested positive in April 2009. That earned him a two-year ban that seemed likely to end his career.

But after his ban he decided he wasn't ready for the scrapheap and he trained himself into prime condition to persuade Saracens to sign him. He repaid their faith with some high-quality performances that earned him an England recall.

Amazingly, he made the World Cup squad, telling the BBC: 'For me and my family it is an amazing story and one I'm very happy turned out well. I know what a special, amazing feeling it is to play for England. I know how important it is to me.'

## 9 David Bishop (Wales)

David Bishop was a man seemingly capable of overcoming any amount of adversity. His first obstacle was a three-year prison sentence. At just 17 Bishop had already made his senior club debut at scrum-half, but his career came to a grinding halt after a violent incident in Cardiff city centre.

A lesser man would have given up all hope of playing test rugby at that point, but not Bishop. On his release he was picked up by Pontypool. He was man of the match when Pooler beat Australia two weeks after he joined. In a twist of fate too cruel to believe, he broke his neck seven games later and was told he might never play again. He was back on the field within eight months, having defied all medical expectations.

The crowning moment of his career came in 1984 when he was called up to the Welsh squad and then picked to play against the Wallabies. Wales lost 27–9, but Bishop scored the only try and was in fact the only man from the Home Unions to complete that feat against the all-conquering Wallabies.

He decided to play league in 1988. 'Before I went north to join Hull KR in October 1988, I was not only the best Welsh scrum half, I was the world's best,' claimed Bishop a few years later. 'Australia's Nick Farr-Jones and Richard Hill of England agreed with me, but rugby's hierarchy were not having me and they broke my heart and I switched codes for £120,000.'

## 8  Alan Tait (Scotland)

When Alan Tait left rugby union to play league in 1988 no one expected him to come back. It would have been getting into the realms of lunacy to believe that he would be able to spend nine seasons playing league and then return to rugby at 32 and become a British Lion at 33. Somehow Tait managed to do exactly that.

He was 23 when he joined Widnes after winning a handful of caps for Scotland in the midfield and, unlike many others who defected to the 13-man game, Tait was an instant success. But when rugby turned professional, he decided he wanted to pick up where he'd left off in 1988 and he joined Newcastle.

Would he have anything left? Would he be able to pick up a game that was vastly different from the one he had known in 1988 and vastly different from the one he had spent the past nine seasons playing?

The answer was an emphatic yes. Tait returned to rugby a tougher player – a better defender, and a supreme attacker. He was a shoo-in for Scotland, and when he effortlessly slipped back into the test arena, he became impossible for the British and Irish Lions to ignore.

Tait's comeback had one more twist. He would play in the tests – as a wing – despite making the Lions squad as a centre. His inclusion was the major selection surprise, but coach Ian McGeechan had no doubt it was the right call: 'He provides more diversity. He can cover the three back positions soundly as well as offering an attacking threat in the midfield.'

Tait was an inspired choice for the Lions and he continued to perform for Scotland, ending his career in 1999 with 27 test caps and a staggering 17 tries.

### 7  Os du Randt (South Africa)

Os du Randt's career was bookended with respective World Cup medals in 1995 and 2007. The amazing thing is that there was a three-year period between 2000 and 2003 when he didn't play.

Having been ever-present in the 1995 Springbok team, du Randt became recognised as a notable scrummager but an even better player in the loose. He was on his way to becoming a Springbok great when he was struck down by injury in 2000. He damaged a knee that just couldn't be fixed. After nearly three years of rehabilitation, du Randt called it quits – he officially retired and gave up all hope of playing again.

But at the end of 2003 former Springbok team-mate Rassie Erasmus, who was coaching Orange Free State, wanted du Randt to give rugby a go again. The big man was reluctant but he tentatively returned and played through the pain. He played so well that by June 2004 Springbok coach Jake White recalled du Randt to the national squad.

'When I returned to rugby in 2003, it was to play for Free State and Free State alone,' du Randt said. 'I didn't think I would wear the Springbok shirt again, ever in my life. When Jake White gave me the opportunity to play for my country once more, it felt like the first time all over again.'

Du Randt became the rock on which the Boks' second World Cup triumph was built. He was 34 but never gave any indication he was too old. He was an 80-minute man, gave the Boks' scrum an edge and he even ran around the field with good effect.

When he did finally retire for good, his team-mate CJ van der Linde said: 'Os is a legend in South African rugby. Even little children know who he is. His name will be mentioned for many years still.'

## 6 Brad Thorn (New Zealand)

When the Crusaders announced in 2008 they had signed 33-year-old Brad Thorn, there was consensus reached that coach Robbie Deans had gone mad. Why was he signing a veteran who had spent the past four years in the NRL and who, prior to that, had only ever been a moderate rugby talent between 2001 and 2004?

It seemed crazy. Thorn had been a sensational league player with the Broncos, having broken into their first team at 17. He left the NRL to have a crack at being an All Black in 2001, which he managed to do in 2003, but was cast adrift the following year when new coach Graham Henry didn't pick him. Thorn was back at the Broncos and surely that was the end of his dalliance with rugby?

Not so. Despite his age and time away from the game, Thorn was not only the best lock in New Zealand in 2008, he was probably the best in Super Rugby. His inclusion in the All Blacks was a formality, and incredibly he would go on to win 60 caps and establish himself as one of the best tight forwards in the world game.

He played three huge games in the knockout rounds of the World Cup in 2011 and retired from test football a universally acknowledged legend of the game.

'It's crazy – I have used that word so many times – but that's what it is,' Thorn told the *New Zealand Herald* when asked about the time between 2008 and 2011. 'I didn't expect it and I'm thoroughly enjoying it.'

## 5 Steve Thompson (England)

Steve Thompson was a beast of a man in his prime and an important part of the England team that won the 2003 World Cup. The bruising 25-year-old was a storming force in the middle of the front row and no one enjoyed playing against him. But he lost his potency after the success of 2003 and began a slow decline after the tournament. As he would reveal: 'I lost that fire in my belly. I didn't want to train any more and I was cutting corners, and that's when I lost my edge.'

It is also when he became prone to injury, and in January 2007 he damaged his spine, announcing his retirement a few months later when he was just 29. He took up a coaching position with the French club Brive, and by the middle of 2008 he began to wonder whether his diagnosis could have been premature. He sought more medical opinions, and the new advice was that he could resume playing. He had to repay the £500,000 insurance payout, and he had an enormous amount of work to do as he had ballooned to 138 kg.

'I trained as hard as I ever trained for three months to come back,' he said. He ended up fitter and faster than before and he earned an England recall in 2009, playing in another World Cup in 2011.

'I'm a lot more relaxed now, it's the second chance, you know? Everything is a bonus, and I'm playing better for it,' he said when he won back his England place.

## 4 Eric Peters (Scotland)

A rangy No 8 who became an integral player in the Scottish and Bath teams of the mid 1990s, Eric Peters encountered some ferocious bad luck. He had captained Scotland in 1999 and appeared, at 30, to be destined to enjoy a glittering closing chapter of an already successful career.

That was until he shattered his kneecap in eight places while playing for Bath. As he was progressing through what would be a year of painful rehabilitation, he felt a pain in his scrotum which turned out to be testicular cancer.

To compound matters, his marriage broke up and he was

at rock bottom. 'My life was in a bit of turmoil at the time and it was worrying,' Peters told the *Scotsman*. He wasn't going to be defeated. It would take him almost three years to overcome the associated problems he encountered. 'The desire to get back and play for Scotland was very much a driving force,' he said. 'My immune system was badly hit and I got an infection in my knee and had to have it washed out. That put me back six months. When I got to play with Harlequins, I made seven or eight games before something snapped in my knee again, and it took another year to get back to anything near full fitness.'

But he did get there, and at 34 years of age he was recalled to the Scotland team in 2002 and added to his tally of 29 test caps.

### 3 Jonah Lomu (New Zealand)

No one who saw Jonah Lomu in full flight at the 1995 World Cup will ever forget it. He was 120 kg of raw power smashing his way through everything. He was just 20 and probably as fit as he'd ever be. That was the tragedy of Lomu – only three years later he was diagnosed with nephrotic syndrome, a deadly disease that until 2003 he was able to manage with a drug regime.

Incredibly, Lomu managed to play test rugby between 1998 and 2002 until he required a kidney transplant in 2004. What was even more incredible is that he was able to play professional rugby after the operation.

At the end of 2003 Lomu cut a heartbreakingly sad figure. He was retaining water and couldn't walk because he couldn't stand the pressure on his feet. He was seriously ill. And yet in 2006 he played for Cardiff in the Celtic League and while he was clearly not the player of old, he was still good enough to play 10 games and set up countless tries, though he scored just one try himself. His stint came to an end after he broke his ankle.

'It was evident on Saturday how much progress Jonah has continued to make over the past six months and it's sad that he will not play again this season for Cardiff Blues,' announced coach Bob Norster. 'Since his arrival in mid-November, we have all been hugely impressed with the sheer determination Jonah has shown to get back to playing top-level rugby.'

## 2  Mario Ledesma (Argentina)

There was little chance of Argentinean hooker Mario Ledesma ever playing in a third World Cup, let alone a fourth. The loveable hooker had been with the Pumas in 1999 and 2003 but was diagnosed with a heart defect in 2005.

It didn't seem like there would be any way back, especially when he was initially told he'd need to have a transplant. On further examination the specialist concluded Ledesma could potentially be fixed with complex surgery, but even if it succeeded he was unlikely to be able to play again. Ledesma didn't hear the last bit – he just heard that his condition could be fixed, and he was back in his beloved Argentinean No 2 shirt in time for the 2007 World Cup. He held on until 2011, playing his fourth tournament at the tender age of 38.

'I never imagined playing to this age,' he told *New Zealand Rugby World* on the eve of the 2011 tournament. 'I underwent some tests that turned out to be very negative. So the heart specialist admitted me to hospital for an angioplasty.

'I felt like I was dying because I was sharing my room with old people who were at the end of their life and the cardiologist also told me at first that I needed a transplant. In the end, he changed his diagnosis.'

## 1  Greg Cooper (New Zealand)

A promising fullback who was on the verge of his Hawke's Bay school's First XV as a 15-year-old, Greg Cooper developed a searing pain in his shoulder while on a family holiday. He was taken to hospital and told he had an inoperable sarcoma. His parents were advised to prepare for the worst – Cooper had maybe six months to live.

When his mum told him the news he burst into tears, looked her in the eye and said: 'I'm not going to die. I'm going to be an

All Black.' He would endure more than two years of radiotherapy and chemotherapy, where his weight would plummet and he would spend night after night on the couch, vomiting. To keep his strength up he would pump iron, envisaging himself making his All Black debut and singing the national anthem.

Amazingly, after all the treatment – and despite being given only a 10 per cent chance of living – Cooper's condition improved. He threw himself into his rugby and in 1986 he was selected to play for the All Blacks, where he scored eight points on debut.

'When I ran out against France it almost felt strange,' he said. 'It was almost as if I had been there before, because the dream had been so vivid. I was on a complete high. I couldn't do anything wrong. Not that I thought it at the time, but maybe I did say to myself, "Now it's over." '

# 10 best team comebacks

## 10 Ireland 29–40 New Zealand, 2001

The fact Ireland have never beaten the All Blacks is not something that escapes the attention of either team. In November 2001 Ireland could sense they had about as good a chance as they were ever likely to have to amend that sobering statistic.

New Zealand had been thrown into a flux when coach Wayne Smith had suddenly resigned after the Tri Nations in August, only to change his mind, re-apply, but miss out to the inexperienced John Mitchell. The Irish test was the new coach's first game in charge and he had already made his mark by selecting the unknown and uncapped 20-year-old Richie McCaw at flanker and his Canterbury team-mate Aaron Mauger at inside centre.

The Irish swarmed the All Blacks and came up with some inventive and clever touches with the ball to lead 21–7 at the break. The All Blacks, disjointed and unable to impose themselves, looked to be in real trouble when Irish wing Denis Hickie crossed early in the second half to make the score 26–7.

But the All Blacks resisted the urge to panic. They held the ball for longer and their composure returned. The Irish wilted and before anyone realised, the All Blacks were in fifth gear. Jonah Lomu, a peripheral figure in the first 40 minutes, was involved in everything and in the final half hour the All Blacks scored five tries to win 40–29.

'Lomu is just devastating,' said Irish centre Brian O'Driscoll. 'Australia have targeted him in recent years, kicking high balls to him and trying to make him turn. I guess he does have some weaknesses, but going forward with the ball in hand he is just something else.'

## 9 England 19–26 Wales, 2008

Wales were hopeful rather than confident that the arrival of Warren Gatland as head coach was going to lead them to a brighter future. They had been dumped out of the 2007 World Cup in the pool stage, leading them to axe Gareth Jenkins and bring in Gatland.

A Six Nations test at Twickenham was a tough opening assignment and Wales appeared to be overawed by the occasion. They drifted through the first half, while England were organised and constructive – and slowly turning the screw. Jonny Wilkinson was kicking the penalties and Jamie Noon carved through to make the score 19–6 with half an hour remaining.

That was enough for Wales to wake up and suddenly remember the game-plan and that they could play. James Hook pulled the strings at fly-half and had the Welsh playing with width and tempo. He also kicked his goals, then created a brilliant try for fullback Lee Byrne, who drew the scores level. The draw was looming until halfback Mike Phillips scorched across the turf and charged down Iain Balshaw's clearing kick to secure a famous win.

'I was confident because we didn't do much in the first half, it was all England and we allowed them to have the ball,' said centre Gavin Henson. 'We hadn't played any rugby but we still had a sniff at half-time. We tend to make it hard for ourselves, but Twickenham is a difficult place to come. It was a big feat we achieved out there and it will give us confidence for the rest of the campaign.'

## 8 Waratahs 29–39 Stormers, 2003

South African teams have notoriously bad away records in Super Rugby. They rarely win in Australasia, and there seemed little prospect of the Stormers coming away from Sydney with anything after they leaked three tries in the first seven minutes. Even by South African standards it was an appalling start, and the statisticians were immediately reaching for the history books to keep an eye on record losses.

But the Stormers somehow managed to find the plug and stop

the leak. Inspired by their enigmatic and belligerent captain Corné Krige, they clawed their way back. At 24–10 at half-time the picture was still bleak, but at least the damage hadn't gotten out of hand. Six minutes into the second half and everything changed. And it changed when, bizarrely, the Stormers were fighting the most severe injury crises that forced them to empty their bench and play with men out of position and some barely able to move because of various leg knocks.

Halfback Neil de Kock went the length of the field to score an unforgettable try and then three more tries followed to cancel out the one scored by Lote Tuqiri. With eight minutes remaining it was 29–all. A try by Stormers wing Egon Seconds clinched it for the visitors in what was one of their proudest victories.

## 7 Scotland 28–28 Wales, 2001

Scotland pulled off one of the greatest comebacks in their history to draw with Wales in 2001, yet felt nothing but frustration that they had failed to win the game. At the core of their annoyance was the fact they had been abysmal in the first half and had allowed themselves to fall 26–6 behind, despite Wales playing little rugby.

Welsh fly-half Neil Jenkins dropped a goal after 46 seconds, dropped two more, then slotted three penalties as the Scots kept needlessly infringing. Meanwhile at the other end of the park, Scottish kicker Kenny Logan couldn't hit a barn door, pushing three kickable penalties wide.

At 18–6 down early in the second half, Scotland had to chase the game, which saw inside centre John Leslie throw a wild pass intercepted by his opposite Mark Taylor, who scored under the sticks.

Half an hour left and Scotland trailed 25–6. But their luck turned. They found space out wide and were suddenly running into huge holes. Burly centre James McLaren scored almost under the posts – Logan missed the simple conversion – to leave Scotland 28–21 down with six minutes to play.

Prop Tom Smith then pulled off the unthinkable. He threw an

outrageous dummy and exploded through the Welsh defence to score from a 40-metre run with a minute left.

Duncan Hodge, who had taken over the kicking duties, nailed the tough conversion to secure the draw. 'It was a point lost,' fumed Scotland coach Ian McGeechan. 'The first half was terrible but it was a super performance in the second. After the first half I felt we just needed to cut out the mistakes. We were getting behind Wales, but we just needed to hold on to the ball.'

## 6 England 32–31 Australia, 2002

England had decided to play New Zealand, Australia and South Africa in consecutive weeks in the autumn of 2002. It was a tough challenge but one they wanted to take on ahead of the 2003 World Cup.

They had defeated a weakened All Black side the previous week and were desperate to follow it up against a full-strength Wallaby outfit. But they were finding it hard to cope with the pace and intensity of the Australians, who scored two stunning second-half tries through Elton Flatley and Wendell Sailor.

England couldn't rely on penalties to claw back the 31–19 deficit they faced with 20 minutes remaining, so had to trust their skills with ball in hand. Captain Martin Johnson ordered a major push in the final quarter for the team to go on the all-out attack and test the Wallaby defence. They stretched the Australians to the point where they had to infringe to prevent England from breaking them. Jonny Wilkinson kicked two penalties, and as the clock reached the 80-minute mark the England first-five slipped the neatest pass to the steaming Ben Cohen, who was able to crash over for a dramatic try.

Wilkinson nailed the conversion – as he always did – and England had set themselves up mentally to win the World Cup.

## 5 Leinster 32–22 Northampton, 2011

Leinster were in danger of slipping out of the Heineken Cup final without anyone knowing they had even been there. The normally imposing and creative Irish side had offered nothing in the first 40 minutes, which is why they found themselves 22–6 behind to Northampton. That was a lot of ground to make up against a quality side full of international players who were in form and full of confidence given the start they had enjoyed.

At half-time, though, a switch was flicked in the Leinster changing room. They decided to throw everything into the next 40 minutes. Fly-half Johnny Sexton was no longer the passenger he had been and was running the show, putting runners into space and tormenting the Saints' defence. He would score tries himself in a total haul of 28 points. The second-half blitz was remarkable – the Irish scoring 27 unanswered points as they ran riot to collect their second title in three years.

Leinster centre Brian O'Driscoll told the *Daily Mail*: 'We had some choice words at half-time, Sexton was phenomenal in the dressing room, he was a man possessed, he was inspirational in the break. We knew we had it in us. The second-half performance was immense.'

## 4  South Africa 24–23 New Zealand, 1998

The All Blacks have a long and treasured history of being precisely the sort of team capable of building a major lead and defending it if needs be. So when they led 23–5 with 20 minutes to go of their 1998 Tri Nations clash with South Africa, they couldn't lose. But 1998 was not a normal year.

The All Blacks had lost their previous four tests – their worst run since 1949 – and were struggling to cope with the unexpected loss of former legends Sean Fitzpatrick, Zinzan Brooke and Frank Bunce. If it hadn't been for bad luck, that uncharacteristic string of defeats might have been broken. At 23–5 and with the Boks strangely quiet, even though they were at home in Durban, the All Blacks had built a lead that all but guaranteed they wouldn't lose a fifth.

That was until Joost van der Westhuizen made a typically strong break and scampered over for a try in the 68th minute. Somehow this one score scrambled All Black minds and sent a surge of hope through the Boks. Bobby Skinstad scored another four minutes later to put the Boks four points behind with a few minutes remaining.

The All Blacks were panicking and conceded a penalty in the last minute which the Boks kicked for the corner. The driving maul was set up after a clean take and James Dalton was carried over, although there is considerable debate as to whether he actually touched down. The record books show he did and the Springboks had pulled off one of the great comebacks.

## 3   South Africa 22–29 New Zealand, 2010

A resurgent South Africa were just three minutes away from ending the All Blacks unbeaten 14-test run. The Springboks had been at their best – physically imposing and aggressive – in their final Tri Nations encounter of 2010. Playing in Soweto for the first time, they were being carried by the most passionate 93,000-strong crowd and by the emotional boost that came from knowing it was also captain John Smit's 100th test.

All Black sides of the recent past hadn't been so good at escaping from situations like this – they were prone to feeling the pressure and making poor decisions. But as they would prove the following year when they won the World Cup, this All Black team was made of sterner mental stuff.

From a scrum 10 metres outside the Bok 22, the All Blacks kept the ball through 11 phases to give Richie McCaw an outside chance wide on the right. The captain barged through three tackles and was adjudged by the TMO to have grounded fairly.

When Carter missed the conversion and the Boks collected the restart, they had two minutes to set up for a drop goal and win the game. But they didn't commit enough bodies to a breakdown and were counter-rucked off the ball. The All Blacks shipped it to Ma'a Nonu who beat Smit on the outside before firing a long pass to the flying Israel Dagg, who scored as the hooter went.

'I can't think I've ever been more disappointed – to lose your hundredth test with a missed tackle at the death and watch a try being scored. It is going to hurt for a very long time,' Smit said.

## 2 Fiji 41–38 Tonga, 2010

The Pacific Nations Cup is a recent addition to the rugby calendar but the participants – particularly the three Pacific island nations of Fiji, Samoa and Tonga – play with an historic dislike of one another. It is full-blooded stuff, with the rivalries as intense as any in the rugby world.

Fiji were understandably a little distraught then to fall 28–0 down to Tonga in as many minutes in the 2010 tournament. This was bad. They were staring down the barrel of a record loss as Tonga were able to score at will.

A converted try and penalty before the break left the Fijians with some hope at 28–10 behind, but it still felt an awful long way back to parity. They obviously didn't see it that way. They went ballistic in the second half, scoring five tries to win 41–38.

Captain Dominiko Waqaniburotu told the Fijian media: 'We knew Tonga would close the ball from going wide, so we just revolved play from the fringes of the ruck and opened it from there. The win proves our bond as a team and working towards a common goal to be able to fight back like that, so we dedicate the win to the team and our fans.'

## 1 Wales 31–24 Scotland, 2010

Maybe more than any other nation, Scotland know how to pluck defeat from the jaws of victory. How they lost to Wales in 2010 will remain a source of angst for years to come.

They were leading their Six Nations encounter 24–14 with three minutes remaining. Yet instead of claiming their first victory at Cardiff since 2002, they were in a state of shock wondering how they had managed to lose 31–24.

Injuries, fatigue and pressure left them with players out of position and one man – hooker Scott Lawson – in the sin-bin. That left them vulnerable, and Wales managed to score in the seventy-seventh minute when Leigh Halfpenny was worked free on the right wing and Stephen Jones struck a glorious conversion. Still, even then…

But Wales were able to collect the restart and hold the ball long enough for Lee Byrne to chip ahead. Referee George Clancy said he was tripped by Phil Godman and awarded a penalty and yellow card to the Scots defender. It was a harsh call but Clancy wasn't going to change his mind. Welsh skipper Ryan Jones asked Stephen Jones to go for goal – which he successfully did to level the scores. 'I put my balls on the line with that call,' said the captain. 'You live or die by decisions like that.'

Scotland coach Andy Robinson sent a message to put the kick-off straight out as time was up, but Mike Blair was told by his captain to keep it in – which he did. Unbelievably Shane Williams would score a try a minute later. 'I've never felt like this after any game I've ever been involved with,' said Robinson. 'International rugby is a ruthless business. The last 10 minutes were sheer madness. We committed suicide.'

# PART 2

# The Worst

---

## 10 worst individual performances

---

**10 Scott Hastings,** Scotland v New Zealand, 1993

Scott Hastings was a double British Lion and, for a time, Scotland's most capped player. His performances in the Scotland shirt were normally outstanding. That was when he was wearing the No 13 shirt.

Strangely, he was asked to wear the No 11 shirt for one day – against the All Blacks – and was sadly exposed for being horribly out of his depth, what with having never played on the wing before.

The All Blacks are not usually the best team to make experimental selections against, given their propensity to be both excellent and ruthless.

To no one's great surprise Hastings was at fault most of the game. He was out of position every time the All Blacks attacked, and his opposite on the right wing – the 19-year-old Jeff Wilson – enjoyed the most fantastic debut, scoring a hat-trick.

The *Independent* in the UK wrote of Hastings: 'He betrayed his inexperience of wing play a couple of times. On both occasions Wilson scored, his first the result of Bunce's craftily weighted pass which he threaded through Hastings' flapping arms, the second when he accelerated on to John Timu's grubber kick behind the defence.'

### 9  Matthew Tait, England v Wales, 2005

Matthew Tait was an unlikely saviour and maybe always destined to end up having a horror debut. At just 18 years old he was selected to play for England against Wales in the opening game of the 2005 Six Nations.

He had pace, elusive running and obvious handling skills, but against that he was small, light, under-powered and barely out of school.

A Six Nations test in Cardiff is a tough enough place for a seasoned professional to make their international debut. It was an impossible place for a hugely inexperienced teenager to make his.

Tait had a nightmare. The Welsh saw him as an obvious target and sent Gavin Henson and Tom Shanklin charging into the middle of the park to see what damage they could inflict. Paul Ackford of the *Sunday Telegraph* wrote of the game, which Wales won 11–9: 'It was almost embarrassing to see how Wales coped with an impossibly callow English midfield. The gulf in class there wasn't entirely the story of the game, but it was almost. Noon and Tait were obvious targets for coach Mike Ruddock's side. Shanklin and Henson ran at them all game and in so doing demonstrated how unforgiving international sport can be.'

Tait was subbed in the second half shortly after Henson had picked him up and driven him 15 metres down the field. It was some time before Tait was seen again in England colours but he remained philosophical about his debut. 'Since I've started playing international rugby, I've been through a few ups and downs, but I'm from the "if it doesn't kill you, it makes you stronger" school,' he told Ackford in 2008.

## 8  Sione Lauaki, New Zealand v Australia, 2008

It's rare indeed for individual All Blacks to have absolute shockers. This is the team, after all, with the best win ratio in any code. They don't pick duff players and they don't show much sympathy to anyone who doesn't play well.

Sione Lauaki found that out the hard way when he had an appalling game against the Wallabies in 2008 after coming off the bench.

Admittedly his team-mates were in the midst of one of their worst collective performances in years, which didn't help. But Lauaki, an enormous loose forward, stood out as being particularly bad. He dropped the ball at the base of the scrum with his first touch.

His second act was to drop the ball again. His third was to concede a penalty for a high shot on Luke Burgess. His fourth was to miss a tackle, and his fifth was basically to give up, or at least show no real interest, in tackling a rampaging Rocky Elsom.

It was such a poor effort that there was good reason to sub Lauaki – the ultimate insult, when a sub has to be subbed for reasons of form. He was spared that indignity as there was no one else left on the bench to take his place.

Due to a lack of alternatives and a desire to rest the frontline troops, Lauaki was given a sympathy outing a few weeks later against Samoa but was never seen again after that.

## 7  Tony Underwood, England v New Zealand, 1995

No one envied England wing Tony Underwood when he was asked to mark Jonah Lomu in the 1995 World Cup semi-final. Poor little Tony was maybe 85 kg dripping wet. Lomu was 120 kg and as quick as your average Japanese train.

The results were about as predictable as their physical statistics would suggest. As Underwood would later tell the BBC: 'Coach Jack Rowell and captain Will Carling may recall it differently, but I remember them asking me if I could handle Jonah on my own.

'I was feeling fairly confident. I'd played well all season and scored a try in the win over Australia, so I was hardly going to say: "I can't handle Jonah." '

Lomu ended up scoring four tries in a performance that was unforgettably good and made him a global superstar. Underwood was catastrophically bad – unable to get a hand on the big man and suffering the ultimate humiliation when Lomu picked him up and swung him around like a rag doll.

'In retrospect, Ian Hunter might have handled it better physically on a one-on-one basis,' admitted Underwood. 'The only saving grace I can take from the whole thing is that I wasn't steamrollered by Jonah for his four tries. I was one of the few Jonah actually ran around rather than through, and it was amazing how he did it.'

## 6 Al Baxter, Australia v New Zealand, 2009

In August 2009 the Wallabies were desperate to keep alive their hopes of winning the Bledisloe Cup. They also wanted to arrest a run of four straight defeats to the All Blacks. They were confident that the second test of the series in Sydney against an All Black side demoralised by two heavy defeats in South Africa would be their best chance to break out of their rut.

They were probably right, as they had the All Blacks in trouble out wide and at the lineout. But unfortunately the Wallabies were being crippled at the scrum where the notoriously suspect Al Baxter was being buckled by his opposite, Tony Woodcock.

It was embarrassing. The Wallabies were being crushed and Baxter was in all kinds of trouble. The All Blacks were either being awarded penalties as Baxter collapsed or were able to disrupt Australia's possession. After just 31 minutes Baxter was taken off by coach Robbie Deans. Baxter, who had more than 50 caps, sat fuming on the bench, knowing that his reputation would never recover from the humiliation of such an early exit. He was right – especially when the Wallabies ended up losing 19–18 and the scrum was extensively blamed.

### 5  Ben Blair, Crusaders v Brumbies, 2004

It's never great when a normally reliable player – an All Black at that – chooses one of the biggest games of the year, a Super Rugby final no less, to have the worst performance of their career.

Sadly that's what happened to Crusaders and four-cap All Black fullback Ben Blair in 2004. In the third minute in the Canberra final, Blair was tested by a high ball. He timed everything beautifully – but his positioning was out by two metres. The ball landed behind him, and while he was flapping about in the air the Brumbies scored.

Another easy seven points followed when Blair, in covering back, inexplicably went to fly-hack the ball into touch but ended up taking an air shot and falling over. Brumbies wing Joe Roff scooped the ball and scored. That was 14 points courtesy of Blair and, with his confidence shot, he was removed just after half-time to prevent him from inflicting any more damage.

'You don't like to be taken off and I would have liked to have stayed out there, but I guess I was fairly shot on confidence by then,' Blair said. 'I didn't get off to a good start and it didn't get any better with that high ball. I was fighting the demons in my head by then. It just wasn't my day. I just feel like digging a hole and burying myself really.'

The final was later dubbed the Ditch Ben Blair Project.

### 4  Rodney So'oialo, New Zealand v South Africa, 2006

Rodney So'oialo was a good All Black. He was an experienced No 8 and part of a capable and imposing loose trio in 2006.

That made his absolute shocker in Rustenburg against the Springboks in late August difficult to understand. It was just one of those games where everything went wrong for the poor guy.

The All Blacks were unbeaten in 15 games and had thumped the Boks the week before. They were confident of making it 16 – until

Rodders had his meltdown. He threw a looping pass inside his own half that Springbok wing Bryan Habana saw coming a good minute before it was launched. Habana intercepted it – of course he did – and cantered in for an easy seven points. The All Blacks slowly recovered and Andrew Hore crashed over for a try just before half-time – except it was ruled out as So'oialo had needlessly blocked the defenders from an offside position. He brought the curtain down when he conceded a lame penalty with two minutes remaining when the All Blacks were leading by two. South Africa won by a point and So'oialo's misery was complete.

'I'll take all that criticism ... I'll go back and work even harder to get back into the team,' he said a few weeks later. 'Everyone's got an opinion. No matter what I do or anyone else in the team, you don't really have a say in it so you just continue doing what you enjoy and what you do, and that's play rugby.'

### 3 Ronan O'Gara, British & Irish Lions v South Africa, 2009

The British & Irish Lions needed heroes in the second half of the second test of their 2009 tour to South Africa. Having lost the first, they were in electric form in the second, leading 19–8 coming into the final quarter.

South Africa fought their way back with a converted try to trail 22–18 with six minutes remaining. By this point Irish fly-half Ronan O'Gara was on the field – he'd been introduced after 65 minutes. His first meaningful act was to miss a critical tackle on Jaque Fourie, which enabled the Springbok centre to barge over in the corner. Then, after the Lions had scrambled with just three minutes remaining to draw the scores level at 25–all, O'Gara played his trump card.

In the final minute he fielded a kick inside his 22 and had these options: thump it into touch to end the game and give his side a crack at drawing the series; or go for broke, try to spark something from deep down.

He kind of went for the latter – but strangely decided to hoist a high kick. O'Gara chased after it, but got the timing all wrong and clobbered the catcher, Fourie du Preez, in the air.

Morné Steyn landed the subsequent penalty to win the test and the series. But O'Gara was unrepentant a year later. 'That decision doesn't cost me a second thought because I'd do the exact same tomorrow. People ask me, "Would you not kick it out?" But it never entered my head to kick the ball out. I couldn't see what a draw would do for anyone.'

## 2 Henry Paul, England v Australia, 2004

It's probably a record – and not one to make him proud – that Henry Paul was substituted in a test match in 2004 after just 26 minutes. He wasn't injured.

Such humiliation was hard for a great league player and improving rugby player to handle. But England coach Andy Robinson felt he had no choice but to make this bold call so soon into the test against Australia at Twickenham.

Robinson's post-match rationale was that Paul, playing at inside centre, had made two glaring errors in those 26 minutes and the balance of the midfield was obviously not right. He felt that if he had left him on, the game could have been over by half-time. As it was, Australia still won, but it was close at 21–19.

'Henry unfortunately made a number of mistakes,' said Robinson, 'and we had a player of Will Greenwood's stature to come on. These are calls you have to make as a coach. I will watch the game again and probably still think it was the right one. I am paid to make those calls and I felt it was the right call.'

Paul never played for England again.

## 1 Stephen Donald, New Zealand v Australia, 2010

There were plenty of eyebrows raised when Stephen Donald was selected in the All Black squad to tour Hong Kong and the UK at the end of 2010.

Donald had been an All Black in 2008 and 2009 and hadn't quite convinced, and after missing most of the 2010 season was a surprise choice.

That risk backfired on the selectors when the 26-year-old came off the bench against Australia in Hong Kong with 20 minutes remaining. Starting fly-half Dan Carter had managed 60 minutes – his fitness not quite there after a lay-off due to ankle surgery. Still, Carter had steered his side into a good position, leading 24–14 when he left the field.

Donald's first act was to chip-kick the ball straight to the Wallabies, and from there they launched a brilliant counter-attack to score through Drew Mitchell. Donald then missed touch from a penalty; he conceded a penalty for a high shot; and, worst of all, he pulled a penalty wide of the posts from 30 metres out almost bang in front with seven minutes remaining. It was a crucial miss as it would have put the All Blacks two scores ahead.

He wasn't done yet though. After surviving a five-minute siege of their line, the All Blacks turned the ball over inside their 22 in the dying seconds. All Donald had to do was boot it out. He booted it straight to fullback Kurtley Beale, the Wallabies scored in the opposite corner, and James O'Connor converted to win the game.

'Obviously there were a couple of poor decisions more than anything,' Donald said. 'To be fair, that's fixable. It's an experience I've got to learn from. As far as confidence goes, I still back myself. I'm in the best physical shape of my life and my skill level is still up there, it's just a matter of making a bit better decisions than I did in Hong Kong.'

# 10 worst team performances

### 10 Scotland 9–8 Australia, 2009

Scotland had won a solitary Six Nations fixture against Italy, which led to the sacking of coach Frank Hadden in August 2009. Morale and confidence were both low when they came to fulfil their November test obligations. New coach Andy Robinson had limited resources and time in which to turn things around.

A comfortable win against Fiji was delivered in his first game at the helm, but the second test was a clash with the Wallabies – the side ranked number three in the world and a side the Scots hadn't beaten since 1982. Australia dominated possession and territory but were unbelievably bad at finishing their opportunities. Kicker Matt Giteau couldn't hit a barn door and the ball was spilled on several occasions with the try-line beckoning.

The Scots led 9–3 courtesy of their resilience and determination, but were unable to prevent the Wallabies from scoring a late try, which should have provided the escape they were after. But incredibly Giteau couldn't land the conversion from the easy angle and the Scots won 9–8.

The Australian press climbed into Wallaby coach Robbie Deans and called for his head. 'The Wallabies are not just the laughing stock of Australian sport,' wrote Greg Growden in the *Sydney Morning Herald*. 'They are also the laughing stock of the international rugby world after suffering their worst loss in decades. This defeat was not as bad as being beaten by Tonga in 1973, but it's not far off.'

## 9 France 21–22 Italy, 2011

France began the 2011 season as defending Six Nations champions and they would end it as World Cup finalists. They were clearly a capable side as they showed when they began their programme with wins against Scotland and Ireland, and a close loss to a vastly improved England team.

When the French headed to Rome to play Italy in their fourth game they were confident of a comfortable win and probably a bonus point to boot. It didn't work out like that, though. Their vaunted scrum was beaten up and the Italians rattled the French with the intensity of their defence. In a performance of relentless bravery aided by some extraordinarily inept and inaccurate work from the French, one of the major shocks of the Six Nations was completed; Italy won the game 22–21.

'To put it mildly, I can say I'm disenchanted,' French coach Marc Lièvremont lamented. 'I had made commitments to some players regarding the World Cup, but everything is up in the air now. Maybe I made some mistakes. I feel like I'm responsible for this, but the players are lacking courage. There is a certain cowardice. When I speak with them, nothing happens. Some of the players maybe wore the France jersey for the last time.'

## 8 Bulls 92–3 Reds, 2007

The Reds were desperate to finish their 2007 campaign. They had been awful pretty much throughout, managing to win just two games. When they headed to South Africa for their final games they were last on the table and had only pride left to play for.

That was the one thing they couldn't afford to lose. Former Wallaby coach Eddie Jones had been prepared to pick youth and back them with a view that after a few tough years they would come good. When the Reds were competitive against the Stormers in Cape Town in their penultimate game, there was confidence they could push the Bulls just as close at Loftus.

The Bulls knew that a bonus point win would guarantee them at least fourth spot. If they could win by 45 points they would jump to third and, ludicrous as it was to even contemplate, they knew that a 72-point margin would see them leapfrog the Crusaders in second place and secure a home semi-final.

The Reds kicked an early penalty and then seemingly gave up. They were so bad it would have been no surprise to learn they had been bribed. The Bulls were able to score at will, running through the Reds as if they weren't even good training opposition. The final score was 92–3 – the biggest margin of defeat in Super Rugby history.

When the Reds won the title in 2011, captain James Horwill, who had played in Pretoria in 2007, said: 'We spoke of the lowest point in Queensland rugby history – that Bulls defeat back in Pretoria. That's probably the lowest point we've ever been as an organisation.'

## 7  Ireland 54–10 Wales, 2002

After a glorious start to his international coaching career, Graham Henry lost the Welsh changing room in the latter part of 2001. The former Auckland coach had been in charge of the British & Irish Lions in the summer of that year – a secondment that saw him develop strained relations with several leading Welsh players who were hurt by not making the composite side's test team.

Wales lost a rearranged Six Nations fixture to Ireland 36–3 in October, then lost to Argentina and Australia in November.

The team were losing their way; they had no confidence in Henry, and when they travelled to Dublin in early February 2002 there was disaster in the air. Wales were abysmal. They couldn't do anything right and appeared to even give up. They lost by 54–10, a record defeat that followed the record defeat in October, and the country was angry.

'Sunday was an abysmal shambles,' said former international Gareth Davies the day after the loss. 'You have to blame the players for a start, but when you have a coach earning nearly £250,000 a year, there has to be some kind of responsibility.'

Henry resigned a few days later, citing the Dublin performance as the final proof he was only having a negative impact on the team.

## 6  Crusaders 96–13 Waratahs, 2002

One of the unexplained mysteries of Super Rugby is what happened to the Waratahs in the final round-robin game of the 2002 competition. They came to Christchurch to play what many felt was a dress rehearsal for the final. Regardless of what happened, the Waratahs were guaranteed to finish second and play the Brumbies in the semi-final in Sydney. The chances were they would be back in Christchurch for the final.

The Waratahs could strike a massive psychological blow if they could beat the Crusaders ahead of that expected clash. To know they could win in New Zealand would be massive, and so the Waratahs came with great intentions on 11 May.

Inexplicably, they were destroyed. They were shredded 96–16 in the most extraordinary effort by both teams. The Waratahs offered nothing and couldn't believe what was happening. They were shell-shocked as the Crusaders ran in 14 tries. Waratahs coach Bob Dwyer was as shocked as everyone else. 'That score is in the history book and we're doing our best to get inside the book and blur the score a bit. Hopefully, some people in years to come will think it's a misprint.'

Sadly it wasn't, and the effect of that mauling was so severe that the Waratahs were hammered 51–10 by the Brumbies the following week.

## 5  South Africa 53–8 Australia, 2008

Australia had serious ambition to win the 2008 Tri Nations after they began their campaign with a solid win against the Springboks and then followed it up with an emphatic destruction of the All Blacks. When the Wallabies then bounced back from a loss at Eden Park in Auckland to beat the Boks in Durban, they were in pole position to win the title. Wins in the Republic had been hard to come by for the Wallabies and new coach Robbie Deans was making an impressive start to his career. Then it all went wrong.

The Wallabies headed to Johannesburg a week after their 27–15 victory in Durban and were royally smashed 53–8. They fell to a record loss because they were barely committed to any of the physical exchanges. Their scrum was crushed, their lineout was a mess and defensively they didn't want to know.

'The guys have always believed in their abilities and finally they showed what they can do,' beamed Peter de Villiers, a happy South African coach. 'We only played to 70 per cent of our potential, but we worked hard out there, created good opportunities and they [Australia] didn't stand a chance against us. All credit to the players. This is what I expect of this group. We didn't want to prove anyone wrong, we simply wanted to showcase our talents.'

##  New Zealand Maori 0–37 South Africa, 1956

The New Zealand Maori team were expected to provide the touring Springboks of 1956 with a fierce challenge. The Maori had enough talent to be considered an unofficial fifth test; they were certainly expected to soften up the Boks.

Instead they were drilled 37–0 and played with little passion or conviction – which was most unlike any previous or future Maori side. The match report in *Te Ao Hou*, published by the Maori Affairs Department, said the Maori tackling was 'ineffectual' and it was a great disappointment to the thousands of Maori people present. 'The score was hard to believe ... the people were subdued, the overwhelming defeat had come as a great shock.'

That result stood as an anomaly in their proud history right up until their centenary year in 2009 when Maori fullback on the day Muru Walters told the *New Zealand Herald* that the team had been asked to play badly. Walters, who became an Anglican bishop, claimed that Maori Affairs Minister of the time, Ernest Corbett, came into the changing room minutes before the game. He allegedly told the team they must not beat the Springboks 'for the future of rugby'.

'What he [Corbett] said was you must not win this game or we will never be invited to South Africa again,' Walters claimed. 'I thought he was joking, but then another official came in and said the same thing ... for the future of rugby, don't beat the South Africans.

That was a pretty destructive message, actually ... and it ripped the guts out of the spirits of our team.'

### 3  Australia 76–0 England, 1998

England had agreed to a schedule where they would play Australia in Brisbane, then two tests against the All Blacks in New Zealand before flying to South Africa for a one-off game against the Boks in June 1998.

It was a mad itinerary, which is probably why virtually every frontline player and then most of the next tier decided they were injured and unable to travel. A crazy challenge like that really needed the very best players, but instead they were having to trawl the net deep to haul inexperienced and under-qualified bodies onto the plane.

While it was apparent England were not genuine test strength when they lined up to play the Wallabies, no one was forecasting the annihilation that followed. England were dire and they tumbled to a record 76–0 loss. They couldn't win the ball; they couldn't tackle; they couldn't do anything – and the ultimate insult was that they earned the pity of the Australians.

Most of the players on the trip – it became known as the Tour to Hell – never played for England again, although it was the making of one, 19-year-old Jonny Wilkinson. 'That experience taught me more in one leap than anything else can, or probably ever will,' said Wilkinson, who went on to become England's leading point-scorer and arguably their best No 10 of all time. 'The intensity of the emotions were massively important to my development. It was a slap in the face at a time when I thought I was getting somewhere and made me realise I had a long way to go.'

### 2  England 53–8 South Africa, 2002

South Africa knew things weren't going terribly well for them on their November tour of the UK in 2002 when they lost to Scotland at Murrayfield. The Scots weren't a team of note at that time. Much worse was to come from the South Africans when they played England at Twickenham a week later.

Prior to kick-off, the team had decided they had no chance and that their best bet was to try to physically damage England by any means they could. Captain Corné Krige led the charge in an astonishing opening 20 minutes where he attempted to smash his forearm into scrum-half Matt Dawson, only to concuss his own team-mate, André Pretorius, by mistake. He then sank a knee into Lawrence Dallaglio, stamped on Phil Vickery and elbowed Jason Robinson in the face.

'I stepped totally out of line and I've got to take the criticism on the chin. People make mistakes in pressurised situations and that's what happened to me,' Krige wrote in his autobiography. 'My team was in dire straits and I allowed myself to be pushed into the wrong decisions.

'We had just lost to France and Scotland so we knew there was no way we were going to beat England. We went out there to ruffle them up and get among them physically.' After 23 minutes lock Jannes Labuschagne was sent off after his second yellow-card offence and the Boks went on to lose 53–8 in a disgraceful performance.

'One of my players got a red card early and things spiralled out of control,' Krige wrote. 'A lot of my guys gave up but I was determined to go down fighting. It was wrong but we were such a poor team there seemed no alternative.'

## 1  Waikato 38–10 British & Irish Lions, 1993

Some insist that the British & Irish Lions' 29–16 loss to Hawke's Bay in 1993 was the worst performance in the composite side's rich history. The 38–10 loss a week later to Waikato was, however, probably worse. The defeat in Hamilton was played between the second and third tests – by which point the so-called 'Dirt Trackers' had given up. The majority of those not in the test side had decided they were already on holiday.

Waikato were the provincial champions but they were amazed at just how soft the Lions' front five was. It was embarrassing how poor they were at the scrum and how little tackling they were prepared to do. Asked after the game why there was such a disparity between the test team and the Dirt Trackers, team manager Geoff Cooke, said: 'I find that very difficult to answer.'

It took test wing Ieuan Evans to say how things really were when he was interviewed in 2005 before the Lions returned to New Zealand. 'As the split between the test team and the rest began to widen to seriously large dimensions, so a number of players decided that they weren't going to let it spoil their fun. They did so to such an extent that some gave the impression they were on holiday.

'The way I saw it, some of those who played didn't give a monkey's. They simply weren't trying. It was as if they were saying to themselves, We're not bothered. We're not going to get a test place so we may as well enjoy ourselves.

'It was safe to say that they drank too much. I don't know whether they were with us in spirit, but they were very much with us in spirits.'

# 10 recidivist offenders

### 10 Andy Powell (Wales)

A fiery No 8 with the capacity to win games with his powerful running, Andy Powell was signed by Cardiff in 2005. But repeat shoulder injuries prevented him from proving himself until late 2007, when he was able to play consistently good rugby and earn a call-up to the national side in 2008.

He stood out against the All Blacks and went on to become a regular and indeed vital member of the Welsh side until 2010. It was after Wales had pulled off an amazing comeback win against Scotland in February 2010 that Powell came off the rails. He woke up at 5 am after a huge night out and decided he needed breakfast – from a petrol station. He jumped into a golf buggy – the Welsh were staying at a resort outside Cardiff – and made the idiotic decision to take it onto the motorway. 'I just wanted some munchies,' he told the *Guardian* a year later. 'I got to the service station without any problems and, in fairness, the police were brilliant. They were quite sympathetic because I admitted I was an idiot.'

He was kicked out of the Welsh team and then moved on by his club. Wasps signed him, but that only lasted a year as Powell and team-mate Tim Payne got into some trouble at a London boozer in early 2011.

'We started singing a few songs and exchanging a bit of banter but then it all kicked off,' Powell confessed. 'I was knocked to the ground by a gang who then started to kick and punch me ... It was pretty scary. I was then hit by a bar stool and lost consciousness after that, but I suffered a pretty bad cut. There was blood everywhere. I think I lost around two pints of blood in the pub. It was just one of those things.'

One of those things that led to him being axed by Wasps.

## 9   Quade Cooper (Australia)

Quade Cooper got himself in a bit of a pickle when he was accused of burglary at the end of 2009. The rising star of Australian rugby allegedly broke into a property and stole two laptops. The story was intriguing and made more so when it emerged shortly before the hearing that Cooper had been disqualified after being picked up by the police for driving on a suspended licence. That wouldn't have been such a drama had it not been for the fact he failed to tell his employer – the Australian Rugby Union – of the driving ban.

The charges relating to the laptops were eventually settled out of court through a mediation process, and Cooper was spared by the ARU as he agreed to undergo personal counselling and quit drinking. They fined him $7500 for inducing negative publicity for the game.

A contrite Cooper spoke on the day his ordeal ended. 'When you think back to all the distractions I had this year, the best that has come of it is that it has made me focus more. People have always said I have good skills on the field, but I guess I have just lacked that focus. Coming out of school and straight into the big time, you are going to have a lot of things going on for you. Once you get that focus and that enjoyment, it all just clicks.'

## 8   Sione Lauaki (New Zealand)

2010 was the year nothing would go right for Sione Lauaki – a 15-test All Black whose last cap had come in 2008. His career had been a sorry tale of under-achievement; at his best he could be devastating, but those days were few and far between.

Chiefs coach Ian Foster made Lauaki captain while regular skipper Mils Muliaina sat out the first four weeks of Super Rugby. It was a brave choice – Lauaki had no experience and little to suggest he was a natural leader. It backfired horribly when Lauaki was suspended for a needless and reckless tackle. A few weeks later he was involved in a late-night incident, sparked by his erroneous belief someone had stolen his drink, that would see him charged with assault.

The final episode came in April when he decided to drive to

Auckland from Hamilton after a Chiefs game. He fell asleep behind the wheel and crashed his car at 4.30 am in the small town of Huntly, damaging his arm.

In fining Lauaki almost $2000 for his assault charge, Judge Philip Connell said: 'You had no idea that he was the person who took your drink but you just decided to get angry and take it out on him ... That's the sum total of the stupidity of your actions. I think the biggest problem you have got is [that] when you drink, you clearly can't control yourself and it's something you need to think about.'

Lauaki took a contract with French club Clermont shortly after.

## 7  Jimmy Cowan (New Zealand)

All Black scrum-half Jimmy Cowan knew he was lucky to survive his third strike. The combative Southlander was forced to give up the booze as a condition of the New Zealand Rugby Union continuing to employ him in 2008.

Such a radical step had to be taken after Cowan was found guilty by his employer of a second serious misconduct charge. Cowan, 26, was charged by police for an incident in Dunedin on 5 April.

He had been warned frequently about his alcohol use but was failing to take heed. The NZRU fined him $3000 and forced him to take alcohol counselling, warning him that if he drank again in the next six months he would be fired. 'We're not going to cast him aside and leave him to sit and wallow in pity about this,' said All Black manager Darren Shand. 'There was a common denominator here, which is his ability to cope with alcohol. When he's assembled with the All Blacks he does things right, he makes good decisions. Outside of this he's been making some bad decisions.'

## 6  James O'Connor (Australia)

James O'Connor is an enormously talented young man who has been hot property since he was 17. Maybe all that attention has made it hard for him to make good judgements off the field – he has been prone to serious lapses, displaying little common sense.

His first significant fall from grace came in June 2009 when he and two other Wallabies engaged in a food fight in their team hotel. O'Connor was fined a significant sum and was back in trouble in late 2010 for a late-night drinking session in Paris where accusations were made that he and team-mates Quade Cooper and Kurtley Beale had been fighting.

His highest-profile shameful act was on the eve of the 2011 World Cup when he was so hung-over that he missed the official unveiling of the Wallaby squad. His 29 team-mates were all at a special function organised by team sponsor Qantas, but O'Connor was in bed when his name was read out and the official team photo was taken. 'I missed a massive event in my life as well, it only comes around every four years,' he said. 'I'm disappointed, there's nothing more I guess I can say, what's happened, has happened. I just want to apologise for letting everyone down.'

He was suspended for one test and heavily fined. He was later digitally added to the official photo.

### 5 Gavin Henson (Wales)

Gavin Henson has never been everyone's cup of tea. His ability to generate headlines off the field has been far greater than his talent on it.

It was in December 2007 that he first got into big trouble – he had been forced to apologise for some venomous remarks in his 2005 biography, but the furore soon died – when he and a few Ospreys team-mates travelled to Wales from London on a train. They were celebrating their victory against Harlequins and playing drinking games. One of these allegedly involved a forfeit of Henson punching his friends in the face, an act in which he reputedly broke his hand. He was also accused of abusing other passengers while one of the group urinated in the carriage.

An enforced two-year sabbatical followed as he struggled to overcome a groin injury, and he quit Ospreys once he recovered to join Saracens, before quickly moving to Toulon. He'd barely played for the French club when his contract was almost terminated. He was accused of bad-mouthing team-mates Jonny Wilkinson and Joe van Neikerk to other team-mates while drinking at a Marseille nightclub.

The argument became a fight and Henson was suspended and seemingly axed before Toulon owner Mourad Boudjellal had a change of heart. 'I consulted my staff, I consulted the group and I decided to return Henson to the line-up,' Boudjellal said. 'We are clear that we're not giving him a second chance, but a final chance. He knows that at the next incident, there won't be any warning shots before the trigger is pulled.'

## 4  Danny Cipriani (England)

Danny Cipriani shot to fame when he cheated on his celebrity girlfriend with a lady who turned out to have originally been a man. He followed that by being suspended for an England test in 2008 after he was spotted in a nightclub at midnight just two days before playing Scotland. He claimed he was there to deliver tickets to a friend, and while he hadn't been drinking, it was hardly the best decision to deliver the goods at such a venue at such a time.

New England coach Martin Johnson had no interest in Cipriani, and the youngster ended up signing with the newly formed Melbourne Rebels in Super Rugby. He arrived with big ambition but wasn't cut out for the rough and tumble of the southern hemisphere. He was, however, cut out for the more laidback lifestyle. In February 2011 he stole a bottle of vodka from a Melbourne nightclub, which earned him a player-imposed one-game ban. He picked up another one-game ban for breaking a curfew, and then he was told to stay at home when the team travelled to South Africa later in the season. Cipriani was accused of various drinking misdemeanours that broke the player's agreed code of conduct.

'I've been misunderstood and judged unfairly by people who don't know me, but I've realised the only way to handle it is by being responsible and accepting it,' Cipriani told the *Melbourne Age*. 'The vodka bottle incident was a silly prank. I should not have done it, but I am not a thief. The nightclub knew I wasn't deliberately stealing. I let the Rebels down at times this year, but next year will be different. I accept I've got to be more responsible off the field for the good of my team-mates. I see myself as a leader of the team on and off the field, and I don't want any more off-field headlines.'

### 3 Wendell Sailor (Australia)

When Wendell Sailor played league his off-field antics were tolerated as he unquestionably delivered on the field. But when he switched codes to rugby in 2001 it wasn't so easy to accept he was high maintenance. He never took to his new code, and his contract would eventually be terminated in 2006 when he tested positive for cocaine. In hindsight it appeared he had always been building to this inglorious finale.

In August 1997 he was acquitted of assault only on the grounds that he did not throw the first punch. He was arrested for being drunk at 5 am in a public place in October 2000; in May 2001 he was fined and ordered to pay compensation for spitting in a woman's face; and in 2005 he was involved in a scuffle with team-mates while in South Africa.

After his two-year ban he returned to the NRL in 2008 a chastened and reformed character. 'Having my sport taken away from me was definitely the lowest time of my life,' said Sailor when he signed with the Dragons. 'I let a lot of people down with that stupid mistake and I just knew I had to make things right. I had the unwavering support of my family and friends, especially my wife Tara and children Tristan and Matisse throughout this tough time, and we all knew that I wasn't finished and that returning to rugby league was the right thing to do.'

### 2 Lote Tuqiri (Australia)

Much like Wendell Sailor, Lote Tuqiri was a high-maintenance league convert who came to union in 2002 and only ever had short periods where he stayed out of trouble.

His first brush with controversy came on a tour to South Africa in 2005 when Tuqiri had an altercation with his Wallaby team-mate Matt Henjak in a nightclub. Tuqiri saw Henjak throw his drink and the two became involved in an unseemly tussle. Henjak was sent home and Tuqiri was later fined $5000 and suspended for two tests. 'It was obviously the wrong thing to do and I'm very remorseful for the fact that we were out, but I can't bring it back now,' Tuqiri said.

In January 2007 Tuqiri failed a fitness test and was sent home from a Wallabies training camp, and during a Waratahs game a few weeks later he pushed over team-mate Sam Norton-Knight on the field and verbally abused him. But there was more to come: in July 2007 he was banned for two matches and fined $20,000 for failing to attend a team medical and registering an alcohol reading at a team breath-test.

And one of his better efforts was that same year when he was out with Waratahs team-mates and took a call from Wallaby selector Michael O'Connor. Tuqiri put the call on speakerphone and asked O'Connor to critique his team-mate Peter Hewat. O'Connor didn't know the situation and made it clear Hewat wasn't in their plans. Hewat, not much liked by Tuqiri, stormed out of the pub.

It all came to an end in September 2009 when Tuqiri's contract was terminated. The specific reasons have never been revealed but speculation was rife that he broke a curfew, disregarded drinking protocol, and then brought a woman back to his hotel room while on duty with the Wallabies.

## Zac Guildford (New Zealand)

It was in the earthquake-torn city of Christchurch where Zac Guildford first had to publicly admit to a drink problem. The All Black wing was forced to apologise for a drunken night out following his horror performance in the final Tri Nations game of 2011. Having played so badly, 22-year-old Guildford drowned his sorrows and was still drinking at 6 am when management were having breakfast. Management were incensed because Guildford had been taken to task by the NZRU for previous alcohol misdemeanours.

The humiliation of that exercise in Christchurch clearly didn't work, as Guildford would be on the front pages a few weeks after the World Cup. Attending a friend's wedding on the Pacific Island of Rarotonga in early November, he lost the plot on a drunken day of carnage.

He reportedly stormed into a bar at about 10 pm, naked and bleeding from a deep head gash, and proceeded to punch two men who came to his aid. It later emerged that earlier the same day he had verbally abused a prominent tri-athlete while she completed a training run, and had followed her on a scooter.

Guildford left the island before his friend's wedding and said on his return to Auckland: 'Firstly, I would like to apologise for my behaviour. I have no clear recollection of the events of that night but there is no doubt that my behaviour was unacceptable and I am hugely embarrassed by what happened. I don't want any sympathy for the situation I have ended up in, but I am thankful for the support I have received so far from so many people. It's obvious that I need help and I want to get home and to get that help as soon as I can. I need to sort myself out.'

# 10 worst rugby league converts

## 10 Barrie–Jon Mather (England)

Named after the legendary Welsh fly-half, there was always an expectation that Barrie-Jon Mather would come to something as a rugby player. He did. He made the England Schools team, but decided he'd rather play league as he could make a professional career out of it.

After finding himself out of a job in 1998 when the Western Reds folded in Perth, Mather returned to England and took up his former code with the Sale club in Manchester. At 1.97 m and 115 kg, he was a huge man – especially so when his chosen position was centre. He earned the most extraordinary call-up to the national squad after just a handful of Premiership games.

He turned up to club training and his team-mates were congratulating him. 'When they told me I was in the England squad I thought they were taking the mickey. I was really apprehensive. I didn't feel like I'd earned it and I was worried what the others thought of me.'

The truth is they were perplexed. No one really knew why the big money was being spent on him. Mather won his first cap in the loss to Wales in 1999 – a game where victory would have won England the Grand Slam. Mather was outclassed and out of his depth, and that was pretty much the story of his union career until he was released by Sale in 2000.

## 9 Tasesa Lavea (New Zealand)

Tasesa Lavea was the NRL rookie of the year in 2000 after leaving school in Auckland and joining the Melbourne Storm. He played for the Kiwis and his future was bright. Auckland Rugby signed him in 2003 believing they had captured gold. Lavea had been part of the famous St Kentigern First XV that had won the Auckland title in 1998 with players such as John Afoa, Joe Rokocoko and Jerome Kaino. Lavea had rugby in his blood and was brought home as a fly-half – with a view to grooming him to replace Carlos Spencer.

But when Spencer left for Northampton in 2005, Lavea failed to nail his spot with either the Blues or Auckland. He just didn't have the skill-set. He played close to the traffic but he had little vision or eye for the holes.

He was regularly booed at Eden Park and ended up being one of the most maligned players of the professional age. 'If I perform then there will not be so much rubbish thrown at me,' he told *New Zealand Rugby World* on the eve of the 2009 Super 14. 'But if I don't perform and the Blues lose, then I guess it's Lavea's fault again.' He joined Clermont following yet another poor campaign with the Blues.

## 8 Lote Tuqiri (Australia)

There's an argument to be made that Lote Tuqiri was far from a failure at rugby. He won 67 test caps, scored 31 tries and played in a World Cup final. Statistically at least, there is reason to believe he was value for money.

Yet that doesn't get anywhere near telling the full story. Tuqiri ended up just like his former NRL mate Wendell Sailor and had his contract terminated in 2009 for various off-field incidents. And just like Sailor, it was maybe no real surprise that things ended the way they did. Tuqiri obviously had massive frustrations with his new code after he converted in 2001.

He had a fight with Wallaby team-mate Matt Henjak in a South African nightclub and was reprimanded for an all-night drinking session with prop Matt Dunning in 2007 that earned him a final warning and also showed how far out of touch he was with the requirements of being an international rugby player.

'Both of these players struggled to understand that they'd done anything wrong and we've just had a pretty mature conversation with them,' ARU chief executive John O'Neill said after disciplining Tuqiri and Dunning.

Tuqiri was a time-bomb from that point, enduring a disappointing World Cup in 2007 and two more underwhelming campaigns with the Waratahs before he was booted.

## 7 Ben MacDougall (Scotland)

The Scottish Rugby Union may have instantly regretted signing the Australian-born Ben MacDougall in 2004. He was unveiled with a big fanfare only for the media to get wind later that MacDougall had served a 22-game suspension from the NRL in 1998 for taking an anabolic steroid.

There were questions raised whether the SRU even knew about this although they claimed they did. A spokesman would only say: 'The decision to sign Ben MacDougall from Australian rugby league club Melbourne Storm was taken in full knowledge of the facts. In particular, that he had failed a drugs test six years ago for taking an over-the-counter purchased supplement, the risks of which were then less well documented.'

The inevitable media frenzy put MacDougall under an unwelcome spotlight and alerted everyone to the fact he wasn't really much good at his new code. Although that was hard to tell, as Edinburgh coach Frank Hadden kept him mostly on the bench and then punted him to rival franchise The Borders at the end of the season.

MacDougall played a bit better after the move, and when Scotland ran into an injury crisis they selected the Australian for two tests. Why they bothered to sign him ahead of local talent – and inevitably pay a premium – was a mystery.

### 6 Wendell Sailor (Australia)

That Wendell Sailor's rugby career should come to such an inglorious end was entirely fitting. Sailor was one of the biggest signings by the Australian Rugby Union – at the time he came across in 2001, he was arguably the biggest star of the other code.

The ARU had to pay a reported $700,000 a season to snare the then 27-year-old wing, but they were sure it was worth it. The euphoria soon died. Rugby may have managed to stick two fingers up at league, but the joy was short-lived.

Sailor always gave the impression he would have been happier playing the 13-man code he knew and loved. His move to rugby was all about the money and he struggled with the defensive nuances, especially having to catch high balls and being expected to kick. It didn't help that he was part of a Reds side that was enduring the most prolonged spell of disorganisation and under-performance. Big Del, as he was known, was a big flop.

He won 37 Wallaby caps, but they were mostly about justifying the money spent on him. He scored 13 tries in his test career – not a great return, and one that didn't really make the investment worthwhile. The worst part of all was that he was high-maintenance off the field, being involved in one unsavoury drinking incident before having his contract terminated in 2006 for testing positive for cocaine.

That led ARU chief executive Gary Flowers to say: 'We have no hesitation in terminating his contract. His actions have been nothing short of irresponsible. He already had a track record for poor behaviour which had seen him called in front of ARU and Wallaby team disciplinary committees on several previous occasions.'

### 5 Timana Tahu (Australia)

The Australian Rugby Union could never resist the temptation to poach players from the higher-profile NRL. League is the big code in Australia, with rugby a distant fourth, so administrators loved the idea of bringing players over – there was instant commercial value and kudos to be gained.

Timana Tahu was one of the men they gladly signed at the end of 2007. A major star of the NRL, the 27-year-old could be just the ticket to grow interest after a disappointing World Cup for the Wallabies.

There was plenty of hype but no substance from Tahu. He was a quiet performer with the Waratahs during Super Rugby in 2008 yet still earned a place in the Wallaby squad. When he made his debut in the record 53-8 loss to the Springboks in South Africa, Tahu was awful. Really awful, and his confidence was shattered.

'I've had a few [heavy defeats] in my career and it's just not the best thing in my debut in the starting side, you get given a chance to prove yourself and it's just shattering,' said Tahu of his nightmare. 'I was looking for a rope to hang myself. The first five minutes everything was going well but after that it felt like we were running backwards all the time. It was probably one of those games where you just want to wake up and think this is a bad dream.'

Unfortunately for him it wasn't a dream, and like so many other high-profile converts, he escaped back to league as soon as his contract expired at the end of 2009.

## 4 Henry Paul (England)

Things never really worked out for Henry Paul in rugby union. He earned six test caps but came across to union hopeful of winning more. His last appearance was cut short after 26 minutes and that epitomised his inability to make the impression he wanted in the 15-man code.

The New Zealand-born Paul decided to leave Bradford Bulls in 2001 and join Gloucester. He'd played rugby as a child in New Zealand so had some familiarity with the code, and there was an expectation he was going to make an immediate fist of things.

He might have settled better if he hadn't been picked for England after just one appearance for Gloucester. That built the pressure and when he came off the bench and struggled, his reputation was immediately tarnished. The hardest part was finding the right position for him; he started at fly-half before shifting to fullback and finally finding a home at inside centre. He ended up on the shortlist for the Premiership's Player of the Year award in 2004, but that was also the same year he played his last test. He came across with ambition to be more than just a handy club player for Gloucester.

### 3 Shontayne Hape (England)

Shontayne Hape was a fair to middling sort of league player. He'd started with the Warriors in his native New Zealand, earned 14 caps with the Kiwis and then took up a contract with Bradford in 2003. A robust creature at 1.87 m and 102 kg, he could be guaranteed to carry the ball straight and hard into the midfield.

When he decided to switch codes in 2008 there was limited excitement – blokes like Hape were easy enough to find: muscular types who could bust over the advantage line and present the ball.

What the English game was crying out for was muscular types who could do all that and play with the ball; men who had the subtle skills and creativity to match their physicality. Hape was never going to be that man, but that didn't stop England coach Martin Johnson calling him up to the national squad in 2010 once he was eligible through residency.

Hape gave England precisely what they already had – physical presence and defensive clout. He offered no variation or threat to opposition defences, and after England had played Wales in a pre-World Cup warm-up game in 2011, renowned rugby writer Stephen Jones of the *Sunday Times* gave Hape a staggering one out of 10 in his player ratings and wrote: 'It is long past time to declare the myth dead and grasp that here is a rugby league disaster.'

### 2 Iestyn Harris (Wales)

The Welsh Rugby Union took what they felt was a calculated risk in 2001 when they signed Iestyn Harris on a four-year deal. Harris was the biggest name in rugby league at the time – a phenomenally skilled and balanced player who was seemingly capable of anything in the 13-man code.

He was paid an extraordinary £400,000 a season, which made him one of the best paid players in the world, and just to make sure he was under maximum pressure, the success-starved Welsh Rugby Union hailed him a potential saviour of the national team despite the fact he hadn't played a senior game of rugby.

Having forked out so much to get him, it was inevitable they would throw Harris into the national team before he was ready. He endured a horror debut at fly-half in late 2001 against Argentina. The Pumas won 30–16 and two of their tries came directly from Harris's mistakes. He was out of his depth, and had to endure Pumas captain Agustín Pichot making the following valid remarks after the game. 'Rugby league is not known for its tactical kickers; we decided to put pressure on Harris whenever we could. It was very difficult for him. Perhaps somebody from league could go straight into a union team on the wing or at centre, but the key positions – eight, nine, 10 – are very difficult. You must know and learn how to manage a game.'

All coach Graham Henry could say was: 'We've got to start somewhere with Iestyn. It wasn't the most positive display, but he will get better – he's a very natural rugby player. With him, we had to go backwards before we could go forwards.'

Harris was a little better when he was shifted to inside centre and won 25 caps. But he never justified the money, and scurried back to league in 2003.

## 1 Andy Farrell (England)

Andy Farrell had been one of the best league players produced by England. When he hinted he fancied switching codes, the Rugby Football Union couldn't get their chequebook out fast enough. They offered a whopping £500,000 a year to bring the 31-year-old to union. It had disaster written all over it; that was a huge investment in a bloke who had been battered for the better part of the past 14 years and was always going to be difficult to fit into a rugby side.

In what position would he play? The RFU saw him at inside centre, yet the club where he ended up, Saracens, who had gone halves with the national body, were going to pick him at blindside. 'Everyone is saying we should pick Andy at 12, but he tends to run across the field and that is the worst trait a centre can have,' said Saracens director of rugby, Alan Gaffney.

It took the outspoken Jeff Probyn to point out what a farce the signing was, and how wrong it had been for Farrell to end up in the England squad after a handful of unimpressive outings at club level. 'I feel sorry for Farrell because he is being given no time to learn what is a completely alien sport for him. He is not ready to play for England now and he will not be anywhere near the required level by the start of the World Cup next year. He has looked a fish out of water in his two games for Saracens, which is hardly surprising, and his presence in the England squad does an injustice to club players in his position who have come through the academy system. It sends out the wrong message.'

Farrell won eight caps in the midfield and never once looked like he was test class.

# 10 wasted talents

### 10 Thomas Castaignède (France)

On a glorious spring day in 1998, the French destroyed Wales 51–0 at Wembley to claim a Grand Slam. The star of the show was Thomas Castaignède, the 23-year-old French fly-half showing a delightful range of skills. He was a rugby genius.

Then in November 2000 he snapped his Achilles while warming up before a test. The next two years saw him undergo several operations, but worse, he became the victim of a legal battle between his English club Saracens and the French Rugby Federation. Saracens ended up paying £300,000 in medical fees the French refused to cover, and the guilt and gratitude were hard for Castaignède to deal with.

He was never the same player again and even had to pay £1500 a test in future to cover his own insurance.

His career should have been full of special memories, but the performance at Wembley signalled the end rather than the beginning. He played on until 2007, only ever a peripheral figure, uncertain of his pace and acceleration – a shadow of the strutting cocksure youngster he had once been.

'It was agonising for a sportsman wanting to prove his worth. I felt a "passenger" and was very depressed about my rugby,' he said after his boots were hung up. 'But Nigel Wray [Saracens owner] was so good to me, offering a new contract when I was still struggling. I will always remember that support and generosity of spirit.'

### 9 James Ryan (New Zealand)

In 2005 it was impossible to watch the Highlanders Super 12 team and not notice the contribution of their ginger-haired lock, James Ryan.

The All Black selectors obviously felt the same way, as they selected the 22-year-old to debut against Fiji that year.

Ryan was rangy, quick and aggressive, and there was a sense that he was going to be a world-class player. But in early 2007 he incurred a serious knee injury playing for the Highlanders. He would miss the World Cup.

He was forced to have three operations in the space of 12 months, but despite the pain his medical team were confident he could return to full fitness. Ryan had different ideas.

'I've decided to have an indefinite break. Some might say that's no decision, but it's been a big decision for me to make,' the then 25-year-old told the *Otago Daily Times*. 'I've had three limb reconstructions in 12 months and that has been pretty frustrating for me to deal with. Four years ago, rugby was just completely everything to me. I wouldn't have expected to be doing what I am now. But it's not money or opportunities that will make me want to play rugby again. I have to really want to be doing it.'

But Ryan has never found the desire. The truth is that he decided in 2007 that rugby was no longer for him and turned his back on being an All Black.

The injury had taken an emotional rather than just a physical toll and he felt it was time to use his law degree. He has been working as a lawyer since 2008 in Wellington and is unlikely ever to play again.

## 8 Paul Sampson (England)

Every now and again the most remarkable things snap even the dreamiest to attention. Like when Paul Sampson was called up to train with the full England squad in 1996 while he was still at school.

For an international coach to put his faith in an 18-year-old studying for his A-Levels, he must have seen something extraordinary.

Sampson was the England schoolboys sprint champion, having clocked 10.48 seconds that year. Lethally quick, not afraid to tackle, he could also read the game. He was set to conquer the rugby world and won his first cap in 1998.

But he had a self-confessed attitude problem and a fixation with rugby league. He drifted in and out of form, never looked particularly quick on the field, and all the early promise never materialised; he only ever won two more caps.

Having married a celebrity, TV host Kirsty Gallacher, that side of life seemed to appeal more. It pretty much summed up his athletic career that he tried out to be a Gladiator in 2008 – the show his wife hosted – but was rejected.

### 7 Andrew Walker (Australia)

Andrew Walker was the ferociously talented dual league and union international of Aboriginal origin. One of 13 children, he came to professional rugby in 2000 after a moderate NRL career.

He was an instant success at the Brumbies, where he scored 13 tries in his rookie year and earned a call-up to the Wallabies. But he ultimately became more famous for walking out of training camps and for his issues with alcohol.

Twice he disappeared without permission while assembled with the Wallabies, and in 2002 he lost his licence for 12 months when caught driving over the alcohol limit.

He won just seven caps before heading back to league in 2004. But that went wrong, too, with Walker testing positive for cocaine and earning a two-year ban at the age of 30.

'Everything was pretty good for the first two years,' Walker confessed after his retirement. 'But then I was pretty lost. The city, it gets you down. Gets a bit too fast for you.'

He was persuaded to give things another go after his ban and ended up playing for the Queensland Reds in 2007. It went a little way to restoring a battered reputation, but really his career is more memorable for what he did off the field than on it.

'The drinking,' his wife Leona said. 'It's not that he drank a lot. But when he did, he hammered himself. He's not a person that would drink every weekend. He'd go a month without drinking. But when he did, he binged.'

## 6 Frans Steyn (South Africa)

Capped by the Springboks on the wing when he was 19 after just 10 Currie Cup games, Frans Steyn was a remarkable prospect.

The following year he showed he could play fullback and fly-half. His talent was unbelievable. At 100 kg and 1.90 m he had the raw pace, defensive clout, physique and micro skills to play across the backline.

He became the youngest player to win a World Cup winner's medal when he made the Springbok starting XV in 2007. Amazingly he wore 12 in the final, having only ever played four other professional games in that position.

His potential to be a once-in-a-lifetime superstar was underlined again in 2009 when he kicked three penalties against the All Blacks from inside his own half. But he chose shortly after to join Racing Métro in Paris and pretty much terminate his test career at the age of 22. He and Springbok coach Peter de Villiers couldn't agree on his best position, and the youngster also gave the impression he felt he needed to be treated with greater reverence.

Steyn and de Villiers sparred verbally in the press with the former launching a bitter attack in late 2010 after he claimed the coach failed to turn up to a long-arranged meeting. 'He was supposed to come to Paris on September 18 but he cancelled the meeting,' explained Steyn to French paper *Midi Olympique*. 'It's not the first time that he's done it. It's a lack of respect for Racing Métro and for me.

'I want to give everything for my club who respect me and take me as I am. I don't expect anything from the Springboks and I've moved on to other things.'

Petulant and moody, Steyn is in danger of sulking away the best years of his rugby life.

## 5 Thom Evans (Scotland)

It's almost ludicrous how much talent is contained within the Evans family. Father, Brian, was a golfer with enough ability to feature in a few Open Championships. Mum, Sal, sprinted and swam for Natal while younger brother Max was a qualified PGA golf professional until he decided to take up rugby full-time and win a regular place in the Scotland team.

Thom Evans also won a regular place in the Scotland team – his first cap coming five years after he quit the boy-band Twen2y4Se7en.

Quick, prepared to back himself, and intuitive, Evans gave the Scotland backline a spark it hadn't had for years. At 23, he was going to be one of the greats; a man to possibly lead Scotland to a brighter future.

Then tragedy struck on the day he won his tenth cap in February, 2010. He incurred a serious neck injury. His cervical vertebrae were so far out of alignment that doctors were amazed Evans hadn't been paralysed for life.

He was forced to retire from the game, leaving everyone to mourn the premature loss of a seriously gifted player.

## 4 Gavin Henson (Wales)

The thing about Henson was that his permanently tanned, almost orange skin, which was always clean-shaven (all over), his immaculate hair, use of moisturiser and desire to be a clotheshorse for anyone who paid, prevented some from seeing the talented rugby player within.

Henson, while probably not world class, could at least play. He was talented, and if he'd had the drive, discipline and professionalism to match, he could have been the sort of player that generations to come would know about.

But his selfishness and courting of the limelight has been to the detriment of his career. Henson is in it for himself. He was harsh about team-mates in his autobiography – written at the absurdly young age of 23, before he had achieved anything. He stormed out of the British Lions camp when he didn't make the test side in 2005 and then spent almost 18 months not playing while he appeared on reality TV shows.

When he did come back he joined Toulon, but his contract was almost terminated after just two games for his part in a brawl in a nightclub with team-mates after a game. Allegedly Henson had bad-mouthed Toulon fly-half Jonny Wilkinson and captain Joe van Neikerk, earning him a punch in the face from Australian scrum-half Matt Henjak.

Toulon owner Mourad Boudjellal had this to say of Henson: 'He has had an attitude which has been difficult to manage. We are not here to back him into a corner. He is a boy who makes mistakes sometimes. He's not the only one in rugby. There are others.

'But at Toulon, as Jonny Wilkinson says, it's 24/7 here. It's a disappointment because he's a great player.'

His legacy will die almost as soon as he stops playing. He'll be famous for not much: for trying ballroom dancing and almost being married to Charlotte Church.

## 3 John Gallagher (New Zealand)

John Gallagher made rugby look effortless. When he came into the line from fullback, it was like seeing a Ferrari reach the outside lane of the autobahn – everything perfectly calibrated, everything designed for precisely that moment.

Strangely, as he wasn't actually a New Zealander – he was born and bred in London, coming out as a teenager to play for Wellington club Oriental-Rongotai – Gallagher looked like he was made to be an All Black. He helped the All Blacks win the 1987 World Cup, won a total of 18 caps and established himself as the best fullback in the world between 1986 and 1989.

Then, at just 25, he defected to rugby league. Rugby union lost something special and its rival code paid top dollar for a bloke who never once came close to being anything. Gallagher was awful at league, and his wasted talent became a source of great pain for many New Zealanders.

## 2 Barry John (Wales)

The tragedy of John's career is not that it was littered with empty years, incorporating a few magic moments. It was his decision to retire at 27 when he was just getting interesting.

Those who saw him play reckon he may well have been the best fly-half of them all. The voice of rugby, the late Bill McLaren, once quipped during a commentary that if anyone ever caught John in a game, they were allowed to make a wish.

That was the perfect way to sum up a player whose skills were sublime and whose control and mastery of the game were almost too good to believe.

Such were John's talents that he tormented All Black fullback Fergie McCormick in the first Lions test against the All Blacks in 1971 to such a degree the New Zealander never played for his country again.

John scored 30 of the Lions' 48 test points in that successful series and earned the nickname 'The King', but the following year, with 25 Welsh caps to his name, he gave it all up. Players like Neil Jenkins and Stephen Jones with barely half John's talent are more widely recognised and more openly revered. The great man didn't leave a great footprint.

## 1 Rupeni Caucaunibuca (Fiji)

Between 2002 and 2004, Rupeni was the best player on the planet. There were even some – not brain-dead types who have to eat with a rubber cork on their fork – who reckoned he was the best player ever.

That's not such a ludicrous claim. Rupeni in his prime could score at will. In the 2003 season playing for the Blues he was devastating. Later that year, when he had obviously existed on a diet of deep-fried everything, Rupeni still stole the show at the World Cup even though he was 10 kg overweight.

He managed another exhilarating campaign for the Blues the following year, but the problem for Rupeni was that being 10 kg overweight became the norm. Blues chief executive David White famously revealed just how much hard work it had been getting Rupeni onto the field in the appropriate shape.

'You have to remember that Rupeni's life in the Islands was so different that it must have been an incredible culture shock when he arrived in Auckland,' says White. 'We really worked hard to put support systems around Rupeni to make sure he could play [to] the best of his ability. We were flexible and forgiving, and even then he had constant challenges around time-keeping and training disciplines. His income in New Zealand was limited but, looking back, you realise just how special a talent he was and can't help but wonder whether he would have been much more successful if he had stayed in Auckland for longer.'

Rupeni shifted from Auckland to Agen in the southwest of France and everything went really wrong. He was homesick and food, booze and fags became his best friends. His life became one ridiculous story after another about why he was not at training, and why he missed national team assemblies. He was forever reporting late for pre-season training, he mislaid his passport and missed a critical test for the Pacific Island team in 2006, and was banned for three months after testing positive for cannabis. Agen eventually terminated his contract in early 2010 when he disappeared without telling anyone where he was going.

His form never reached the heights it did for the Blues – didn't even get close – and the truth about Rupeni is that he never delivered after he turned 24. He could have been the biggest star to ever play the game.

# 10 coaching disasters

### 10 Mike Brewer, Sale, 2010

Former All Black flanker Mike Brewer was euphemistically referred to as an 'old-school' coach. Roughly translated that meant he was out of touch with modern methods and thought belittling his players in public would lead to improved performance.

That method gains little traction these days, as Brewer discovered when he lasted only eight months at English Premiership club Sale. Hired in April 2010, Brewer was booted out in December.

The club were lying tenth at the time, just one place above the relegation zone. The bigger problem was that his relationship with star man Charlie Hodgson had broken down. Brewer overlooked the sometime England fly-half for the captaincy, then publicly criticised him following a defeat to Wasps.

After Brewer was fired, Hodgson told the *Daily Mail*: 'Having stated what he did in the press when he criticised me after the Wasps game, that was it. Job done. Beforehand, a big part of the squad were not happy. The fact that [Sale owner] Brian [Kennedy] has made his decision [to fire Brewer] has uplifted the place. People don't get abused every day, and it's a nice place to come to work.'

### 9 Kiwi Searancke, Glasgow, 2002–2003

The turbulent world of Scottish rugby was forever attracted to volatile characters in the early years of professionalism. Money was tight, so both Edinburgh and Glasgow were looking for bargains.

Glasgow felt they had found value for money in June 2002 when they hired the New Zealander Kiwi Searancke as head coach. A likeable, dry character, the former Waikato coach was asked to give the side steel. They hoped his abrasive, call a spade a spade philosophy would toughen a talented but underachieving side. Good theory but bad in practice, as Searancke ended up going too far.

He was critical of his players too often. Almost weekly Searancke would publicly remark about their poor basic skills and questionable attitudes. If he thought it was a neat reverse psychology, it proved to be anything but. Glasgow fell further in the 2002–2003 season and were mired at the foot of the Celtic League. When they were thumped 45–3 by Sale in the Heineken Cup, Searancke received an official warning for verbally abusing the sponsorship manager.

When Glasgow continued to lose games, Searancke was fired in April. In announcing the decision, Scottish Rugby Union director Jim Telfer said: 'I think Kiwi is a very good coach but in hindsight it was the wrong decision and an error of judgement on our part. But what he said about Scottish rugby is actually true. He's very open and very honest, but it was the way he said it that backfired on him. I've seen him and his assistant, Steven Anderson, coach and speak and they were probably in the wrong culture.'

## 8  Jed Rowlands, Blues, 1999

When Graham Henry suddenly left the Blues in late 1998, the Auckland Super Rugby franchise were left scrambling for a new coach. Henry had won the first two Super Rugby titles and taken the Blues to the final in 1998, so the new man would be under pressure to deliver. Taranaki coach Jed Rowlands appeared to be the weakest of the candidates, who included the more experienced John Boe, Maurice Trapp and Mac McCallion. Yet it was the less experienced Rowlands who landed the post.

The former schoolteacher had a tough time engaging with a squad full of international players. The senior players didn't believe in Rowlands; he lacked credibility in their eyes and as the campaign, which had started badly, continued to fall apart, the players voiced their concerns.

After finishing ninth they held a meeting with the New Zealand Rugby Union, reported the *New Zealand Herald*. 'The players then excluded all officials and Blues staff from the room, discussed the season's dramas and after a unanimous discussion wrote down their unflattering resume of Rowlands' debut coaching season and asked for that to be forwarded to the NZRU,' said the paper.

Rowlands was gone a few weeks later.

## 7 Wayne Shelford, Saracens, 2002–2003

It wasn't easy for anyone to enjoy Buck Shelford's forays into the world of coaching. He was a classic example of a great player making an ordinary coach. Saracens should have had some idea they were getting an inferior product as Shelford had consented to a documentary being made about his time as North Harbour coach. The programme did not present his methods and ideas in a flattering light, but that did not deter the big-spending London club, who were desperate to get the best out of a star-studded squad.

The club felt that too many big names had come for the money and were coasting. Shelford was precisely the man to provide the hard edge that was missing. Shelford's first interview was a bit of a giveaway as to what was coming. 'A lot of players over here are too soft. Just because someone has played for France doesn't mean they are going to deliver,' he said.

That was followed by a week-long training camp with the Army. That brutal mentality persevered all season and failed to deliver improvements. Shelford flogged the players and they didn't respond. When a new chief executive, Mark Sinderberry, arrived at the end of the season, Shelford's tenure ended.

'When I arrived, Wayne Shelford was in charge,' said Sinderberry. 'Wayne was a fantastic player and a fantastic bloke. Nobody had a bad word to say about him. But very early on, we recognised that he wasn't the right person for the role and made the only decision we were able to make.'

## 6 Greg Smith, Bay of Plenty, 2009

Even the worst coaches have managed to stay in charge until the season proper has actually started. Not former Fiji and Waikato hooker Greg Smith, who was booted by Bay of Plenty on the eve of the 2009 provincial championship in New Zealand.

Bay of Plenty were desperate to stay in the top flight, which they knew was going to be cut from 14 to 10 teams at the end of the season. They had spent big to strengthen their squad and would be facing financial ruin if they were relegated. Smith, contracted for one year, had coaching experience at professional level in Japan and was seen as a rising star. But he was sacked just four days before the Steamers played their first game.

There was concern about the performances in the warm-up games – the Bay were defeated by Counties 28–19, then thumped 35–7 by Hawke's Bay. It seemed crazy to sack the coach so close to the start of the season, but the board concluded that the damage caused by keeping Smith on would be greater.

Smith arrived at training on 27 July and, after a meeting with chief executive Jeremy Curragh, drove home, leaving his assistants to take the session. 'We've got some concerns [about] the way the Steamers are tracking in such a critical season and we're working as hard as we can to get things back on track,' Curragh said when word leaked out about the day's drama.

'We've agreed with Greg that he should take a few days off and Steve [Miln] and Sean [Horan] will continue to take training in his absence, holding the fort.'

Smith never came back.

## 5 Matt Williams, Scotland, 2003–2005

No stranger to tough periods, even Scotland were shocked at just how bad they had become with Australian coach Matt Williams in charge of the national team.

Appointed in late 2003, Williams took Scotland through one of their worst 18 months in history where they won just three out of 17 tests. Williams had previously coached the New South Wales Waratahs and Leinster without any great success. Still, Scotland were convinced he was going to be their saviour.

He wanted to build a 'Fortress Scotland' mentality where players returned to Scotland to play their club football and hinted that those who didn't would not be picked for the national team. The second plank of his strategy was to lower expectations by reminding the public just how poor his players were. His final offering was to have virtually no idea how to build a game-plan or select a team.

Scotland actually had a handful of promising players, but they were either not picked or were asked to play in a vague style that made little sense. When crowds began to dwindle at Murrayfield and the national union could see it was heading into even more financial trouble, the decision was made to fire Williams in August 2005.

'I'm quite glad that the SRU are being accountable for the first time in a long time,' former lock Doddie Weir said when Williams was fired. 'It's nice to see them stand up and try to get some credibility back. Scottish rugby is at rock bottom just now and getting credibility back meant removing Matt Williams.'

## 4 Brian Ashton, Ireland, 1997–1998

In 1997 Ireland appointed Brian Ashton on a six-year contract. Ashton was seen as one of the more visionary and cerebral characters in English rugby, having helped transform Bath into the strongest club side in Europe on the back of an expansive game-plan.

The Irish players were excited to be coached by one of the more forward-thinking men in the game, but team manager Pat Whelan wasn't so keen. He and Ashton clashed and had several public disagreements and obviously a few more in private. The tension had an impact on the players – and undermined Ashton.

Ireland were thumped by Scotland and England in the Five Nations, and stories appeared in print on the eve of the 1998 championship about disharmony between Ashton and Whelan. 'Of course, differences arise in the normal course of events, but there are no serious problems between myself and Brian Ashton,' Whelan insisted.

His view was supported by Ashton, who said a week before the Irish opened their campaign against the Scots in Dublin: 'There are bound to be differences of opinion on some topics. After all, I'm

English, Pat is Irish and there were one or two points to be resolved. But that has been done.'

This charade fooled no one, and after Scotland won 17–16 Ashton resigned for 'personal reasons', his six-year contract over after just one year.

### 3 Laurie Mains, Highlanders, 2002–2003

At his peak – in the early 1990s – Laurie Mains was an excellent coach. But when he returned to the Highlanders in 2002 after a stint in South Africa, he had not evolved. The players no longer accepted the authoritarian, dictatorial ways of the past and cultures in New Zealand were inclusive.

The Highlanders were dominated by big-name players at the time – Carl Hayman, Anton Oliver, Carl Hoeft, Simon Maling, Josh Blackie, Taine Randell, Byron Kelleher and Tony Brown – and by early 2003 they had lost faith in Mains. When the 2002 campaign ended, the senior players had sat down with Mains and asked for more rugby-specific training, more work to be done on the game-plan and less time spent being physically battered. They had little patience for his methods and peculiar, arbitrary declarations on various matters such as what they could eat.

Oliver would reveal in his autobiography: 'After the 2002 season, many of the players were extremely unhappy; some were disillusioned. They felt Laurie was too often petty, needlessly picky about some matters, and was manipulative in ways that frequently left them feeling uneasy and insecure. The rule was no fat, no cheese, no eggs, no mayonnaise, no butter, but margarine was okay, for some reason ... I found Laurie's food-restriction fixation excessive and plainly ridiculous.'

By the middle of 2003 the squad called in the New Zealand Rugby Players' Association pleading for help. A letter was drafted to the New Zealand Rugby Union outlining all their concerns, and when the Highlanders failed to make the play-offs after a promising start, Mains left at the end of the season. Most of the players celebrated his departure.

## 2  Alex Wyllie and John Hart, All Blacks, 1991

Politics were to blame for the catastrophic decision to send the All Blacks to the 1991 World Cup with co-coaches. The idea of two men sharing power was novel and it was possible to make a theoretical case for it being a good idea.

In 1987 the All Blacks had a head coach – Brian Lochore – and two assistants, Alex Wyllie and John Hart. When Lochore retired in 1988, Wyllie, a gruff Cantabrian, took over and the basic but effective character of his coaching took the All Blacks through 1988 and 1989 unbeaten.

When the All Blacks ran into issues in 1990 – they dropped their captain Buck Shelford and lost their first game for three years – a strong Auckland lobby in administrative circles argued for the elevation of Hart to share the national coaching post. Never much of a player, Hart was an articulate and intelligent coach who had forged a strong career in the corporate world.

It was a desperately bad idea. The two men were barely on speaking terms. Tension spread through the team – a team that was poorly selected, as many of the players were either past their peak or brought in without having proved their worth. They struggled through their pool before being dumped out by Australia in the semi-final in Dublin. They were aloof and arrogant, with their two-man leadership team working against each other.

All Black flanker Paul Henderson would later comment: 'I never thought I'd say these words, but I wish I hadn't been picked for this [World Cup]. It's the worst experience I've ever had in rugby.'

## 1  Clive Woodward, British & Irish Lions, 2005

It was hard to see by the end of the British & Irish Lions tour of New Zealand in 2005 how coach Clive Woodward could have got things more wrong. His appointment was initially hailed as a victory for common sense – he was no longer in charge of a test side, having resigned from his English job in 2004 – so was ideally placed to devote his time to the Lions.

But he had some crazy ideas. He took 45 players, with some of them, such as Welsh scrum-half Gareth Cooper, restricted to less than an hour of game time. He took former UK Prime Minister Tony Blair's spin doctor Alistair Campbell, and he took a handful of players like Ollie Smith and Andy Titterall who weren't remotely close to being test class.

His other giant mistake was to cling to the erroneous belief that an aging core of England World Cup winners from 2003 should form the basis of the test team. Having bumbled their way to a victory against a mediocre Otago side a week before the first test, Woodward would famously claim: 'I've just got a really warm feeling about what's going on. Those of you at home, you should get on a plane and come over, even without a ticket. I've got a feeling something good's happening and don't miss it. It's been a great trip. No bullshit.'

The Lions lost the series 3–0 – the second test a record 48–18 thumping – and Woodward hasn't worked as a rugby coach since.

# 10 worst signings

## 10  Christian Cullen (Munster)

In his prime, Christian Cullen was one of the greatest attacking fullbacks the world had ever seen. Sadly, when Munster got him in late 2003 he was some way off his prime.

What irked the Irishmen about Cullen was that they just didn't see he was about to fall apart. He had recovered from a serious knee injury incurred in late 2001 and was unfortunate not to have forced his way into the All Black World Cup squad.

He showed enough in 2003 to suggest Munster were getting good value for the €300,000 a season they were forking out.

But Cullen arrived in Ireland with a bung shoulder that needed an operation. Then he had more issues with his knees. Then his pace seemed to desert him when he did return and no one in Ireland could understand what had gone wrong.

Munster got almost nothing out of Cullen, and when his three-year contract expired, they offered him a pay-for-play deal. He stayed for one more year – out of guilt to try to give the club something. He didn't magic much, and in four years with Munster he managed 45 appearances and 14 tries.

## 9  Waisale Serevi (Leicester)

It was understandable, maybe, why Leicester moved for Waisale Serevi. The diminutive Fijian was a recognised genius at Sevens and could make the impossible seem possible. No one ever laid a hand on him in the abbreviated game and his skills were outrageous.

Leicester thought he'd be able to bring that Pacific flavour to the Premiership and blow everyone away with his ability to be unconventional. Nice idea, but in practice Serevi hated the cold, despite his protestations to the contrary when he first arrived. 'I've just played through three Japanese winters and I know all about snow,' he told the *Independent*. 'I admit to feeling the cold during the World Cup Sevens at Murrayfield in 1993, but even the New Zealanders were moaning that weekend. It was freezing.'

Tigers coach Bob Dwyer was also keen to justify the decision to bring the Sevens expert to the English Midlands. 'They turn out on absolute mud-heaps in Fiji, you know. Either that or on something resembling concrete. He'll be fine, I promise you.'

He wasn't fine. In the mud of the English Premiership where oversized forwards lurk down every dark alley, Serevi was a disaster. He had no tactical appreciation, no real desire to be thumped in contact and, within a few weeks of him arriving in Leicester, it was fairly obvious things weren't going to work.

Initially signed on a two-year deal, Serevi was released after one and no one, other than the accountant, noticed he had gone.

## 8   Jason Little (Gloucester)

As professionalism took hold, big-name foreign stars became the must-have accessories of all the ambitious English clubs.

Gloucester decided in 2000 that they needed to get involved in the transfer market and spent up large on former Wallaby centre Jason Little. Still only 30, and having been part of the successful 1999 World Cup squad, Little didn't seem such a risk.

But Little didn't settle. He didn't have much talent around him and the Gloucester faithful, passionate about aggressive forwards and scrummaging, couldn't understand why some Australian was being paid massive amounts to flap his handbag in midfield.

Gloucester didn't get the results they wanted and there was also an undercurrent of rumours that the coach, former French international Philippe Saint-André, was no great admirer of Little's. Confirmation of sorts that relations were strained came at the end of Little's first season when he chose to leave and join Gloucester's arch-rivals Bristol.

### 7 Rico Gear (Nelson Bays/Tasman)

Struggling to get game time at the Blues, Rico Gear was going to sign with Canterbury at the end of 2004 to make himself eligible for the Crusaders.

But Canterbury also bought Mose Tuiali'i and Kevin Senio that year, the latter becoming an All Black (for 10 minutes) and scuppering Gear's move due to regulations that restricted transfers to two test players per season.

So Nelson Bays, in Division Two at the time, but aligned with the Crusaders, stepped in to buy Gear. They had to pay the All Black wing a signing-on fee of $100,000 and then another $100,000 in wages.

Gear made the move purely to make the Crusaders and ended up playing just seven games in two years. Nelson Bays (they became Tasman in 2005) effectively paid Gear $42,000 a game and, to show his gratitude, he refused to play for them in 2007 and wriggled out of his contract. After a public saga he signed with Canterbury as his wife wasn't happy in Nelson.

The following year Tasman had to be financially bailed out by the New Zealand Rugby Union. They were broke. In 2010 Tasman chief executive Peter Barr confessed his regret at the deal. 'I was involved in bringing Rico Gear here [initially for Nelson Bays] and the purpose of bringing [him] here was, because [Nelson Bays] were vying for a position in the top echelon of New Zealand rugby. We wanted to show the NZRU that we could attract good players to this region and so we did that.

'The fact that he didn't provide other value to us [attend sponsor functions and generally promote the game in the region] is probably because he had no affiliation to the province. He was more interested in playing for the Crusaders and also for the All Blacks.'

### 6 Riki Flutey (Brive)

England regular, Riki Flutey, decided to leave London Wasps in the summer of 2009, lured to France by a vastly improved pay packet.

He joined Brive and became one of many leading England players to sign with French clubs. It was all about the money – the French were able to pay significantly more on account of not being restricted by a salary cap.

Brive were confident they were buying a ball-playing inside back who could run their game for them from either 12 or 10. What they actually got was a bloke who was badly busted and spent the entire season having various operations. Flutey played just nine games for Brive before he decided life was better back in Blighty after all and returned to Wasps.

'Because of my injuries we were spending as much time in Britain as in Brive,' said Flutey when he was safely back in London counting his loot. 'We'd be there for a couple of weeks, back here for three, in Brive for four then in Britain for six. It was crazy and there was no way that my family could settle. That was the reason I left.'

## 5   Wendell Sailor (Australian Rugby Union)

The Australian Rugby Union became obsessed at the turn of the millennium with chasing the biggest names in the NRL. Someone in power became convinced that rugby, Australia's fourth football code, could make huge leaps in popularity by pillaging from league. So the ARU got out the chequebook and went after Lote Tuqiri, Mat Rogers and Sailor.

Sailor was the biggest name – a huge man who had made a huge contribution to the success of the Brisbane Broncos. The ARU had to pay unprecedented sums to get Sailor in 2001 – reportedly A$700,000 a season. The problem was Sailor never took to rugby. He couldn't turn quickly and wasn't much chop under a high ball. He didn't really know how to go looking for the ball either. Ultimately he was chosen for the Wallabies – but that was really about making his enormous salary seem worthwhile.

He always gave the impression he'd have been happier back in league, which is where he ended up. In 2006, after he tested positive for cocaine, his contract was terminated and a two-year ban was thrown in on top.

## 4  Ben Castle (Toulon)

For most of his career in New Zealand, Ben Castle had been recognised as a fairly solid if limited prop. When it was announced he'd be leaving the Chiefs in 2008 to join Toulon, no one was particularly surprised. Castle would be yet another journeyman New Zealander infinitely better paid by a foreign club.

But Castle barely lasted six months in France, where the scrum is everything. He was eaten alive. He'd managed to hide his technical deficiencies pretty well in the pass-and-catch world of Super Rugby. The French found him out in minutes. He joined in October 2008 and by January 2009 it was announced he would be joining the Western Force in Perth.

Incoming Toulon coach Philippe Saint-André had seen enough – Castle was never going to make the grade.

## 3  Geo Cronje (Harlequins)

There was considerable surprise, to put it mildly, when Harlequins announced in October 2004 that they had signed Geo Cronje.

The former Springbok lock had made headlines the previous year when he was sent home from a World Cup training camp for refusing to share a room with Quinton Davids, a black team-mate.

A reclusive figure who disliked leaving home and rarely spoke English, Cronje seemed an odd choice for the notoriously well-heeled Harlequins, a club renowned for City types. But they justified his arrival on the grounds that at just 24 and with test experience, they were buying a potentially world-class player who was big, rangy and aggressive.

Cronje, though, didn't even manage one game. He arrived with a damaged knee that wouldn't come right and after weeks of it swelling, it was announced he needed an operation that would keep him out of rugby for five to nine months. Harlequins released him immediately.

Harlequins manager Mike Scott tried and failed to find some positives about the deal: 'We are bitterly disappointed and his efforts to get fit have been tremendous. I know he is very frustrated. He wanted to play for Quins and he wants to play rugby. But the injury is an unusual problem and they have taken some cartilage out.'

## 2 Juan Martín Hernández (Natal Sharks)

After enormous speculation, Juan Martín Hernández signed a one-year deal to play for the Natal Sharks in the 2009 Currie Cup and 2010 Super 14. The Sharks had to dig deep into their coffers to get the man who starred at the 2007 World Cup with the Pumas, and was recognised as being of similar calibre to world greats like Dan Carter, Jonny Wilkinson and Matt Giteau.

The Argentine fly-half/fullback managed the first part of his contract, but not the second. He damaged his back on the eve of the Super 14 – the main reason he was in South Africa – and was ruled out for the whole tournament. The Sharks had to draft in England international Andy Goode, and while no one doubted the seriousness of Hernández' injury, suspicion grew he desperately missed France.

He signed for Racing Métro in May 2010, revealing to *Midi Olympique*: 'I miss Paris. I fell in love with this city and I realise it now.'

## 1 Dan Carter (Perpignan)

In their desperation to win the French Top 14 for the first time since 1955, Perpignan were prepared to pay All Black fly-half Dan Carter €650,000 for a six-month contract.

Carter was granted special dispensation by the New Zealand Rugby Union to play offshore between January and June 2009 in what was one of the best-paid sabbaticals ever seen. The New Zealander was at the peak of his powers, and Perpignan figured that as long as they were in the running when Carter joined (which they were), he'd be able to guide them to the title.

But Carter arrived on the back of a full season that had seen him play his first game in February 2008 in Christchurch and his last, a test match against England, in late November. It wasn't, then, a great surprise that in his fourth game for Perpignan, Carter's Achilles was damaged and he would not play again for the French club. Their €650,000 bought not quite 300 minutes.

And the greatest irony of all – Perpignan went on to win the title without Carter.

# 10 worst ideas

### 10 England running the ball, 1991

It's wishful thinking on England's part and spiteful gloating by everyone else, but the men in white probably would have won the 1991 World Cup if they had stuck to their game-plan.

England had made it there on the back of stoic, up-the-jumper stuff. Their set-piece was superb, they rolled the mauls beautifully, tackled expertly and played the most effective, tight, driving-grinding-kicking game.

It was what they were good at. It was what they had the players for. Inexplicably, come the final, they tried to run the ball from everywhere. They were reacting to some goading in the press by Australian wing David Campese who said they just weren't capable of playing pass and catch.

Rather than ignore the notorious motormouth, England reacted, had a team meeting and decided to prove him wrong. 'On the day, given the amount of ball the forwards won and the way we dominated up front, I think we should have won by about 50 points,' lamented tight-head prop Jeff Probyn years later. 'I remember we had a meeting before the game to discuss tactics and it was decided we would continue to play a forward-orientated game but open up when we could. But as soon as we got on the field the game-plan seemed to fall apart.'

Campese laughed all the way up Twickenham's steps to collect his winner's medal.

### 9 All Blacks reconditioning programme, 2007

In 2005 and 2006 the All Blacks were just about untouchable. They won 23 out of 25 tests, in many of which they used their second team. Those victories included a 3–0 series clean sweep against the Lions and a 47–3 demolition of France. On their end-of-year tour in 2006, they scored 40 points plus against England, France and Wales. The All Blacks were the best team in the world; their B side was the second best team in the world.

But the coaches worried about burnout ahead of the World Cup so decided to keep their 22 best players out of the first seven rounds of Super 14 in 2007 to rest and recondition.

In theory, it was a good idea. In practice, it was a terrible idea, with blanket programmes enforced, expectations and communication badly handled, and individuals left frustrated and angry at not being part of their respective Super Rugby campaigns.

Most of the players reached June short of games, out of form and their confidence shot. The All Blacks were knocked out in the quarter-final of the World Cup – their worst-ever result – and were barely a shadow of the side they were in November 2006.

## 8 Experimental Law Variations, 2008

In terms of spectacle the 2007 World Cup was horribly lacking. The final left the spectators in need of resuscitation, such was its ability to suck the life out of people.

In reaction, the International Rugby Board decided to see if they could fast-track their plans to introduce some experimental new laws. The southern hemisphere, always a sucker for any idea marketed as being for the rugby cavalier, volunteered to introduce the so-called Experimental Law Variations into the 2008 Super 14.

Australian Rugby Union chief executive John O'Neill highlighted the desire for change down-under when he suggested that without global adoption of all the new laws, the hemispheres could fall out irreparably. 'What would a World Cup be like without Australia, New Zealand and South Africa in it? No one wants to see two games, but unless there is a degree of reasonableness, it could happen,' he threatened.

But that just made the northern hemisphere more determined to dig their heels in and wait until later in the season before introducing change. The southern hemisphere players had to learn the ELVs in Super 14, then play the June tests under the old laws, the Tri Nations under the ELVs and the November tests under the old laws. Confused?

The players certainly were, and by the end of the year rugby was in a shambles. The failure to universally introduce the ELVs was a disaster for the sport and most of them were rejected anyway. It took until 2010 for rugby to be worth watching again.

## 7 Scotland's orange change jersey

Between 1998 and 2000 there were two man-made things visible from the moon: the Great Wall of China, and the Scotland rugby team's change shirt.

Someone, clearly with insufficient cranial synapses connected, decided that rather than persevere with the classic white alternate jersey, Scotland should adopt a luminous orange one.

It did in fact look like the colour of late-night vomit – the alcohol-induced kind. It was truly hideous, and the funniest part was the logic behind the change: the Scottish Rugby Union were convinced that switching to orange would boost replica sales.

It would be a surprise in the extreme to learn that anyone was daft enough to make a purchase.

## 6 World Rugby Corporation

Ross Turnbull nearly stole role rugby in 1995 when, armed with Kerry Packer's money, or supposedly armed, he came after the best players in the world and just about got them. His concept was World Rugby Corporation – a professional global tournament.

It was all a bit vague, but seemed to be suggesting that teams would be created in various parts of the world which would then play each other. Oh, and the players would have to forfeit their right to play international rugby. Hey presto – a competition.

Well, not really. The principles of all good competitions are consistent: they have to induce loyalty; fans have to identify with their team and feel connected. Opponents need to be relevant and preferably local to create some meaning, and in rugby especially, test football has to remain sacrosanct – the kingpin lording it over provincial contests so there is something more than money for which the players can strive.

WRC was soulless, spiritless and thankfully doomed when the IRB finally got its act into gear and responded by allowing the game to become professional.

## 5 Rejecting eligibility law changes

In 2009 the IRB had to vote on a proposal to change the eligibility laws to allow players from a Tier One Nation – New Zealand, England, Australia and the like – to be able to stand down and play for a Tier Two nation if they were qualified – Samoa, Fiji, Georgia and the like.

Overnight, the Pacific Island teams as well as the Eastern Europeans could be greatly strengthened to the extent that World Cup pool rounds could actually become interesting.

But wait a moment, some of the established chaps cried, that would run the risk of teams like, oh, say Scotland, Ireland and Wales becoming vulnerable against the likes of Samoa, Fiji and Tonga. Exactly.

So the Celts used their six votes to block the move and make sure that the world order of international rugby stayed just how it was. After all, the game, surely, wouldn't grow commercially if it had more genuinely competitive countries? No way.

New Zealand Rugby Union chief executive Steve Tew, who had been instrumental in getting the proposal to a vote, was dejected. 'The optimists thought we might get it through. The reality is there is a group of northern unions that is very nervous about strengthening the island nations,' he said.

## 4 England's Grand Slam Nike advert

It was understandable that England's key commercial partner, Nike, wanted to have a TV advert ready to run immediately should their client have beaten Ireland and secured a Grand Slam in the final Six Nations game of 2011.

But England's rugby bosses should never have agreed – the capacity for egg to splatter all over faces was enormous. They didn't think of that, however, and they allowed several of their leading players to be filmed for such a purpose in a truly cringe-worthy production.

And egg did indeed go splattering all over faces when England lost 24–8. Things went horribly wrong when somehow the ad was leaked onto the Internet and the world was able to see the likes of Ben Foden, Toby Flood and Mark Cueto prance around in celebration of being Grand Slam champions 2011.

Ooops!

'It is disappointing that details of Nike's internal planning has got into the public domain,' offered an RFU statement way too late to save face. 'In no way did the RFU or the England team underestimate the challenge that the Ireland team would pose. We were well beaten by a team who played better and we have the utmost respect for [Ireland coach] Declan Kidney and the Irish players.'

## 3 Dancing with the Calcutta Cup

It might have been the frustration of being involved in what was the single most tedious international game of rugby ever played. Or it might just have seemed like a good idea at the time.

Whatever, Scotland flanker John Jeffrey and England No 8 Dean Richards decided after a dire 9–6 victory to England in a 1988 Five Nations test at Murrayfield to take the Calcutta Cup out on the sauce with them.

Magic – the old trophy would surely love the chance to let its hair down and take in some of Edinburgh's seediest nightspots. What it didn't appreciate was being used as a football in the early hours. Obviously the worse for wear, the two players kicked the trophy through Edinburgh's cobbled streets and returned it badly damaged in the morning.

The upshot? One massive repair bill, a six-month ban for Jeffrey and curiously, somewhat unjustly, a one-week standdown for Richards.

'Myself and Dean did take it out on the town, and it came back damaged,' said Jeffrey. 'For that we have to hold our hands out and take our punishment, it's not something I'm particularly proud of, but what riles me is the disparity in the punishment between myself and Deano.'

## 2 New Zealand Rugby Union agreeing to apartheid

Everyone gets that South Africa and New Zealand became the fiercest of rivals in the 20th century and had the healthiest rugby respect for one another.

But everyone also knew that the South African Government had in place an abhorrent apartheid policy that meant Maori players wouldn't be able to travel to the Republic. Of course the All Blacks wouldn't agree to that – they would either take who they wanted regardless of background, or stay at home.

Er, no. The New Zealand Rugby Union rather gutlessly left their Maori players at home for the respective tours of 1928, 1949 and 1960.

In 1976 they travelled to South Africa again – this time the likes of Billy Bush (Maori) and Bryan Williams (part Samoan) were allowed to travel as 'honorary whites'. But New Zealand travelled against the advice and wishes of the rest of the world and 26 African countries boycotted the Montreal Olympics in protest.

In 2010, the centenary year of Maori rugby, the NZRU finally said sorry. 'We apologise to the families of those players and to the wider Maori community who were affected directly or indirectly by the decisions taken to not include Maori players. It was a period in which the respect of New Zealand Maori rugby was not upheld and that is deeply regretted.'

## 1 Kamp Staaldraad

Springbok coach Rudolf Straeuli thought his troops would benefit from attending a no-frills boot camp ahead of the 2003 World Cup.

He left the team's bodyguard, Adriaan Heijns, to take care of the details and the former SAS officer relished his task. The Boks headed to a police camp in the bush near the town of Thabazimbi.

The list of activities included players having to crawl naked into fox holes and have icy water poured over them. Once down there, they were asked to sing the national anthem while loudspeakers boomed God Save the Queen and the All Black haka.

They also had to crawl naked over gravel and spend a night in the bush where they had to catch and kill chickens but not eat them. Footage from the camp was leaked by the team's video analyst Dale McDermott, who was ostracised by many in South African rugby as a result, which led to his becoming depressed and later committing suicide.

Needless to say, the Boks suffered a dismal World Cup where they were hammered by England in the pool rounds and the All Blacks in the quarter-final.

Straeuli lost his job, and images of terrified Boks, standing naked in the dark holding rugby balls in front of their private bits, became the enduring images of the World Cup.

'When I heard the reports I thought the training methods were barbaric and outdated. If we want to be counted as one of the rugby superpowers again we will have to be a lot more scientific,' was South African Rugby Union chairman Rob van der Valk's rather understated reaction after stories of what happened began to leak. 'The time could have been better used promoting skills to get us back into the top three of world rugby, which is South African Rugby's performance measurement.'

# PART 3

# Countries

---

## Australia

---

### 10 best players

#### 10 Chris Latham (1998–2007)

It's tempting to describe Chris Latham as mercurial but that does him an injustice. His bad play was infrequent and never that bad either. He was able to score spectacular tries and produce rugby that was sometimes too hard to comprehend. His bravery gave him an edge and he had this ability to pull off the outrageous.

#### 9 George Smith (2000–2009)

It was a pity that the career of George Smith overlapped that of All Black openside flanker Richie McCaw. The excellence of McCaw often made it hard for Smith to earn the accolades he deserved. He was incredible on the ground – his ability to win turnover ball was better than McCaw's. Smith was a world-class player who held his own against the best and kept the Wallabies in tests they would otherwise have lost.

### 8  Phil Kearns (1989–1999)

One of the select crew to have won two World Cups, Phil Kearns was the ideal modern hooker. He was a big unit yet managed to get around and he was dynamic when he carried the ball. He was a noted scrummager and loved the rough and tumble.

### 7  George Gregan (1994–2007)

George Gregan played a silly number of tests – 146 to be exact – and for much of his last five years there was a vocal Australian lobby calling for him to stand down. But they could never get their way: Gregan was always the best halfback available. A sharp passer and deceptively strong, Gregan made everything happen around the tackled ball.

### 6  Michael Lynagh (1984–1995)

Michael Lynagh was a vastly underappreciated runner and backline orchestrator and it was only after he retired that the Wallabies came to realise what they had in Michael Lynagh. He was not only a technically proficient fly-half, but his hands were fast and soft and he could open teams up.

### 5  Stephen Larkham (1996–2007)

Stephen Larkham went from being a scrum-half at third-grade senior club rugby to Wallaby fullback in 18 months. He would then shift to fly-half after a few tests, because everyone could see he was an extraordinary talent with the skills to play in traffic and challenge the line. He was one of the best running No 10s since Barry John.

### 4 Nick Farr-Jones (1984–1993)

Intelligent and tough, Nick Farr-Jones was a cussed beast in his Wallaby No 9 jersey. He saw the game before it happened and was always one step ahead of opponents yet perfectly in tune with his own team. A towering captain and inspirational performer.

### 3 Tim Horan (1989–2000)

Tim Horan is one of only a handful of men to have won two World Cup medals. Few players have been as gifted. The powerfully built inside centre could jink or blast depending on what he fancied. He hammered on defence and he played with enough composure and all-round skill to comfortably slot in at fly-half on occasion.

### 2 David Campese (1982–1996)

The first Wallaby to win 100 caps, the greatest tribute to Campese was the respect in which he was held in New Zealand. The Kiwis knew Campese was rugby gold and admired the way he could score tries from anywhere and play with such vision. Campese was always dangerous.

### 1 John Eales (1990–2001)

John Eales earned the nickname 'Nobody' as in 'nobody is perfect'. There was nothing this bloke couldn't do. He was brutal in the collisions, one of the best lineout forwards in history, a tactically astute captain and a goal-kicker if required. There may never be another player quite like him.

# 10 best games

### 10 Australia 19–18 Ireland, 1991

Australia pulled off a miracle to reach the 1991 World Cup semi-final, and it was due to the calm and calculated brilliance of fly-half

Michael Lynagh. His level-headed approach typified the Wallabies of that era, and when he stood in for injured captain Nick Farr-Jones, he refused to panic when Ireland took the lead late in the quarter-final. With three minutes left, Lynagh orchestrated a brilliant move that led to him scoring to break Irish hearts.

## 9 Australia 32–15 France, 1989

This game marked the beginning of the Wallabies' recovery after the series loss to the British & Irish Lions. The key component was the hard edge brought by their forwards, something they felt had been missing earlier in the year. They held the French physically and then let their natural talents out wide do the rest.

## 8 Australia 24–3 France, 1993

The Wallabies were like a vet putting down a beloved pet when they played France in 1993. They were functional, cold and clinical in the way they dissected France in front of the Parc de Princes faithful.

## 7 Australia 22–10 New Zealand, 2003

Having ripped the Wallabies apart on the same ground only a few months earlier, the All Blacks were favourites to win the 2003 World Cup semi-final. But they encountered a tactically smart Wallaby team who out-thought and then out-fought the All Blacks. It was a performance of guile and ingenuity.

## 6 Australia 26–3 South Africa, 1992

The Boks had just been welcomed back out of isolation and began their assimilation with a test against the All Blacks. The following week they played the world-champion Wallabies and had their root pulled firmly out. The Wallabies gave the Boks nothing, rattling them hard and leaving them in no doubt that they had a massive amount of ground to make up if they wanted to have any impact at the 1995 World Cup.

## 5 Australia 28–7 New Zealand, 1999

A few months out from the World Cup, the Wallabies established their credentials with a stunning blitz of the All Blacks. The Wallaby forwards turned up angry and dealt to the New Zealanders, and the score remains a record defeat for the All Blacks.

## 4 Australia 51–15 England, 2004

When the Wallabies encountered a dry ball and fast track in Brisbane in their first encounter with England since their epic World Cup final battle, they decided to make the most of it. They hit England out wide, found space and were deadly; their backs ran riot.

## 3 Australia 40–15 England, 1991

The Wallabies never felt they played at their best at the 1991 World Cup, largely because they had set an incredible benchmark earlier in the year when they blew a good English side away in Sydney. The pace and movement were frightening and the ball zipped about leaving England chasing nothing.

## 2 Australia 59–16 France, 2010

This was the test when a young Wallaby backline showed the full range of their skills. Given a decent platform from their forwards, they were able to cut loose, scoring brilliant tries that were reliant on pace, precision, timing and confidence.

## 1 Australia 49–0 South Africa, 2006

It couldn't have been more emphatic. The Wallabies were fancied to win this Tri Nations encounter in Brisbane but not like this. They had free rein of the field, total control of the football and didn't stop to think why.

# 10 iconic moments

## 10 Victory on the Highveld

The Wallabies hadn't won at altitude in South Africa for 47 years when they played the Springboks in Bloemfontein in 2010. They were on track to sort that out when they led 31–6 after half an hour, but an incredible comeback saw the Boks lead 39–38 with one minute remaining. The Wallabies were handed one last chance with a penalty in the final minute, just inside the Bok half and wide on the right. But up stepped Kurtley Beale to land an incredible pressure kick.

## 9 Campo throws it away

The 1989 series between the Wallabies and British & Irish Lions was locked at one test each. The third was desperately close until the brilliant wing David Campese decided to launch a counter-attack on his own goal-line. He threw a terrible pass to Greg Martin, and Lions wing Ieuan Evans pounced on the loose ball to win the test. Defeat in the series led to the Wallabies ripping everything up to rebuild their team. They won the 1991 World Cup, with coach Bob Dwyer citing the series loss to the Lions as the catalyst.

## 8 Poetic justice

Steve Tuynman appeared to have scored a legitimate try in the second Bledisloe Cup test of 1986. But referee Derek Bevan didn't give it, which saw the Wallabies lose 13–12 and the All Blacks square the series. It was a painful blow as the Wallabies had never won a series in New Zealand. That injustice fuelled them to a huge performance in the third encounter at Eden Park, which they won 22–9.

## 7 Full bake in the cake tin

The All Blacks thought they were going to open the newly built Cake Tin stadium in Wellington with a victory in 2000 – they led the Wallabies 23–21 in the final minute. But they gave away a penalty and up stepped captain John Eales. The crowd were howling, the wind was blowing and four million people were willing him to miss. But Eales didn't flinch – he secured the win that ushered in a prolonged period of Wallaby dominance over the All Blacks.

## 6  Scottish sabotage

Australia came to the UK in November 2009 hoping to emulate the achievement of the great 1984 side that completed a Grand Slam against the four Home Unions. The opportunity was blown when they drew with Ireland, but worse was to come when they lost 9–8 to a lowly ranked Scotland team. The Wallabies had the chance to win it – Ryan Cross scored a try on full-time to give Matt Giteau a simple conversion. The fly-half missed, falling to his knees, aware that not only had Australia suffered a humiliating defeat but that this was pretty much the end of his test career.

## 5  Ella's personal Grand Slam

It was a delicious collaboration among the prodigiously talented Mark Ella, Roger Gould and David Campese that led to the first of them pulling off the unprecedented feat of scoring a try against every opponent on Australia's 1984 Grand Slam tour. The Wallabies swept their way past the Home Unions with stunning rugby, and when Ella collected an inside pass from Campese to crash over in the second half at Murrayfield in the final game, history was made.

## 4  The great escape

The Wallabies had lost their last 10 encounters against the All Blacks and were staring at defeat number 11 when they met in Hong Kong in October 2010. The All Blacks led 22–17 and, after holding out for a five-minute siege, turned the ball over inside their 22. All Black fly-half Stephen Donald just had to kick it out – but he kept it in, and James O'Connor ended up scoring and then kicking the tight conversion. It was a victory that intensified an already bitter rivalry and one that led to significant numbers of Wallabies extending their contracts in the belief that Australia's future was golden.

### 3 A double touch of class

The 1991 World Cup semi-final in Dublin was won by the Wallabies on the back of two flashes of genius. Both came from David Campese, the greatest wing they ever produced and the man who ignited the Wallabies in the 1980s and 1990s into being the world's best attacking force. Campese created one try with an outrageous no-look pass and scored the other himself with a brilliant acute dash across the face of the All Black defence.

### 2 The ultimate steal

The 2001 series with the British & Irish Lions was tied 1-1, and in the final minute the tourists had the chance to win the series. They had a lineout on the Wallaby five-metre line and had the forward power to drive over if they took possession. But Wallaby lock Justin Harrison took the brave call to challenge for the ball in the air, getting in front of Lions captain Martin Johnson and pulling off the most important steal of his career.

### 1 The big drop

Stephen Larkham dropped just one goal in his career – and what an impact it had. The 1999 World Cup semi-final was in danger of going on forever until deep into extra time, the scores still locked, Larkham dropped this low flapper that scraped over. It was an ugly way to win, but with France spent from their efforts beating the All Blacks in the semi-final, that drop goal effectively won the World Cup for the Wallabies.

# England

## 10 best players

### 10 David Duckham (1969–1976)

The blond-haired David Duckham played rugby the way many felt it should have been played. He had an incredible side-step that would see him go one way and his shock of hair the other. He could beat players one on one and scored tries that required pace and balance.

### 9 Andy Ripley (1972–1976)

Andy Ripley will never be forgotten by anyone who saw him play. He was an angular athlete – a man who probably could have won Olympic track and rowing medals if that had been his dream. He had an incredibly high knee-lift and a long stride which allowed him to be one of the great corner-flagging No 8s.

### 8 Jeremy Guscott (1989–1999)

Jeremy Guscott wasn't one of the best defensive operators but he was up there with the best offensive threats. He could glide onto the ball and drift into space. He scored plenty of tries but was also a talented kicker, which he showed with some well-timed drop goals throughout his career.

### 7 Stuart Barnes (1984–1993)

Stuart Barnes was never given a fair go by England – the selectors preferred the stoic talents of Rob Andrew. But Barnes had the skills and vision to play a game Andrew never could; Barnes was a runner and a player, Andrew was a pocket man and a kicker.

### 6 Jonny Wilkinson (1998–2011)

There have been better all-round No 10s than Jonny Wilkinson, but no one could match him as a tactical navigator and kicker. He was a machine who in his prime was the ideal fly-half for England. His kicking game hurt teams, and he knew when to flick the switch and back himself with a run. Probably the best defensive fly-half ever seen.

### 5 Will Carling (1988–1997)

The English captain was a deadly runner and a better defender than many realised. He was deprived of the ball for long stretches of his career as England pursued a forwards game, but there were always flashes of Carling's acceleration and ability to bust holes.

### 4 Peter Winterbottom (1982–1993)

An athletic open-side whose accuracy was legendary. As was his commitment and willingness to hurt for the cause. Winterbottom was fit in an age when many of his peers weren't, and he was single-minded in his pursuit of excellence. He would have made a lot of money if he'd been around in the professional era.

### 3 Richard Hill (1996–2007)

The quiet man of the England pack was versatile and uncomplaining. He made big tackles, won collisions, held bodies up and linked the play. It is easy to see why he was so highly regarded by his fellow professionals who knew he was a hard man.

### 2 Lawrence Dallaglio (1994–2008)

Lawrence Dallaglio made his first international appearance of note at the 1992 World Cup Sevens where he helped England win the title. He had the pace and ball skills to revel in Sevens, and he brought all that, plus rabid ferocity, to his work in the 15-a-side game. Dallaglio was colossal at times – almost unstoppable when he charged from the base of the scrum.

### 1 Martin Johnson (1993–2003)

A borderline thug but a brilliant player, Martin Johnson brought the same sort of intensity to the field as the legendary All Black captain Buck Shelford. Johnson was a mean operator – he never took a backward step and dealt with problems head-on. Could play a bit of rugby as well and had a neat range of skills.

# 10 best games

### 10 England 60–26 Wales, 1998

No wonder Wales were looking for a new coach shortly after this defeat. England destroyed them – it was humiliating at times, as the English were able to do what they wanted, when they wanted. It was a performance that showed England were on their way towards becoming an excellent side.

### 9 England 15–9 New Zealand, 1993

The All Blacks were confident they would do to England what they had to Scotland the week before – rip them apart. But the All Blacks were never able to cope with the power of the English forwards and couldn't get their hands on the ball. England were tactically astute and every one of them gave everything they had.

### 8 England 27–15 France, 1982

It took everything England had to beat a good French side so easily in 1982. It wasn't common for England to be so in control, so much quicker around the park and sharper to the ball. But they enjoyed 80 remarkable minutes to win with plenty to spare.

### 7 England 32–15 South Africa, 1994

South Africa were still feeling their way into test football after years in isolation in 1994 and learned a harsh lesson when they encountered a rampant England team who had aggressive and skilled forwards. England never let the Boks settle and turned a hostile crowd quiet.

### 6 England 16–10 New Zealand, 1973

This was a random result no one saw coming. The All Blacks had never lost a test to England in New Zealand before and the tourists weren't considered much chop. But they played well on the day, got their tactical approach right and executed superbly. They wouldn't win in New Zealand again for another 30 years.

### 5 England 25–6 Wales, 1991

It had been 28 years since England had won in Cardiff and they had to break that hoodoo. There had been a couple of draws in that period, but there was never going to be any other outcome than a deserved England victory in 1991. They squashed Wales – sat on them like a big brother, and used that performance to push on to win a Grand Slam.

### 4 England 15–13 New Zealand, 2003

England came to New Zealand in 2003 with the aim of psychologically damaging the All Blacks a few months out from the World Cup. They did just that when they managed to destroy the All Black pack – despite only having six forwards on the field at one stage. England were in control for the entire game despite only winning by two points.

### 3 England 25–14 Australia, 2003

A week after they had beaten the All Blacks, England flew to Melbourne and belted the Wallabies in a performance that was even better. That was England at their deadly best, the forwards both physical and athletic and the backs capable of finishing. England were the red-hot World Cup favourites after this game.

### 2 England 30–18 Scotland, 1980

England secured a Grand Slam in Edinburgh when they beat Scotland 30–18. And they beat the Scots with a potent mix of expansive back play and brutal work from the forwards. Wing John Carlton scored a memorable try and Bill Beaumont was in his element as captain.

### 1 England 42–6 Ireland, 2003

This was the game that finally secured England the Grand Slam that had evaded them on the final days of 1999, 2000 and 2001. They were ruthless and powerful. Their scrum was huge and they moved the ball when it was on. Ireland were glad it was only 42 they conceded.

# 10 iconic moments

### 10 Burton's Brisbane bombshell

Mike Burton made headlines around the world in 1975 when he became the first Englishman to be sent off in a test. The fearsome prop was given his marching orders in Brisbane after he hit Australian wing Doug Osbourne late. The tackle was more clumsy than malicious, but it earned England and Burton a reputation they could never shake.

### 9 Pumas bite at Twickers

It takes a lot for a home crowd to turn on their own, but the Twickenham faithful did just that in 2006 when they roundly booed at the end of the game. England had lost to Argentina – the first time the Pumas had won at the hallowed ground – and it was the latest in a string of poor performances by England. Coach Andy Robinson was sacked shortly after.

## 8 Bracken stays on

England selected the relatively unknown Kieran Bracken at scrum-half to play the All Blacks in 1993. The 21-year-old was five minutes into his debut when his ankle was deliberately stamped on by All Black flanker Jamie Joseph. The injury was severe – Bracken would be out of the game for three months – but he hobbled on; he decided he needed to show some bulldog spirit and his bravery inspired his senior team-mates to deliver a huge performance that enabled them to win.

## 7 Sheridan goes on the rampage

The sight of an angry Andrew Sheridan in 2005 may haunt the Wallabies for some time yet. The giant English loose-head was in such destructive form that first he forced off Wallaby prop Matt Dunning, then Al Baxter followed shortly after. Both Wallaby props had been buckled by Sheridan in one of the best scrummaging performances ever seen.

## 6 Picking Tonga's finest

In 2007 New Zealand-born Tongan national Lesley Vainikolo made his England debut. His presence on the England wing highlighted how desperate England were to claim any player as their own. Vainikolo qualified through the three-year residency rule and his presence opened the way for swathes of non-Englishmen to play for England. There were 12 non-Englishmen in the 45-man 2011 World Cup training squad.

## 5 Losing control

England came to Murrayfield to secure a Grand Slam in 1990 and were confident the job was already done. So confident they already had T-shirts printed. But 15 minutes into the game they were under pressure and captain Will Carling was losing control. He was being overruled by the forwards, who wanted to go for a pushover try when Carling wanted to kick the points. The bickering was a bad sign and the Scots ended up escaping from a series of scrums on their line without conceding. England knew then that they were in desperate trouble. They lost 13–7.

## 4 The hand of Campo

England surprised everyone – even themselves – with their expansive approach in the 1991 World Cup final. It was probably a bad call in the end when they had so little experience, but they were still in the game when David Campese seemingly deliberately knocked down what would have been a try-scoring pass late in the game. A penalty try was a realistic option but they were denied justice.

## 3 Big Lol's bust

England thrashed Wales 46–12 in 2000 and the try everyone remembers – the try that closed out the game – saw No 8 Lawrence Dallaglio pick up and drive from a five-metre scrum. Dallaglio was electric and powered through the first tackle and then kept going even though there were Welshmen hanging off his back. It was raw power at its best.

## 2 Arise Sir Clive

England made the brave and radical decision to appoint the inexperienced and relatively young Clive Woodward coach in 1997. It also turned out to be an inspired decision as he delivered the best sustained period of success in England's history. He turned England into a fiercely professional set-up that culminated in them winning a World Cup in 2003 as well as frequently defeating the best in the southern hemisphere.

## 1   Jonny's strike from heaven

With one minute of extra time left in the 2003 World Cup final, England's forwards took control of the ball and smashed their way into the right place. England fly-half Jonny Wilkinson fell into position and dropped a goal off his right foot to win the World Cup. Really, there will be no more memorable kick than that.

# France

## 10 best players

### 10 Jean-Luc Sadourny (1991–2001)

Having produced Serge Blanco, it seemed a little greedy of France to be able to introduce a player almost as good in Jean-Luc Sadourny. He was electric across the ground and played three steps ahead of everyone else, scoring tries few other players could.

### 9 Fabien Pelous (1995–2007)

There were undoubtedly better locks to play for France, but Pelous has to be recognised for his longevity and consistency. To play 118 tests in that position is remarkable, both for the pounding he took and for the fact he was able to win selection in a competitive berth for as long as he did.

### 8 Pierre Berbizier (1981–1991)

The pint-sized Pierre Berbizier was often compared to Napoleon. It was easy to see why; Berbizier was a tactical genius, knowing instinctively where opponents were strong and where they were weak. He was the beating heart of the French team for a long time, pulling every string they had.

### 7 Olivier Magne (1997–2007)

In his prime Olivier Magne was a freakish talent on the openside. He had the look of a 400-metre runner with that rangy stride of his. Huge engine, huge heart and probably skilled enough to play in the midfield.

### Pierre Villepreux (1967–1972)

Had an incredible tactical brain that allowed him to torment opponents with both his running and kicking game either from fullback or fly-half. It was at fullback where he excelled, his love of the counter-attack inspiring a generation to see the berth as one for the creative and visionary rather than the defensively sound. His knowledge enabled him to become a successful coach with both France and Italy.

 ### Jo Maso (1966–1973)

Jo Maso was the manager of the French team forever. It was a position he was able to hold between 1999 and 2011 because of the respect in which he was held. And that respect was earned as a player with a range of skills that cut open any midfield he encountered. Maso had time on the ball and always made the telling pass or the right decision.

 ### Jean Prat (1945–1955)

Unfortunately named but blessed in every other way, Jean Prat was the man who put French rugby on the map. Before he arrived they were a sporadic bunch. But Prat gave them structure, belief and a touch of magic. He was a fearless flanker who earned the nickname Monsieur Rugby.

 ### Laurent Cabannes (1990–1997)

Laurent Cabannes was the sort of player every coach in world rugby would have loved to have had. A natural athlete who could roam with purpose, he could also win lineout ball, make big tackles and link the play. He was a No 7 to treasure.

## 2 Philippe Sella (1982–1995)

To many astute judges Philippe Sella remains the best centre to ever play the game. He was comparatively small by modern standards but lacked nothing in power. He was quick and agile and yet rock-solid on defence. He had the total game; he was the total player.

## 1 Serge Blanco (1980–1991)

Everyone loved Serge Blanco. He played with adventure and spirit, as if anything was possible, which it usually was when he was involved. He glided across the turf, found holes where there weren't any, and made the game look ridiculously easy. Not bad for a bloke who smoked 80 fags a day.

# 10 best games

## 10 France 20–12 Scotland, 1994

Normally wins against Scotland don't set the pulse racing or have anyone believing they have pulled off a miracle. But this victory in 1994 was critical as it was the first time in 16 years the French had won in Edinburgh. It was a massive psychological hurdle for them to clear. Since making the breakthrough they have seen an uplift in their Six Nations away form.

## 9 France 20–13 South Africa, 2009

The Boks came to France in November 2009 on the back of a 3–0 series win against New Zealand. They were in imperious form and France smashed them. They took them on physically and won; they took them on out wide and found holes; and when it came down to it, they had more desire and more ability.

### 8 France 31–6 England, 2006

This equalled France's record win and all victories against England are to be savoured. Admittedly England were awful, but the French were largely responsible for that: they didn't let England settle, harassed them and intimidated them, and then took all their chances.

### 7 France 9–5 South Africa, 1958

Not many teams win a test in South Africa, let alone a series. But the French managed to do both in 1958 with a 9–5 victory at Ellis Park in Johannesburg. That followed a 3–3 draw in the first test. France were still relative newcomers on the big stage following their late entry into the Five Nations, and to put their achievement into perspective, the All Blacks only managed to win their first test series in South Africa in 1996.

### 6 France 20–18 New Zealand, 2007

Having lost to Argentina in the opening game, France ended up playing the All Blacks in Cardiff in the 2007 World Cup quarter-final. They were desperate to avoid being eliminated from their own tournament in Wales, making an incredible 300-plus tackles, scoring two great tries and then holding the All Blacks out for the last 12 minutes.

### 5 France 22–8 New Zealand, 1994

It takes an enormous performance to beat the All Blacks in New Zealand and that is exactly what France gave in the first test of the 1994 series. They had the All Black scrum under pressure, were winning lineout ball at will and had plenty of good ideas about what to do with the ball. It wasn't even close.

## 4  France 8–3 Wales, 1928

There was reluctance among the Home Unions to allow the French entry into what was then the Four Nations. And France struggled for a long time before they were able to regularly win games. One of the major milestones was the 8–3 defeat of Wales in 1928. That was their first against the Red Dragons and the beginning of the French renaissance.

## 3  France 16–9 Wales, 1977

The Welsh were the dominant force of Five Nations rugby in the 1970s so the fact France were able to defeat them and go on to clinch a Grand Slam was a major achievement. The championship was clinched in Ireland but it was the 16–9 win against Wales in Paris that was critical. The French were dynamite, taking no prisoners, and their multiple hard men in the pack made sure the Welsh resistance was broken.

## 2  France 51–0 Wales, 1998

This was one of those days when the French were at their spellbinding best. Playing at Wembley, they found their rhythm early and were in the mood to fulfil their considerable potential. The forwards were brutal, the backs beautiful. Wales didn't stand a chance.

## 1  France 43–31 New Zealand, 1999

This was maybe the greatest game of rugby ever played. France were given no chance beforehand and even less than that when they were 24–10 down a few minutes after half-time in the 1999 World Cup semi-final. Then something happened. They went ballistic, scoring 33 points in 27 minutes. No one really knows how that happened but it was glorious, glorious, glorious.

# 10 iconic moments

### 10 The human tricolor

In the build-up to the 2007 World Cup quarter-final there was endless debate among France, New Zealand and the IRB about what colour jerseys the teams would wear. It put both teams on a war footing – which became obvious when the French faced the haka. Each player wore a red training top, with their white match shorts and blue socks. They were human tricolors – their passion and emotion quite stunning.

### 9 Chabal's big hit

The French took a 'B' squad to New Zealand ahead of the 2007 World Cup. It was one last chance for fringe players to force their way into the picture. Only one man was able to do that – Sébastien Chabal. The French were hammered by the All Blacks in both tests, but the big No 8 became a celebrity and the highest-paid player in France when he knocked down and briefly knocked out his opposite man, Chris Masoe, in what would be a contender for tackle of the century.

### 8 Seeing red

In 1992 France were out for revenge when they played England in Paris. The two had fought a bloody battle in October 1991 at the World Cup, which the English won. France decided they were going to fight their way through the 80 minutes; Gregoire Lascube was the first to be sent off for kicking lock Martin Bayfield in the head. Then Vincent Muscato went for causing mayhem in a scrum. Reduced to 13 men, France were hammered 31–13 and the sight of referee Stephen Hilditch being escorted off the field by police was unforgettable.

### 7  Capital kick

In 1968 France played the All Blacks in Wellington with the capital enduring one of its infamous hurricane-strength winds. France were awarded a penalty well inside their half and opted to kick for goal. The crowd was bemused, but fullback Philippe Villepreux toe-poked the ball almost 70 metres with the wind at his back for one of the great long-range efforts.

### 6  Bleeding for the cause

It was an image that summed up the commitment of Jean-Pierre Rives. Playing against Wales in 1977 wearing the French alternate white shirt, the blond-haired Rives was bleeding profusely from a head wound, his white shirt looking like it had been put through a coloured wash such were the stains from his blood.

### 5  Try of the century

In a Five Nations clash at Twickenham in 1991, England kicked for goal to try to increase their 6–0 lead. The ball drifted past the uprights. Serge Blanco should have touched down for the 22 but instead he decided to run. He made a neat pass to Jean-Baptiste Lafond and three more passes would see the French in space. Fly-half Didier Camberabero gathered his own chip ahead and then booted back into the middle of the field where left wing Philippe Saint-André gathered and scored – English fans would later vote it Twickenham's 'Try of the Century'.

### 4  Drama in Durban

The semi-final of the 1995 World Cup was delayed by two hours while organisers tried to sweep rain off the field at King's Park, Durban. France and South Africa battled through 80 minutes on a heavy field, the game tense and brutal. The French – trailing 19–15 – laid siege to the Boks' line in the last five minutes. No 8 Abdel Benazzi seemed to crash over and touch down through a mêlée of bodies. Was it a score? No, said referee Derek Bevan. It broke French hearts and was of the most contentious decisions in World Cup history.

### 3 Serge's late surge

Only France could have scored the try that saw them defeat Australia in the semi-final of the 1987 World Cup. It took belief, confidence, inordinate skill and daring to keep the ball alive for so long and score in the corner. The try was brilliant – but it was really the reaction of scorer Serge Blanco that was memorable. Having blasted in at the corner to win the game, he tried to stand up, fell down to his knees, looked to the heavens, put his hands in the air and roared with elation.

### 2 Sella's century

While it was commonplace in football, no rugby player had won 100 test caps until Philippe Sella was selected to play against the All Blacks in Christchurch 1994. It was a huge moment for him, France and world rugby. It was made all the more special by the fact the French won.

### 1 Try from the end of the earth

The French had beaten the All Blacks in the first test of their 1994 series, but were left with only a couple of minutes to win the second and make history. It seemed unlikely they could pull off the salvage operation – but when All Black fly-half Stephen Bachop missed touch with a clearance, the French began a counter-attack deep inside their territory that was breathtaking in its execution, fluidity and skill. They ended up scoring through Jean-Luc Sadourny to win their first series in New Zealand – and it became known as the 'try from the end of the earth'.

# Ireland

## 10 best players

### 10　Tony Ward (1978–1987)

A lively and gifted footballer, Tony Ward was unfortunate to overlap with the more pragmatic and prolific Ollie Campbell, whose boot came to be Ireland's key weapon. The romantics always wanted Ward to be at fly-half – to bring Ireland alive with his acceleration, adventure and guile.

### 9　Keith Wood (1994–2003)

There was never a dull moment when Keith Wood played for Ireland. His gleaming bald head buzzed around with great effect. He was a touch mental in the way he had no regard for his own safety, and he was highly skilled. Desperately quick and agile, he never failed to surprise by what he could pull off. One of the great hookers of the professional age, he would have had an even greater impact had it not been for multiple injuries.

### 8　Tony O'Reilly (1955–1970)

Selected for Ireland when he was just 18 and then for the Lions at 21, Tony O'Reilly enjoyed the longest test career in Irish history. He had the pace and bravery to finish from anywhere on the field and was inducted into the Hall of Fame in 1997.

## 7 Willie John McBride (1962–1975)

More famous for his work in the Lions jersey, Willie John McBride still did plenty for Ireland – he clearly wouldn't have been selected for four Lions tours otherwise. A quiet, thoughtful man off the field, he was controlled fury on it.

## 6 Fergus Slattery (1970–1984)

There was a touch of the crazies about Fergus Slattery, a man who would definitely be considered one of the game's 'good bastards'. Quick as a wing, he punished teams from the openside with his pace and instincts. He was also famously committed, and that combination won him 61 caps for Ireland and a place in the 1974 Lions back-row that is considered one of the best of all time.

## 5 Tom Kiernan (1960–1973)

Tom Kiernan held just about every record imaginable by the time he retired. He was Ireland's record cap-holder, record points-scorer and was also the man who had captained Ireland (24 times) more than anyone else. A fullback with punch and goal-kicking accuracy, Kiernan also read the game superbly from the backfield.

## 4 Paul O'Connell (2002–)

Paul O'Connell continues a great Munster tradition of producing bone-hard, physical forwards who are happy to throw themselves about legally or otherwise. A thundering big man, he is technically polished and mobile yet never one to shirk the core jobs. His captaincy of the Lions in 2009 proved his standing as one of the great locks of the modern era.

## 3 Jackie Kyle (1946–1958)

Inducted into the International Hall of Fame in 1999 and named the Greatest Ever Irish Rugby player by the Irish Rugby Union in 2002, Jackie Kyle holds a special place in his nation's heart. A supremely talented fly-half, he was so skilful that barely a hand was laid upon him in 46 tests.

### 2 Mike Gibson (1964–1979)

For a long time the Irish didn't think they would produce a better player than Mike Gibson. His test career spanned 15 years and he pretty much played across the backline. Throw him a jersey and he'd excel. Elegant and subtle, direct and deadly, he had everything he needed.

### 1 Brian O'Driscoll (1999–)

Tough, durable and deadly accurate, O'Driscoll was the world's best centre for most of the first decade of the new millennium. He scored tries, made tries, tackled hard and captained the Lions as well. The best.

## 10 best games

### 10 Ireland 13–12 England, 1994

None of the Celtic teams have enjoyed much luck at Twickenham. But in 1994 Ireland produced 79 minutes of perspiration and one minute of inspiration when a brilliant backs move sent flying wing Simon Geoghegan in at the corner for a famous win.

### 9 Munster 11–0 New Zealand, 1978

There isn't really a more famous game in Irish folklore than this one. Everyone in Ireland apparently was there, and it ended up with a play being written about a game no one wants to forget. Ireland have never beaten the All Blacks, so the fact an Irish province has is something quite special.

### 8 Ireland 15–10 South Africa, 2009

The Springboks had been the world's number one team for most of 2009. They were the masters of kick-and-chase rugby, which was all the rage that year. But they encountered an Irish team at Croke Park in late November that could match them physically and stretch them out wide. Five Johnny Sexton penalties were enough to get the job done – this was a classy win.

### 7 Ireland 18–9 Australia, 2002

This was the performance that clarified Ireland had a golden generation of players; they had shed their amateur past of underachievement. They were better than the world champions across the park and turned their opportunities into points. The Ireland of old would have run out of steam in the final quarter, but this brave new professional Ireland – they had belief and got the job done.

### 6 Ireland 43–13 England, 2007

It's rare indeed for England to fall by such a heavy loss to any side, let alone Ireland. But they stood little chance in Dublin when the Irish made a compelling case to be taken hugely seriously ahead of the World Cup. They did everything right and played with such pace.

### 5 Ireland 54–10 Wales, 2002

Admittedly this record win had plenty to do with Wales' incompetence, but it still took a classy performance by Ireland to make it as convincing as it was. They were on fire in the second half, playing from touchline to touchline like they were the All Blacks.

### 4 Ireland 11–8 France, 1952

Obviously the Irish didn't know it at the time, but they wouldn't win another test in Paris until 2000. It was probably only in that

28-year gap that the quality and scale of the achievement in 1952 came to be appreciated.

### 3 Ireland 15–6 Australia, 2011

This was the game that turned the 2011 World Cup upside down. On a wet Auckland night, the Irish forwards beat up the Wallabies for 80 minutes, smashing them off the ball at every collision and then buckling their scrum. It was brave and relentless, tactically smart and composed.

### 2 Ireland 15–8 Australia, 1967

A supreme piece of opportunism by Mike Gibson was the catalyst for this famous win. Gibson was at his best, managing to fire out of the defensive line to intercept a pass on the Wallaby 5-metre line and crash over. Gibson was at his peak – inspirational in the most infectious way.

### 1 Ireland 20–14 England, 2001

For the third consecutive year England reached the final day of the Six Nations with the Grand Slam in sight. In 1999 it was the Welsh who surprised them, in 2000 the Scots, and in 2001 the Irish played party-poopers. Their victory was built on a defensive effort that may rank as the best in their history. England were overwhelmed by green jerseys and the pressure was too much for them.

# 10 iconic moments

### 10 The baby-faced assassin

On a glorious spring afternoon in Paris the Irish were given no chance against an in-form French team in 2000. But the men in green lifted to incredible levels and the baby of their team, 21-year-old Brian O'Driscoll, scored three memorable tries. Everyone knew then – they had a special talent in their midst.

### 9 Rough justice

Ireland had the All Blacks rattled in Dublin in November 2001. They were leading 16–7 late in the first half and were pushing hard for another try. They created an overlap but the last pass was slapped down by All Black lock Norm Maxwell, who was offside. The crowd held their breath – a penalty try was on the cards, but referee André Watson decided against it. It was one of those moments; if it had been given, Ireland most likely would have pushed on for their first win against the All Blacks. Instead the All Blacks saw it as a turning point and scored five second-half tries to win 40–29.

### 8 Night of the long knives

Ireland appeared to be on their way to a brighter future in late 2001, having pushed the All Blacks much closer than the 41–29 scoreline suggested. But despite that encouraging performance, coach Warren Gatland was suddenly sacked shortly after, stabbed in the back by a divided Irish Rugby Union. There were certain administrators with power who wanted Gatland out so they could promote his assistant Eddie O'Sullivan.

### 7 Fingering the All Blacks

The All Blacks were heavily fancied to win their 1995 pool clash with Ireland, which of course only served to fire up the underdog and have them barking wildly by kick-off. When prop Gary Halpin scored an early try for Ireland he celebrated by turning to the All Blacks and giving them the 'fingers' with both hands. There was some glee and spite when he did it, too.

### 6 The ugliest kick in history

In 59 years of trying the Irish had never beaten South Africa and were heading for a draw in 1965. The scores were locked at 6–6 with only a few minutes remaining, but a powerful Irish scrum on the Springbok 10-metre line earned a penalty. Fullback Tom Kiernan stepped up, full of confidence, to scud the ugliest kick in history just over the cross bar to secure the victory.

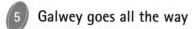

## 5 Galwey goes all the way

An overconfident England came to Lansdowne Road in 1993 certain they were going to win and take out the Five Nations. They were also confident they would be rewarded with a huge number of places in the Lions squad named the following day. Instead they encountered a rampant Irish side at their passionate best; Eric Elwood was immaculate at fly-half and kicked 12 points. But the defining score came from man of the match Mick Galwey, the Munster lock going over in the corner after Will Carling had been hammered in midfield and had spilled the ball.

## 4 Crowning glory

Ireland were attempting to win a Triple Crown in their final game of the 1985 Five Nations, having beaten the Scots and Welsh. They were only a whisker away from a Grand Slam, as they had drawn 15–all with France in their previous game and were staring at another draw with the score at 10–all against England in the final minute. But a lineout drive by Donal Lenihan took them deep into England's 22 and Michael Bradley fired it back to Michael Kiernan, who struck the winning drop goal.

## 3 BoD breaks the record

It was fitting that Brian O'Driscoll, having been one of the great figures to feature in the Six Nations, should become the tournament's record try-scorer in 2011. In a typically committed Irish performance against England on the final weekend, O'Driscoll roared over early in the second half for his 25th Six Nations try. It was also critical in hammering one more nail in England's coffin, Ireland winning easily 24–8.

## 2 Off the long run

With six minutes remaining of a tense World Cup quarter-final in 1991, who could ever forget the sight of Irish openside flanker Gordon Hamilton scoring in the corner of Lansdowne Road? His legs tying up, the Wallaby defence catching ... he held on for a try that let a nation believe for three glorious minutes they had pulled off the greatest win of their history.

## 1 Ending the agony

Having waited 61 years for a Grand Slam, it's not likely that anyone Irish will ever forget the moment in 2009 when Ronan O'Gara dropped a goal with three minutes remaining against Wales to secure the clean sweep. Under incredible pressure, he kept his head down and never looked like missing.

# New Zealand

## 10 best players

### 10 Don Clarke (1956–1964)

The big Waikato fullback became a lethal weapon in a period when pitches could be heavy and games unable to flow. His massive right boot could bang the ball over from prodigious distances, and Clarke won the All Blacks several test matches on the strength of his ability to convert pressure into points.

### 9 Frank Bunce (1992–1997)

Frank Bunce didn't win his first All Black cap until he was 30 but he made the most of his opportunity once he was in the team. He was a cussed player, a hardened campaigner who played with his wits about him. A brilliant distributor with innate timing, Bunce brought his back three into the game. He also became a good finisher himself, his strength on his feet being the key to his game.

### 8 Colin Meads (1955–1971)

The rugby player within Meads was always more impressive than the thug he could sometimes be. Meads was a raw athlete who famously used to run with the ball gripped in one hand. He was powerful and rangy, capable of winning the ball and using it. The All Blacks tended to win the collisions when he was playing.

### 7 Sean Fitzpatrick (1986–1997)

Sean Fitzpatrick became known as a great captain, which he was. But that sometimes meant his role as a player was overlooked. He was a great hooker in his final few years. His throwing was faultless, his scrummaging low and aggressive, and he became expert at knowing when to lurk on the wing and use his pace and bulk to bash over for tries.

### 6　Zinzan Brooke (1991–1997)

Zinzan Brooke was a footballer of rare class. He was more talented than most backs and full of tricks – he could throw huge backhand passes, flip the ball out of contact and he could drop goals. But none of this was at the expense of his core skills. He was tough and uncompromising, happy with a wet or dry ball.

### 5　Christian Cullen (1996–2002)

Christian Cullen scored a hat-trick on debut and pretty much continued in that vein. His record of 46 tries in 58 tests says it all. He was a fullback who could change direction at top speed without losing any momentum. He was deceptively strong and capable of knocking men down on defence despite an obvious lack of bulk. The try he scored in Dunedin in 1997 when he burst clear from his 22 and left George Gregan tied in knots was pure class.

### 4　Dan Carter (2003–)

There has never been a fly-half with the all-round skills of Dan Carter. He can do everything and he can do it to world-class standards. He's a magical runner, has a huge boot, reads the game expertly and tackles hard. He's cool under pressure and has the gift of time – he never looks hurried.

### 3　Jonah Lomu (1994–2002)

The exploits of Jonah Lomu are presumably known the world over. He was the man who put world rugby on the map with his performances at the 1995 World Cup and again four years later. He was 120 kg of lean beef in his prime – quick enough to run

100 metres in 11 seconds flat and curiously nimble. Lomu could run over anything or around them if he could be bothered.

## 2 Michael Jones (1987–1998)

Nicknamed 'The Iceman', Michael Jones was as quick as a wing, as strong as a lock and as agile as a fly-half – a never-before-seen package. His tackling was destructive and intimidating, yet he was so much more than a hit man. He was athletic and skilled, comfortable on the ball and more than capable of using it effectively.

## 1 Richie McCaw (2001–)

New Zealand has been able to produce an outrageous number of good opensides, but the king of them all is Richie McCaw. Three times he's been the IRB Player of the Year and it probably could have been more. He can run with the ball, win it on the ground and tackle. He's never had a bad test and is deemed to have played two perfect games: in Brisbane in 2006 and in Cape Town in 2008.

# 10 best games

## 10 New Zealand 29–9 France, 1987

This game was significant more for the result than the performance. The All Blacks were functional and clean in the way they dissected the French in the World Cup final. There was nothing fancy or showy – just good adherence to the basics and a cast-iron will to not feel any pressure.

## 9 New Zealand 19–0 South Africa, 2008

This was the only time in South Africa's history they have been held scoreless at home. They couldn't break a relentless defence and they couldn't break it because they couldn't get their hands on the ball. Richie McCaw played the game of his career, even setting up a try with a grubber kick.

## 8 New Zealand 20–6 Australia, 2011

The All Blacks took charge of the 2011 World Cup semi-final from the first seconds. The Wallabies put the kick-off out on the full and the All Blacks crushed them from there. New Zealand's scrummaging was brilliant and their ability to deal with the high ball unfailingly accurate. They were inventive and controlled, playing with aggression yet discipline.

## 7 New Zealand 30–18 British & Irish Lions, 1993

The All Blacks had been awful in the second test, which had kept the series alive and also put the hosts under enormous pressure. They bounced back with a commanding display that was everything they weren't the week before. They controlled every aspect of the game and left no doubt they were the better side.

## 6 New Zealand 52–3 Wales, 1988

Sometimes things just click for rugby teams – this was the case in 1988 when Wales, admittedly not a great team, were belted by an All Black side that could do no wrong. This was the All Blacks at the peak of their powers during a three-year undefeated stretch. It was high-tempo, brutal rugby that blasted big holes in the Welsh psyche.

## 5 New Zealand 33–26 South Africa, 1996

This victory took courage. The All Blacks had to weather an initial Springbok storm, then a late siege. It took composure to make sure all opportunities were converted and it took enormous belief and confidence to blot out the occasion; the All Blacks had never won a series in the Republic and this was the clincher – a game many of the players felt was bigger than the World Cup final.

### 4  New Zealand 48–18 British & Irish Lions, 2005

Dan Carter and Richie McCaw were at their imperious best and helped by a big game from captain Tana Umaga. The rugby was played at tempo and with width, and the gulf in skills was enormous.

### 3  New Zealand 45–29 England, 1995

Emphatic doesn't even get close to describing this victory. The All Blacks played the best half of rugby in World Cup history to lead 25–3. Jonah Lomu would end up scoring four tries, Zinzan Brooke dropped his goal on the charge and England were shell-shocked.

### 2  New Zealand 43–6 Australia, 1996

Playing in atrocious conditions, the All Blacks made just three unforced errors in what is widely considered to be the best performance of wet-weather rugby ever produced. The Wallabies didn't fancy the howling gale and lashing rain, but the All Blacks were in their element – they were scarily good.

### 1  New Zealand 39–35 Australia, 2000

Many consider this the greatest game of rugby ever played. It was an impossible game to follow. The All Blacks scored three tries in the first eight minutes to lead 24–0. Yet it was 24–all at the break. The Wallabies were leading 35–34 with a minute left, then Lomu broke free down the left, swatted handfuls of Wallabies out the way, stayed infield (just) and touched down for a breathtaking winner only he could have scored.

# 10 iconic moments

### 10  Outrageous fortune

At the 1995 World Cup the All Blacks, despite not winning the final, were playing different rugby to everyone else. They were fitter, faster, more aware and their skills, to a man, were better. That was demonstrated in the semi-final when No 8 Zinzan Brooke dropped a goal from 45 metres. That was the act that confirmed the All Blacks have innate skills that everyone else can only gawp at.

## 9  A united front

The British media had gone nuts about the tackle made on Brian O'Driscoll in the first minute of the first test between the All Blacks and Lions in 2005. When Umaga eventually fronted the media three days later, a few seconds after he sat down, the entire All Black squad filed in and stood behind their skipper in a show of solidarity. A few days later Umaga was in top form, leading the All Blacks to a 48–18 victory that clinched the series. The British media had provided the ultimate emotional fuel.

## 8  Annus horribilis

1998 was a bad year for the All Blacks – a stain on a proud record. That was the year the All Blacks lost an unprecedented five tests. They had lost three key men at the end of 1997 – Sean Fitzpatrick, Zinzan Brooke and Frank Bunce – and struggled without them. The fifth loss was in Durban and came courtesy of a dubious try to Springbok hooker James Dalton in the last minute.

## 7  The Baby Blacks

In 1986 All Black coach Brian Lochore was left with no choice but to pick what became known as the 'Baby Blacks'. The majority of the country's frontline talent were banned for two tests, a punishment that was inflicted after they played in a rebel tour of South Africa. It was a huge ask for so many inexperienced players to take on France, but they did, and they famously beat them, causing more ructions when the first-choice players became available.

## 6  Stirling steals the show

Having failed at the 1991, 1995 and 1999 World Cups, the All Blacks were determined to make amends in 2003. Once again they were favourites and came into their semi-final fancied to beat Australia. But mid-way through the first half, fly-half Carlos Spencer threw a flat pass inside the Wallabies 22 that, had it gone to its intended target, would have seen the All Blacks score a try. Instead it was intercepted by Wallaby centre Stirling Mortlock, who went the length of the field to change everything. That was the catalyst for a famous Wallaby win, and yet more World Cup agony for New Zealand.

## 5  The Invincibles sign off

The Victoria Ground on Vancouver Island is not rich with rugby history, but it is the venue where the 1925 All Blacks, dubbed 'The Invincibles', won their 32nd match of a five-month tour. It was an incredible feat that went a long way to establishing the aura of the All Blacks. The only shame of that tour was that they were denied a Grand Slam as Scotland refused to play due to a wrangle over expenses.

## 4  Richie cracks the century

When Sean Fitzpatrick was forced to retire on 92 caps, there was a feeling no New Zealander was every going to crack the century. It was too hard – the competition in the All Blacks was so fierce that no one could hold their spot long enough to win 100 caps. So when Richie McCaw became the first All Black to that landmark in 2011, it was a big, big deal. A psychological barrier had been broken and New Zealand had another reason to see McCaw as arguably the greatest player the country had produced.

### 3 Breaking the pattern

In 2007, after being knocked out in the quarter-final of the World Cup – their worst result – the All Blacks were expected to sack coach Graham Henry. No other coach had survived a failed World Cup campaign. But the New Zealand Rugby Union defied history and retained Henry, arguing he deserved a second chance. The move was initially unpopular but paid off when Henry led the All Blacks to World Cup glory in 2011.

### 2 The first Grand Slam

For a variety of reasons – financial disputes, political troubles and poor form – it took the All Blacks six attempts to secure a Grand Slam against the four Home Unions. It was only in 1978 that they finally managed to get the job done, and even then they nearly didn't. Scotland's Ian McGeechan had a drop goal charged down in injury time – it would have tied the scores at 12–all – allowing Bruce Robertson to pick up the loose ball and score a try at the other end. It was a dramatic play, one that allowed the All Blacks to tick a box that had bothered them for some time.

### 1 The breakthrough

It took the All Blacks until 1996 to win a test series in South Africa, and when they finally did it led to a number of grown men, hard men, weeping openly. The iconic image as the final whistle blew at Loftus Versfeld was of an exhausted captain Sean Fitzpatrick crumpled on his knees, looking to the heavens in a mix of exhaustion and euphoria.

# Scotland

## 10 best players

### 10 Colin Deans (1978–1984)

A dynamic and energetic hooker, Colin Deans has admirers all around the world for the way the way he played. He was a hooker who liked to get his hands on the ball and be involved, and he was happy to play that bit wider to have more impact.

### 9 Jim Renwick (1972–1984)

Jim Renwick was a touch deceptive because of his prematurely balding pate. No one really expected to be confronted by such searing acceleration and poise. But that was Renwick – a balanced and direct runner who could scythe through defensive lines and create opportunities.

### 8 Gordon Brown (1969–1976)

Gordon Brown was one of Scotland's best locks. He was a strangely mobile beast who was quite a sight when he was at full tilt. He was an aggressive and uncompromising player, yet a fun-loving, good-natured rogue off the field.

### 7 Scott Murray (1997–2007)

He was built like a piece of string, but Scott Murray was a physical player. He was spring-heeled and probably the best lineout forward in Europe in the late 1990s and early 2000s. He was athletic and robust, the perfect lock for modern rugby and unlucky not to have made the 2001 British & Irish Lions test team.

### 6 David Sole (1986–1992)

David Sole never held a global reputation as a strong scrummager, but was always able to make up for that with his mobility and ball-carrying around the field. A ferocious and focused loose-head prop with the discipline and dedication many modern professionals would kill for, he could have played flanker.

### 5 Gregor Townsend (1993–2007)

If Gregor Townsend had been born in New Zealand or Australia he would have been sensational. But this magical player was often hindered by the lack of quality around him. He was a maverick operator who played a test in nearly every backs jersey but was always happiest at No 10. He could find holes in any defence and was never afraid to chance his luck.

### 4 Finlay Calder (1986–1991)

Former Scotland and British & Irish Lions coach Jim Telfer had charge of many great players, but few impressed him like Finlay Calder, who was rangy and fearless. Calder could roam about and do the tough stuff, and always had an awareness of what was going on, which is why he captained the Lions in 1989.

### 3 Gary Armstrong (1988–1999)

Gary Armstrong is the toughest man to play for Scotland. A scrum-half who was built like a loose forward, he had no qualms about hurting for the cause. He was a damaging runner and lethal around the fringes, while his tackling was always destructive.

### 2 Gavin Hastings (1986–1995)

Gavin Hastings was a player for every occasion. He was solid on defence, could kick like a mule and was surprisingly deceptive when he was at full steam. Unusually big for a fullback in that era, Hastings was also comfortable being used as a crash man. A gentleman off the field, Hastings was a natural leader.

### 1  Andy Irvine (1972–1982)

There was something hypnotic about Andy Irvine in full flow. He was one of the first dashing fullbacks on the world stage, and his love of the counter-attack was as breathtaking as it was refreshing. He was multi-skilled – a great kicker, a great runner, a great reader of play – and had a great instinct for the try-line.

# 10 best games

### 10  Scotland 13–9 Argentina, 2010

When the Scots beat the Pumas in Mar del Plata in 2010 the significance of their victory was huge. They had won a series in Argentina – something few teams have managed. It took courage to sneak past a Pumas side that could hold their own against any forward pack.

### 9  Scotland 9–8 Australia, 2009

There has never been a defensive effort quite as brave as this one. The Scots had to make close to 300 tackles and only made one collective lapse all game to allow Wallaby centre Ryan Cross to score in the last minute. Their bravery and tenacity to stay in the game with so little territory or possession was incredible.

### 8  Scotland 32–3 Ireland, 1984

The Triple Crown was up for grabs in Dublin. Everyone was expecting a tight encounter between the two Celtic nations. That was until scrum-half Roy Laidlaw played out of his skin to score two tries that inspired Scotland into a flowing performance that was inventive and creative and far too good for Ireland.

## Scotland 12–7 Australia, 1982

Amazing as it is, excluding the Pacific Islands and Argentina, Scotland have won just one test in the southern hemisphere. A good Scottish team, who had played expansive and high-tempo rugby throughout the Five Nations in 1982, managed to beat the Wallabies in Brisbane. In many ways the performance didn't really matter – it was all about the win.

 ## Scotland 21–6 South Africa, 2002

Scottish wins against southern hemisphere opponents are rare indeed and every one is cherished. In heavy rain in Edinburgh, the Scots fronted. They held firm in the set-piece, played the conditions superbly and slowly ground the Boks into submission.

 ## Scotland 22–12 England, 1983

Having only won three times at Twickenham in their history, the Scots are never likely to forget the occasions they have been victorious in London. In 1983 they had played well but had narrowly lost their opening two games. At Twickenham they got off to a good start, enjoyed a bit of luck and took every opportunity that came their way.

 ## Scotland 36–22 France, 1999

No one could believe their eyes when Scotland began carving up the French in Paris in the final Five Nations series. The Scots played with precision and a *joie de vivre* more commonly associated with their hosts. The backs were outstanding and the flow and rhythm have rarely, if ever, been repeated.

## Scotland 34–18 Wales, 1982

The Scots had suffered more than most at the hands of the glorious Welsh throughout the 1960s and 1970s, and hadn't won at Cardiff for

20 years when they played there in 1982. They ended their drought in emphatic style with champagne rugby that delivered memorable tries and great passages of play.

### 2 Scotland 33–6 England, 1986

This was the game Scots never wanted to end, as they had shattered England mentally and physically. The final 20 minutes were about as good as it gets – the ball was being moved everywhere as the Scots could see England just wanted the game to be over. The final try was one of the best scored by a Scotland team at Murrayfield.

### 1 Scotland 23–21 France, 1995

For 26 years the Scots wondered if they would ever be free of grainy footage of former captain Jim Telfer scoring the winning try in Paris, 1969. That was the last time the Scots had won in France until Gavin Hastings inspired a brilliant come-from-behind win in 1995.

# 10 iconic moments

### 10 The surprise kicker

The older brother of Lions lock Gordon, Peter Brown was a never-to-be-forgotten creature for the way he goal-kicked. Brown would tee the ball up and then turn his back on it and stay that way before turning to begin his run-up. It was the most unusual technique, but he landed a pressure kick in 1971 to beat England at Twickenham after a last-minute Duncan Paterson try. That was the centenary game between those two nations, and Scotland would beat England again a few weeks later in the Five Nations.

### 9 Thirty seconds of madness

It had been a struggle, but with eight minutes to go in their 2011 World Cup pool clash, Scotland appeared to have finally gained control against the Pumas. They were leading 12–6 and neither side had looked remotely like scoring a try. But in a sudden flash, Argentine wing Lucas Amorosino was able to avoid three weak tackles and score a try, which was converted. When the Scots recovered to set themselves up for a field goal, Pumas captain Felipe Contepomi was able to come from an offside position to charge down Dan Parks' attempt, but there was no penalty forthcoming from referee Wayne Barnes. That was it – the Scots were effectively eliminated.

## 8  Bravehearts do it again

2000 had been a miserable year for Scotland. They lost to Italy in their opening game and were staring at a whitewash when England came to Murrayfield on the final weekend. A Grand Slam was at stake for the visitors, but in a perishing wind and icy rain Scotland found their braveheart spirit and suddenly came good. When fly-half Duncan Hodge crashed over from short range and fist-pumped in euphoria, a nation had its image to preserve.

## 7  Smith saves the day

The Scots were in danger of being bundled out of the 2003 World Cup when two spectacular tries by Rupeni Caucaunibuca saw Fiji lead the critical pool clash with only minutes remaining. The Scots, who had never failed to make the quarter-finals, dug deep and were able to save face when prop Tom Smith burrowed over two minutes from time to win the game.

## 6  Heart and Sole

Ridiculed by his English opposite Jeff Probyn for not being a strong scrummager, Scotland captain David Sole exacted the best revenge in 1992. The Scots had a 5-metre scrum and Sole called for the ball to stay in, and when they went for a second shove they pushed England over the line. Scotland had done the unthinkable and scored a pushover try, and Sole made sure he let England see his joy.

## 5  The foreign invasion

Matt Williams became the first foreign coach of Scotland in late 2003. The Australian had enjoyed moderate success with the Waratahs and Leinster, but turned out to be a total disaster. He dragged Scottish rugby into the Dark Ages – winning just three of 17 tests, which saw home crowds and interest in the game plummet. The union is still dealing with the financial fallout from the Williams era.

## 4  Big Gav's big miss

The tension at Murrayfield was electric in 1991 when England travelled north to play the World Cup semi-final. The English had been to Edinburgh the year before and famously lost. When Scotland were awarded a penalty in front of the posts on the 22 with four minutes remaining, history was on track to repeat. But Gavin Hastings, one of the best and most reliable goal-kickers in world rugby, inexplicably pushed the ball wide. England scored a drop goal two minutes later to win 9–6.

## 3  Bevan's bad call

In a proud history of hard-luck stories, one stands out: Scotland were hurt by Welsh referee Derek Bevan in 1990 when he awarded the All Blacks a penalty they should never have had. Scotland were in control of the game at Eden Park, and when Gavin Hastings caught a high kick he should also have been awarded a penalty, as the tackler, Mike Brewer, was miles offside. But Bevan penalised Hastings for holding on and the mistake allowed New Zealand to escape 21–18.

## 2  Jim Calder's famous flop

There was more than a hint of Jim Calder being offside when a stray lineout throw landed in his arms midway through the second half of the 1984 Grand Slam showdown with France. But the Scotland flanker caught it and flopped over – the try was given and Scotland knew then they had all but secured a 21–12 victory to win their first Grand Slam in 59 years.

## 1 The Battle of Hastings

Scotland had five minutes to hang on to secure a famous Grand Slam at Murrayfield in 1990 when England wing Rory Underwood appeared to have broken free. The Englishman was the fastest player on the field, but centre Scott Hastings somehow managed to catch Underwood by the ankles and haul him down to save the score. It was an unforgettable tackle.

# South Africa

## 10 best players

**10** **Frik du Preez** (1961–1971)

Frik du Preez was versatile way before players were encouraged to be versatile. He was equally comfortable at flanker or lock, and just as happy dropping goals as he was making tackles and cleaning bodies out the way. A freakish all-rounder who was blessed with innate rugby skills.

**9** **Hennie Muller** (1949–1953)

There is no bigger tribute to Hennie Muller than the fact that more than 50 years after his last test, youngsters around the world are subjected to 'Hennie Muller's' in pre-season training. This is a lung-bursting sprint session that Muller supposedly invented to establish himself as the best No 8 in world rugby. He was extraordinarily fit, playing with his head up and incredible anticipation.

**8** **Bryan Habana** (2004–)

An IRB Player of the Year and World Cup medal winner, Bryan Habana has the silverware to justify his reputation as one of the deadliest wings. Terrifyingly quick and alive to the intercept, Habana was a supreme finisher in his early years, becoming a better all-round player as he matured.

**7** **Bernie Osler** (1924–1933)

If anyone wants to know why the Boks have been able to produce generations of technically proficient fly-halves with booming kicking games, the answer lies with the excellence of Bernie Osler. He was the original kicking No 10 and nudged his team around the fields of the UK in 1931 and 1932, when the Boks collected a Grand Slam.

### 6 Francois Pienaar (1993–1996)

Francois Pienaar is recognised more for his contribution as captain than player. He led the Boks to World Cup victory in 1995 in a campaign made famous by the film *Invictus*. The fact that Pienaar was played by Hollywood star Matt Damon is the ultimate accolade: the Bok captain was an inspiration to his team and nation during his tenure.

### 5 Danie Gerber (1980–1992)

Unfortunate to have been at his prime when the Boks were in isolation, Danie Gerber would otherwise have been recognised more widely than he was. A stunning hat-trick against England best illustrated all that he was: forceful, direct, elusive and dangerous.

### 4 Joost van der Westhuizen (1993–2003)

Quick enough to play on the wing (as he originally did), and big enough and strong enough to play in the back row, it was never possible for any team to take their eyes off Joost van der Westhuizen when he was at scrum-half for the Boks. He scored memorable solo tries and was the tactical general for a decade. One of the great scrum-halves.

### 3 Morné du Plessis (1971–1980)

Morné du Plessis is still widely viewed as the best captain the Boks ever had. He was a thoughtful, intelligent operator whose measured opinions earned him huge respect as well as the role of Springboks manager for their 1995 World Cup campaign.

### 2 Victor Matfield (2001–2011)

Few would dispute that the Springbok lock Victor Matfield was the best lineout operator in history. No one studied the lineout in as much depth, and Matfield reaped his rewards. He hardly ever lost his own ball and frequently stole possession. He was more than just an aerial player, however. He was mobile on the ground and capable of playing with the ball in hand.

### 1 Danie Craven (1931–1938)

Imagine being talented enough to play tests at scrum-half, fly-half, centre and No 8. That was Danie Craven, a name that still looms large over South African rugby. He was noted as a player of extreme vision and understanding , which is why he went on to coach the Boks and hold influential executive positions within the rugby union.

# 10 best games

### 10 South Africa 96–13 Wales, 1998

This result was an anomaly – one of those days where everything the Boks did came off. They scored 15 tries and would have hit the century if they hadn't emptied their bench early in the second half. The defeat scarred Wales for some time and gave the Boks the confidence to push on to equal the world record for consecutive victories.

### 9 South Africa 6–3 Scotland, 1932

The Boks had to grind and graft for this win – a victory that was significant because it secured them a Grand Slam against the Home Nations.

## 8   South Africa 68–10 Scotland, 1997

This was South African rugby at its best. They were a heady mix of athleticism, brutality and creativity. They ran riot at Murrayfield, leaving the Scots hopelessly outclassed and desperate to get off the field. It was boys versus men.

## 7   South Africa 35–9 England, 1985

A brilliant Dannie Gerber hat-trick was the highlight of this commanding performance by the Boks. The burly centre was at his thrusting best and England had no answers. One team played ball-in-hand rugby that was all about good angles and finding the space. The other team didn't.

## 6   South Africa 44–0 Scotland, 1951

For a long time, this 11-try victory stood as the biggest defeat for any established rugby nation. This was Scotland's day of rugby shame but they needn't have beaten themselves up. It was a loss that was as much to do with South Africa's excellence as it was about their own incompetence. The Scots gave the inch ... the Boks took the mile.

## 5   South Africa 36–0 England, 2007

Incredibly, these two sides would clash again in the final of the 2007 World Cup. Incredible because the gulf in class during their pool encounter was massive. The Boks were full of good ideas and underpinned their game-plan with excellence in the set-piece and at the collisions. England had no idea what had hit them.

## 4   South Africa 30–28 New Zealand, 2008

Despite having won the World Cup in 1995 and 2007, the Boks hadn't won a test in New Zealand since 1998. They were beaten up by the All Blacks in Wellington in their first Tri Nations encounter in 2008 but gained their revenge the following week when scrum-half

Ricky Januarie scored a spectacular solo try six minutes from time.

### 3 South Africa 12–9 France, 1968

The Boks had been able to subdue the All Blacks – in fact, they beat them many times even in New Zealand in the first 60 years of the twentieth century. But it took until 1968 for them to win their first test in France. They had to claw their way to the tape, hold their own against a French pack ready for trouble and take their opportunities when they came.

### 2 South Africa 28–25 British & Irish Lions, 2009

The Springboks had won the first test of the series but looked to be gone for all money in the second when they were being run off their feet by the Lions. They were 11 behind in the final quarter but struck back with brilliant tries by Jaque Fourie and Bryan Habana. At 25–all it was heading for a draw until Lions replacement Ronan O'Gara infringed in the last minute and Morné Steyn landed the winning penalty to clinch the series.

### 1 South Africa 15–12 New Zealand, 1995

The World Cup final of 1995 was going to be New Zealand's crowning glory. They had been the outstanding team leading into the game and with Jonah Lomu in devastating form, they were fancied to win. But the Boks delivered one of the great defensive performances where they swarmed Lomu. Their passion was incredible and when Joel Stransky kicked an extra-time drop goal, he delivered one of the most heroic and significant victories of all time.

# 10 iconic moments

### 10 Reaching the never land

With South Africa having hosted the FIFA World Cup earlier in 2010, the Springboks made the bold decision to play the All Blacks in the newly built Soccer Stadium in Soweto. The Springboks had been the symbol of division in the apartheid years, hated by the black population, and Soweto had been one of the most volatile centres during the troubles. It was a sight many thought they would never see – the Boks in Soweto, in a state-of-the-art stadium in a test that would also see captain John Smit make his 100th appearance. The only shame was the stunning late comeback pulled off by the All Blacks to win.

### 9  The gold run

All good things have to come to an end, and 5 December 1998 will be remembered with both fond and bad memories for South Africans. They lost to England at Twickenham that day, failing as a consequence to secure what would have been a world-record eighteenth consecutive victory. Still, it was in defeat that they could come to appreciate the magnificent run which had equalled that of the All Blacks of 1965–69.

### 8  Five of the best

The Springboks have never been fussy about how their points come. But they took that philosophy to extremes at the World Cup in 1999 when fly-half Jannie de Beer kicked a record five dropped goals in the quarter-final victory over England. No one had seen anything like it.

### 7  The long shot

For a brief second, Springbok fullback Frans Steyn thought about it. South Africa had been awarded a penalty in their 2009 Tri Nations clash against the All Blacks in Hamilton. It was barely 10 metres outside their own 22 and Steyn considered going for goal from 75 metres or more. Ridiculous? Possibly not. Only a few minutes earlier he'd landed one from 65 metres that was still going strong when it went over the bar. He nailed three from inside his own half, disillusioning the All Blacks who knew too late that they were in danger of conceding points if they infringed even that far into Bok territory.

## 6 Home comforts

In the 2007 Tri Nations the Springboks made the bold but unpopular move to keep their best players at home for the away leg of their campaign. Rather than fly the top XV to Australia and New Zealand, coach Jake White sent the second-stringers and lost both tests. Accused of treating the Tri Nations with disdain, White proved the genius of his strategy when the Boks won the World Cup later that year. The All Blacks were clearly inspired, as they did much the same thing four years later.

## 5 Commonwealth boycott

In 1976, against concerted international pressure, the All Blacks toured South Africa. They arrived shortly after the Soweto uprisings and earned condemnation from 28 other countries who protested by boycotting the Summer Olympics. The tour highlighted the international disgust at apartheid and the commitment to force change, and the following year the Commonwealth signed the Gleneagles Agreement to discourage future tours and sporting contact with South Africa.

## 4 A hero is found

South Africa were looking for a hero in 1995 to spark their World Cup campaign and to persuade the nation to unite behind the team. That hero was found in the quarter-final when Chester Williams, the only black player in the team, scored four tries against Samoa. It was a poignant and powerful moment – a black Springbok hero being cheered by other black South Africans.

### 3  In from the cold

On 15 August 1992, the Springboks were formally welcomed back into international rugby. The legal apparatus of apartheid was abolished, paving the way for the Boks to begin international competition again. They returned to action in a thrilling game against the All Blacks, whom they had not played since the infamous flour-bomb test of 1981. It was a game that marked the beginning of a new history for both the Springboks and the South African nation.

### 2  The final nail

South Africa were largely in control of the 2007 World Cup final but couldn't quite put England away. They were leading 12–6 when it looked like England's Mark Cueto might have scored a try to change everything. But he was ruled to have put a foot in touch, and a few minutes later Frans Steyn landed a long-range penalty. That was the decisive score, the moment everyone knew the Boks had their second title in the bag.

### 1  Plane sailing

It broke every flight safety regulation in the book, but those who saw the jumbo jet pass over Ellis Park at a dangerously low altitude say it was unforgettable and set the mood. The shadow and deafening noise engulfed the stadium shortly before the 1995 World Cup final and it sent the crowd into a frenzy. As a result, even before the kick-off, there were millions of South Africans suddenly believing they could win.

# Wales

## 10 best players

### 10 Mervyn Davies (1969–1976)

Known as 'Merv the Swerve', Mervyn Davies was the right mix to be a high impact No 8. He could take the direct route or use his athleticism to roam around in the wider spaces. He was also a gifted ball player – something that was critical in allowing Wales to play their open game.

### 9 Neil Jenkins (1991–2002)

Maligned for not being a natural passer or runner, Neil Jenkins often surprised with his ability to find holes and take on defences. But his main skill was his unerring boot. He was the first man to score 1000 test points and if ever there was a kicker for the big occasion it was him.

### 8 Scott Gibbs (1991–2001)

Scott Gibbs was a bull of a man. He looked like a hooker but ran like an inside back – a deadly combination – and for the better part of a decade he made sure Wales were always able to get over the gainline and usually a good bit further.

### 7 Gerald Davies (1966–1978)

A stylish and elegant wing who knew his way to the try-line, Davies was small in stature but big on impact. He scored tries no one else could because he had the raw pace to back himself to take the outside channel. He was lively on his feet and always aware of the space.

### 6 Cliff Morgan (1951–1958)

Dubbed 'Morgan the Magnificent' by the South African press, it was an apt title for one of the great fly-halves. Cliff Morgan had balance and daring – he was strong and open to opportunity, yet technically proficient. He set the benchmark for all future Welsh No 10s.

### 5 JPR Williams (1969–1981)

There probably won't be another fullback quite like JPR. He was tough enough to play flanker in a test, and there were plenty of grizzled forwards who were wary of him. He could run and he was ambivalent as to whether it was around people or through them. His bravery was endless – the perfect man to have at the back.

### 4 Shane Williams (2000–2011)

It was scarcely believable that Shane Williams could survive in professional rugby for as long as he did. He would usually be conceding 20 kg or more to the men he marked but he was never exposed defensively. He retired with 58 test tries – a tally much bigger, more powerful men could only dream of. Williams was agile and elusive, and deserved to be IRB Player of the Year in 2008.

### 3 Phil Bennett (1969–1978)

Phil Bennett was much like Barry John but more reliant on his incredible step than any ethereal ability to drift past defenders. Against a broken defence Bennett was deadly – he could step his way past anyone and often did. His partnership with Gareth Edwards was the key to Wales' golden era in the 1970s.

### 2 Barry John (1966–1972)

Commentator Bill McLaren once said that if any player ever managed to catch Barry John on the field, then they were able to

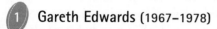

make a wish. That pretty much summed it up – in a line of great fly-halves he was maybe the best. He ran like a ghost.

### 1 Gareth Edwards (1967–1978)

It wouldn't have mattered in what era Gareth Edwards had been around – he'd have been a superstar. He was the complete rugby player and could have played in almost any jersey in the backline. He was fast, brave, agile, skilled, clever, visionary and committed.

# 10 best games

### 10 Wales 26–19 England, 2008

It had been 20 years since the Welsh had won at Twickenham when they began their Six Nations campaign there in 2008. History and form were against them, and after a dire first 50 minutes they were trailing 19–6. Then they launched the most astonishing comeback where they threw the ball about with precision, shredded England at will and scored 20 unanswered points. They went on to win the Grand Slam that season.

### 9 Wales 27–3 England, 1979

It was amazing that England would win a Grand Slam a year after this hammering in Cardiff. They met a Welsh team that was in the mood to get the job done. There was no fussiness or softening-up period – Wales went for the jugular and played England off the park for 80 minutes. This was a good old-fashioned doing.

### 8 Wales 21–19 Australia, 2008

It took courage and discipline for a heavily fatigued Welsh team to hold on to their deserved lead in late November 2008. The Wallabies were doing all they could to claw their way back from 21–13 but Wales clung on. Their defensive line refused to buckle and they tackled themselves to a standstill.

## 7　Wales 22–10 Ireland, 2011

The Celts were both in great form when they clashed in the 2011 World Cup quarter-final. Ireland were favourites but they never stood a chance when they encountered a Welsh pack that stood up everywhere. Wales opened with a brilliant try, scored a clever solo effort through Mike Phillips and then clinched it when Jonathan Davies coasted through the Irish backline.

## 6　Wales 25–20 Scotland, 1988

This was rugby at its best. Welsh wing Ieuan Evans scored one of the best tries ever seen in Cardiff when he evaded six tackles after some stunning handling from the rest of the backline. Jonathan Davies scored a try almost as good and then Paul Thorburn kicked a goal from 70 metres. A good day's work all round.

## 5　Wales 28–3 Australia, 1975

This is still Wales' record victory against the Wallabies and was secured on the back of a ruthless display from the pack. Gareth Edwards was brilliant at scrum-half and wing JJ Williams scored a hat-trick. A performance that was befitting of a team considered one of the best in rugby history.

## 4　Wales 34–33 France, 1999

Even in their pomp – their golden era throughout the 1970s – Wales struggled to win regularly in Paris. They famously won in 1975 but would have to wait 24 years before they would do so again. But it was worth waiting for – Wales won in 1999 in the most incredible, breathtaking game that saw both sides run from everywhere. Wales broke out of their 22 in the first minute and things escalated from there. There were seven tries, but the greater accuracy of Wales' goal-kicking secured the win.

### 3  Wales 43–35 France, 2001

A bit like buses – you wait for ages and then two come along in quick succession. That was the story for Wales in 2001 when they returned to Paris after breaking their 24-year drought there in 1999. They were well off the pace in the first half hour but sprung to life after Rob Howley made an 80-metre break for a special solo try. They would score two more before Neil Jenkins managed to break free for a last-minute try to win the game and take his personal tally to 28 points.

### 2  Wales 13–8 New Zealand, 1953

Wales' 13–8 win against the All Blacks in 1953 has come to be treasured. The Welsh haven't beaten New Zealand since in 24 attempts. The Welsh were behind 8–5 with 15 minutes to go when back-rower Clem Thomas kicked diagonally from the flank, a move that threw the All Black defence, and wing Ken Jones gathered the ball and dived over for a clever score.

### 1  Wales 29–19 South Africa, 1999

There was double cause for celebration when Wales beat the Springboks in June 1999. It was the first game played at the revamped Millennium Stadium – previously it had been Cardiff Arms Park. But more important, the 29–19 victory was the first time Wales had beaten South Africa in 13 attempts. Wales were organised, dynamic and ruthless.

## 10 iconic moments

### 10  The great debate

It made for unforgettable TV when Wales captain Gareth Thomas clashed with former captain and media commentator Eddie Butler live on air in early 2006. Coach Mike Ruddock had suddenly stepped down despite winning the Grand Slam the previous year, citing family reasons for doing so. Butler had written that day in his column for the *Observer* that the players had pushed him out and Thomas took exception. The presenter lost control of a debate that was heated and personal.

## 9   Thermal wonderland

One of the great games of the 1987 World Cup was the Bronze Medal final in Rotorua between Wales and Australia. Usually this game is treated as a dead rubber with neither team really up for it, but this inaugural effort was a belter. Wales, amazingly – as they had against Scotland in 1971– scored through Adrian Hadley in the last minute. Paul Thorburn, like John Taylor 16 years earlier, stroked the ball through the posts from the touchline.

## 8   Holding their ground

In 2009 Wales hosted the All Blacks at the Millennium Stadium. The anthems out of the way, the All Blacks performed the haka with Wales respectfully lined up on the 10-metre line. But when the All Blacks finished, Wales didn't move. They stayed as they were, so the All Blacks, unsure what to do, decided to stay where they were. Neither team moved for close to a minute. It was brilliant theatre and set the tone for a bruising Welsh performance where they were unfortunate not to claim a draw.

## 7   Pacific thunder

The joke in Wales for some time was that they were thankful they hadn't had to play the whole of Samoa. Humour was the only way such a proud nation could react to the humiliation of losing to Western Samoa in Cardiff at the 1991 World Cup. Wales were left stunned by the brutality of the South Sea Islanders, who won 16–13, the defining image being Welsh lock Phil May sitting aghast on the bench in his number ones, having been forced off in the first half with a dislocated shoulder.

## 6  The ghost try

In 1969 the great Barry John scored a try against England where he seemingly transformed into a ghost. Picking the ball up on England's 22, he danced and weaved his way past five Englishmen without anyone laying a hand on him. It was the work of a genius and the platform for Wales to post a 30–9 humiliation of their old foe.

## 5  Welcome to international rugby

England, as always, came to Cardiff in February 2005 confident they were going to start their Six Nations campaign with a victory. They had picked 18-year-old Matthew Tait in their midfield and felt he was going to lead them to a bright future. But early in the game Tait ran onto a flat pass and was hit in the midriff by his Welsh opposite Gavin Henson, picked up and driven back before being deposited on his backside. Wales knew then it was going to be their day – it was a tackle to inspire the win and a Grand Slam.

## 4  Cardiff train smash

Wales were chasing a Grand Slam in 1976, and their last game was in Cardiff against a rampant French team who were also unbeaten at that stage. The French were beginning to wind things up and put the heat on with their ferocious pack. They looked destined to score and take the lead late in the game when they sent giant wing Jean-François Gourdon seemingly clear with the line at his mercy. But Welsh fullback JPR Williams appeared from nowhere to smash Gourdon into touch and then stand over him, both fists clenched, roaring at the fallen Frenchman. Wales won 19–13 thanks to that tackle.

## 3  The red mist falls

Wales came into the World Cup semi-final in 2011 with a realistic chance to progress. They were in cracking form. France weren't. But just 17 minutes into the game, captain Sam Warburton was sent off for a dangerous tackle. That was the moment that killed a nation's dream. They gallantly dug in to lose by only a point, but having a man down, and their captain and openside at that, meant that red card will haunt them forever.

## 2　Roaming in the gloaming

In 1971 Wales would secure their first Grand Slam in 29 years. The key victory came in Edinburgh when Wales were trailing 18–13 with only a minute remaining. But the electric wing Gerald Davies was able to score a dramatic try in the right-hand corner. Flanker John Taylor had to nail the kick from the touchline – the wrong side for a right-footer – but he banged it over and Wales had escaped 19–18 to keep the dream alive.

## 1　Coming of age

Wales hosted the last ever Five Nations match in April 1999, but the game was actually played at Wembley in London as the Arms Park in Cardiff was being rebuilt. Their opponent was England, who were chasing a Grand Slam. What Wales managed to do was take the fortress of England soccer and turn it into a pocket of the Principality for the day. Max Boyce and Tom Jones sang before the game and it was a magnificent celebration of all things Welsh. It was the day a nation came of age, especially when they pulled off the most dramatic late win with a spectacular Scott Gibbs try.

# PART 4

# World Cup

---

## 10 best games

---

**10** Wales 16–17 South Africa, 2011

Wales will wonder for some time how they failed to win this game. They played spectacularly good rugby in patches that stretched the brilliant defence of the South Africans. It was gripping from start to finish with a bit of scandal and an epic closing five minutes. Shortly before half-time Welsh fullback James Hook appeared to land a penalty but as it was higher than the posts, neither touch judge was sure. Referee Wayne Barnes could have gone to the TMO but chose not to, declaring the kick had missed. 'I did not ask the referee to consult the television match official but in hindsight maybe I should have,' said Hook. 'I knew the ball was over, which is why I ran back to my own half. I had no doubt. The TMO would have been the best solution but it was not to be.'

The ruling was critical given the final score but Wales had plenty of other chances to win. After seeing their 16–10 lead overturned when replacement Francois Hougaard scampered through a loose defence, Rhys Priestland missed a dropped goal in front of the posts and then Hook missed another easy penalty in the final minute. Springbok coach Peter de Villiers confessed: 'We were lucky to get through it.'

'We have to take it on the chin,' admitted Wales coach Warren Gatland. 'We had chances to win the game late on but missed a drop goal and a penalty. In the end we were not quite good enough.'

## 9　Samoa 35–12 Argentina, 1991

Everyone remembers Samoa's defeat of Wales in 1991, but the South Sea Islanders actually played their best rugby against Argentina in their final group game. It turned out to be a ferocious encounter. The Pumas, aware by then of the phenomenal explosive power of the Samoans, were determined not to be intimidated. It became a highly combustible affair littered with violence and astonishingly brave and creative rugby.

It helped no end that Samoa's lock Matt Keenan was sent off, as was his opposite Pedro Sporleder. With a little extra room on the field, both teams played with width and offloaded out of the tackle – particularly the Samoans, who showed they had natural flair and talent to complement their defence. They scored six tries and had Scotland more than a little concerned ahead of their looming quarter-final clash.

## 8　England 25–22 Australia, 1995

A big and well organised England pack set about beating up the Wallabies in the 1995 quarter-final in Cape Town. The English were brutal and had the Wallabies on the ropes at half-time when they led 13–6. But one minute after the break Wallaby wing Damian Smith caught a high ball for a miraculous try and belief flooded through the defending champions. The Australians weren't ready to give up their title and for the next 39 minutes clawed and scrapped with an amazing tenacity and courage.

The scores were locked at 22–all after 80 minutes and there was no telling what would happen in extra-time – the game was so tense and tight.

A lineout just inside Australian territory was won cleanly by England and then driven by lock Martin Bayfield. Scrum-half Dewi Morris fired a huge pass to fly-half Rob Andrew, who attempted the drop goal from 45 metres. The ball stayed in the air for an age before eventually clearing the bar. England coach Jack Rowell summed up the moment. He said: 'People jumped 10 feet when that went over. When they came down to earth, they were crying.'

## Tonga 19–14 France, 2011

Ranked number five in the world, France were expected to dispatch Tonga with some ease when they met in their respective final pool clash in 2011. Tonga had been put away by the All Blacks and had also lost to Canada, and were far from the force they had been in 2007.

But the form book went out the window and the French, who had been so-so in their previous games, were under enormous pressure. The Tongans clicked – their forwards carried the ball like they were angry and their set-piece was immaculate. They began to find space in the midfield and their creativity and power was too much for a fragile French defence. Tonga's victory could and should have been much bigger as they squandered several golden opportunities in the second half. They didn't really care, though. They had pulled off a famous win by playing brilliant rugby and had humiliated the French.

'You probably don't know what it means to me and the people back in Tonga,' Tonga coach Isitolo Maka said. 'In Tonga right now they're going crazy and we are going to get a lot of support when we get to Auckland.'

In stark contrast, French coach Marc Lièvremont was being quizzed about whether he would resign. 'I have absolutely no intention of giving up. I've got my share of responsibilities, but do you sincerely think that it is because of my management that we failed to be committed against Tonga? There is a lack of collective dynamism. For now, there is no divide in the group, even if it may look like it.'

## 6 Australia 19–18 Ireland, 1991

For three glorious minutes, Ireland thought they were in the semi-final. They looked to have pulled off the improbable with a try six minutes from the end by flanker Gordon Hamilton that pushed them 16–15 ahead. The crowd – in fact the whole country – had gone delirious when Hamilton had been on the end of a break from inside the Irish half. The ball was moved wide from a scrum, fullback Jim Staples booted ahead, and wing Jack Clarke gathered the loose ball, stayed on his feet for an age and then off-loaded to the openside Hamilton who just had the legs to make it home from 35 metres. When Ralph Keyes landed the conversion the Wallabies had three minutes to salvage their World Cup.

They had been in control for most of the previous 76 minutes, but Ireland had bravely dug in and somehow stayed in touch through the boot of Keyes. 'The Ireland game was when the tournament ignited for us,' Wallaby captain Nick Farr-Jones, who had come off injured during the game, would later recall. 'It captivated people back home. I heard endless stories of people kicking their cats or booting the dog after Gordon Hamilton scored. I'd come off injured and, sitting in the stands, thought we were done.'

But the Wallabies didn't lose. They amazingly held their composure. They used a string of penalties to kick their way deep into Irish territory and scored a try through stand-in captain Michael Lynagh in the last minute. 'Michael Lynagh treated the situation very differently to how I would,' said Farr-Jones. 'I would have read the riot act but he asked the ref how long was left and then said he would kick long. That took guts and the rest is history as he went on to score.'

## 5  New Zealand 55–37 Wales, 2003

Both New Zealand and Wales had qualified for the quarter-finals when they clashed in the pool round in 2003. The Welsh decided to write the game off – they picked their second team so their first team could rest before playing England. It was an admission that they felt they had no chance of beating the All Blacks.

Except the second-stringers saw it differently – they wanted to push for places in the top team and thought that if they played without fear, they would at least ask some tough questions of the All Blacks. They did more than that – they rattled the tournament's joint favourites by scoring four brilliant tries to lead 37–33 with 20 minutes remaining after being 21–10 down in the first quarter.

The rugby from both teams was breathtaking. It was high-tempo, creative thrust and parry. The All Blacks finally woke up in the last 20 minutes to score four tries and restore order. 'We will learn a lot from this about how to defend against sides who can recycle the ball quickly,' said All Black coach John Mitchell. 'I think we had a few issues with quick recycling, not getting into the right position in defence subsequently.'

## 4  France 30–24 Australia, 1987

Australia began the inaugural World Cup as favourites and were expected to have too much firepower for their semi-final opponent France. When the Wallabies went 9–0 up and were controlling the game, no one had any reason to doubt that perception. But the second half erupted – the rugby from both sides was sublime. Australia scored two tries, France scored three, and with a few minutes remaining Australia led 24–21. French fly-half Didier Camberabero was hit late in a tackle and had to pick himself up to land one of the great pressure goals to force the game into extra time.

'This great match was the perfect advertisement for international rugby,' wrote the *Guardian's* David Frost. 'It had everything: great skill, challenges offered and taken up, the lead fluctuating, and a dramatic finish.'

That dramatic finish saw France scramble the ball into Australian territory and then keep it alive in a way only they could. The ball was worked to Serge Blanco who had the pace to outstrip the cover. There were only seconds left on the clock when Blanco dived in for the famous win with Camberabero converting for a 30–24 victory. 'The team that did it today can do it again,' said the Australian coach, Alan Jones. He was right that the French had been brilliant, but they were blown away by the All Blacks in the final.

### 3  Fiji 38–34 Wales, 2007

The incredible thing about this game was that the Welsh, having just about been dead and buried after 30 minutes, appeared to have fought back to escape the humiliation of defeat. In an incredible opening 15 minutes Fiji scored 25 points. It was scarcely believable as Wales looked much too good on paper.

'Wales should beat Fiji handsomely in Nantes and progress to a quarter-final against South Africa if they play with the adventure that produced 11 tries against the Japanese,' suggested the *Guardian*. But the Welsh stayed composed – Alix Popham scored a try six minutes before half-time and in a replica of the first half, Wales scored three tries in the first 11 minutes of the second to lead 29–25.

Even when Fiji fly-half Nicky Little landed two penalties to push his side 31–29 ahead, the Welsh looked stronger. Flanker Martyn Williams intercepted inside his own half with six minutes remaining and had the legs to score and push Wales 34–31 ahead. Surely that would be it? But no. Somehow Fiji ground the ball to the far end and prop Graham Dewes scored the deciding try with three minutes remaining. The game doubled as the 100th cap for the long-serving Welshman Gareth Thomas. 'Life goes on,' was his laconic response, except for coach Gareth Jenkins it didn't – he was sacked two days later.

## 2 New Zealand 45–29 England, 1995

From as early as February 1995 the All Blacks were certain they would be playing England in the semi-final of the World Cup later that year. Their premonition turned out to be right and the two clashed in Cape Town. It was almost a surreal experience for the All Blacks, who had been preparing for the better part of six months. They had a detailed game-plan that was all about keeping the ball away from the bigger English pack and trying to create space out wide.

The All Blacks had done their homework and had decided that England centre Jeremy Guscott was defensively weak. 'He was a talent for sure,' said All Black centre Frank Bunce of his opposite. 'But we thought he might be a bit frail so we set out to intimidate him. We didn't think we could unsettle Will Carling like that, but we did Guscott.' The All Blacks ripped England apart in the first half. They kept the tempo high and continually moved the ball wide to Jonah Lomu on the left wing, who gave one of the greatest individual performances. He scored four tries and the All Blacks had the game won after 50 minutes before they eased off and let England restore some respectability.

'Suddenly the world saw that international rugby didn't have to be dull,' said All Black coach Laurie Mains. 'We showed it didn't have to be low-scoring. We set on the structure to get quick ball and to give our inside backs the freedom to play and to get it wide. It was a style the players really enjoyed playing and it changed the face of professional rugby.'

## 1 New Zealand 31–43 France, 1999

To this day, and probably forever, it will remain a mystery what precisely happened to the respective combatants in the second half of the 1999 World Cup semi-final. The All Blacks were just about home and hosed five minutes after half-time. They hadn't been super slick but Lomu was in strong form and they were beginning to stretch and regularly break France.

Having gone 24–10 ahead, the All Blacks were poised to run riot but instead France dropped two quick goals through fly-half Christophe Lamaison, which would start the most unbelievable 27 minutes where they would score 33 unanswered points.

'I was doing the radio commentary for that game,' recalled All Black squad member Ian Jones. 'At 24–10 I was speaking with a lot of enthusiasm and all the radio guys around us were pretty confident. I was dumbstruck in those final 30 minutes. I didn't say anything. It was so sudden. We lost control of the game in those 25 minutes.'

Diminutive wing Christophe Dominici had the pace to chase after a kick down the left and score after Lamaison's drop goals. Centre Richard Dourthe caught another Lamaison chip to score the second try and with five minutes to go Philippe Bernat-Salles put the game beyond the All Blacks. A sixth tournament try from Jeff Wilson in the last minute counted for nothing: France had won 43–31 and New Zealand, indeed the whole of the world, was stunned.

# 10 World Cup controversies

**10** Swapping balls

England played their first two games of the 2011 World Cup at the 'indoor' stadium in Dunedin. Goal-kicker Jonny Wilkinson struggled horribly in the opener against the Pumas – missing five shots at goal. There was discussion in the media whether there was a problem with the new ball that had been introduced on the eve of the tournament.

This unsettled the English, who took matters into their own hands by their third game, against Romania. On at least two occasions after England had scored tries, they managed to slip a different match ball onto the field for the conversion. The rules are clear – the conversion must be taken with the same ball.

The controversy was inflamed because the IRB seemed indifferent, while the Rugby Football Union conducted their own review and lamely stated that kicking coach Dave Alred and fitness coach Paul Stridgeon had mistakenly believed there to be a problem with one of the match balls and had therefore, according to a statement: 'Taken it upon themselves to substitute balls during the match in contravention of both the laws of the game and the spirit of the game. The RFU fully accepts that the action of those team management members was incorrect and detrimental to the image of the tournament, the game and to English rugby.'

Alred and Stridgeon were not allowed to be at Eden Park for England's next game.

## 9 The final insult

The 2011 World Cup was the best run in the tournament's history, providing endless good rugby that was played in exactly the right spirit. It had been a risk taking the tournament to New Zealand as the financial returns to the IRB were considerably down on the profits made in both 2007 and 2003, which is why the governing body were not keen for anything to sully such a great six weeks.

That's the only explanation that can be found to justify why they were so reluctant to investigate what appeared to be a deliberate and brutal eye-gouge on All Black captain Richie McCaw in the final few minutes of the epic final. Video footage clearly shows French centre Aurélien Rougerie diving into a ruck where he puts his hands on McCaw's face. The All Black skipper emerged in obvious pain with his eye bruised and damaged, yet he stayed quiet during the post-match celebrations. He would say a few weeks later: 'The French are worse when they are scared ... they were as bad as they have been and were going for the eyes. My eye was a bit sore for a while and I was struggling to see for a bit. I was surprised they didn't cite him.'

The IRB didn't want to know about it, preferring to pretend it hadn't happened and citing technicalities as to why the incident wasn't investigated.

## 8 Biting Boks

The Springboks came to life in their 1995 quarter-final against Western Samoa. This was the game they showed their champion potential, building a platform with their set-piece and aggression at the breakdown and capitalising on that by playing with width and enterprise. It was also the game the Boks found the hero they were after – left wing Chester Williams scored four tries and the feel-good swept through the whole of South Africa.

The Samoans were crushed 42–14, but some of the players were sporting bite marks on various parts of their bodies and there were rumblings, supported by video evidence, that they had been subjected to verbal and physical abuse that was way beyond acceptable.

Some of the players wanted to go public, but they were persuaded not to by Samoan management who feared that if they complained they would almost certainly lose any chance of being invited into the soon-to-be created Super 12 and Tri Nations. They stayed quiet and, predictably, they were still not invited into either the Super 12 or Tri Nations, which was unveiled a few weeks after the World Cup.

### 7 Tana Umaga's phantom knee

It was incredible bad luck that 23 minutes into the All Blacks' first game at the 2003 World Cup, Tana Umaga should pick up a serious knee injury. He was looking to come back on the cut when his own fly-half, Carlos Spencer, tripped and fell into Umaga, causing the accidental damage.

Initially the All Blacks thought they had lost their key back for the tournament, but it turned out to be posterior cruciate damage rather than anterior, which meant Umaga was able to slowly regain his fitness and was passed fit to play in the quarter-final by team doctor John Mayhew. The All Blacks needed him back – they had lost faith in Umaga's understudy Ma'a Nonu and were playing fullback Leon MacDonald at centre in the interim.

But while Umaga had the green light to play, he wasn't picked and nor was he selected for the semi-final against Australia. The decision not to pick him backfired – Australia's centre, Stirling Mortlock, was the central figure, scoring a critical try and exposing MacDonald. The scandal in New Zealand was huge – coach John Mitchell chose not to play a world-class centre in a semi-final and instead went with a fullback.

'To this day I don't know whether they really didn't want to play him [Umaga],' said Mayhew in 2006. 'He [Tana] perceived Robbie Deans [All Black assistant coach] didn't rate him as a player.' Mitchell was sacked a few weeks after the failed campaign.

## 6 French resistance

Many people in France were unsure whether they should be angry that France, as hosts, had lost their opening game to Argentina in 2007, or angrier that the pre-match team talk had been hijacked by politics. French coach Bernard Laporte was stepping down after the World Cup to become minister of sport. He had read to the team a letter written by 17-year-old Guy Môquet, a resistance fighter, the night before he died in 1941.

This piece of writing was a favourite of President Nicolas Sarkozy, who ordered all schools to read it to their classes each year. There was resistance throughout France to Sarkozy's request to enforce the reading of the letter. Those with a centre-left political leaning felt the President was trying to create a patriotic myth and was manipulating the legend of Môquet, who was executed by the Nazis, for his own nationalist purposes.

The French players didn't like being caught in the political spotlight and felt that Laporte, a close friend of Sarkozy, had abused his position. Several schools, such as Robert de Luzarches lycée in Amiens, northern France, protested: 'We, the teachers at Robert de Luzarches, have collectively decided not to read this letter by Guy Môquet. We refuse to allow this letter to be used as a political propaganda tool by removing it from its historical context and by participating in a ritual gathering a thousand times removed from the intimate concerns that this document covers.'

## 5 Paddy power

In 2007 the Tongan team became the darlings of the tournament when they almost beat South Africa in their opening game and then beat Samoa and the USA. They managed to do this despite being broke – struggling for all sorts of training kit while the players were being paid a pittance. Irish bookmaker Paddy Power had taken pity and made a five-figure donation.

As a thank-you, and as something of a tribute to their Irish benefactor, the Tongans wanted to dye their hair green for their final pool game against England. But the IRB got wind of it and threatened to fine the Tongans if they went ahead. They also began investigating another payment that had been made to the Tongans earlier in the tournament from a non-official sponsor. 'The Tongan team and officials have agreed that they will appear normally and have been reminded of the importance of the match,' an IRB spokesman said.

Inoke Afeaki, one of Tonga's senior players, said the team had been told by the IRB that they were 'overstepping the mark'. He added: 'There's been a lot of kiboshing going on. We wanted to do it as a show of unity and togetherness.'

## 4 Losing the plot

When France made the semi-final of the 1999 World Cup there was a little disbelief. They were there courtesy of a soft draw and one of the worst refereeing performances in the tournament's history. New Zealand referee Paddy O'Brien would later write a chapter in his autobiography about the pool game between France and Fiji – citing it as the greatest embarrassment of his otherwise illustrious career. He called it a 'train crash of a game'.

O'Brien was guilty of many small errors and three giant ones that cost the Fijians a victory and safe passage through to the last eight. First he denied Fiji a legitimate try. They had caught the French fullback in a pincer tackle, the ball jolted loose and they hacked on and scored. O'Brien, though, saw a knock-on no one else in the world did. Then he missed three blatant forward passes in the build-up to a French try and, amazingly, with Fiji under pressure on their own line during a series of scrummages, he awarded a penalty try after French hooker Marc Del Maso popped up.

Those decisions allowed the French to win the game 28–19, with O'Brien telling journalists after the game: 'I lost the plot.' Working as a pundit for British TV, All Black captain Sean Fitzpatrick, the king of understatement, said of O'Brien's performance: 'He will look back on this and learn from his mistakes.'

## 3 The Channel tunnel incident

Things are never easy or without drama when the French are involved, and that was certainly the case in 1991 when they lost their quarter-final to England. That defeat hurt them – they hate losing to England anyway, and the pain was more acute given this was a World Cup quarter-final in Paris.

It was an ugly, violent game full of nasty stuff with scuffles every few minutes. Even Serge Blanco, the legendary creative genius at fullback for France, let loose with a flurry of punches on England wing Nigel Heslop. The French had hoped to intimidate England but it didn't work, and the longer the game went on, the more irate the French became. Worse still, they felt New Zealand referee David Bishop was working against them; he did admittedly miss a forward pass in the build-up to one of England's tries.

After the final whistle French coach Daniel Dubroca made his way to the tunnel where he accosted Bishop, grabbing him by the throat and screaming in his face that he was a cheat. He is alleged to have also spat on the referee. 'I simply went up to congratulate him and said bravo,' a contrite Dubroca would later say. 'I have known the referee for a while and I just went to give him a hug.' Dubroca immediately resigned and apologised for his actions and because of that, the IRB tried to sweep the whole business under the carpet.

## 2 England find extra man

If England had tried this against any of the major nations there would have been more serious consequences than the slap on the wrist (a £10,000 fine) they did receive. England's crime was to play almost one minute of their pool game against Samoa in 2003 with 16 players on the field. An accident? Probably, but still ... it is hard to imagine the All Blacks or Wallabies would have seen it that way had they been England's opponent.

In the final minutes England wanted to replace Mike Tindall, but instead of waiting for him to come off, replacement Dan Luger ran onto the field before he was allowed. He was told to get on by

England conditioning coach Dave Reddin, who ignored the protests of fourth official Brett Bowden. For 34 seconds, with England leading 35–22, they had a man advantage. Really it was cheating, yet the IRB didn't fancy having to properly discipline the tournament favourites by docking them points or forcing them to play the test again.

'There were a range of mitigating circumstances, including a clean record, character evidence and an apology,' said the IRB's judicial officer Brian McLaughlin after the fine was handed down. 'But this was weighed against a number of factors including the fact that the directions of the match official were ignored and the need to maintain the integrity of the match officials.'

## 1  Benazzi tries in vain

If only the Television Match Official had been part of the armoury in 1995, one of the great injustices might have been avoided. France, after their semi-final defeat to South Africa, had an entirely legitimate sense of betrayal at the 1995 World Cup.

The pitch at King's Park Durban was barely playable due to torrential rain that had delayed the kick-off. A classic arm-wrestle on a heavy pitch ensued and at 19–15 down, the French spent the last five minutes of the game camped on the Boks' line. They appeared to have scored through No 8 Abdel Benazzi, who had smashed through the throng of bodies to touch down at the base of the posts. That would have seen the hosts knocked out, but Welsh referee Derek Bevan ruled Benazzi had come up short. It was a 50:50 call but took on a sinister hue at the end of the tournament.

At the closing dinner South African Rugby Union president Louis Luyt made an appalling speech where he said: 'There were no true world champions in the 1987 and 1991 World Cups because South Africa were not there. We have proved our point.'

He then asked Bevan to come up to accept a gold watch for being 'an outstanding referee'. Bevan joined the mass walkout, later saying: 'It was something I could have done without. It came out of the blue: I have no idea why he singled me out. It could be misconstrued, and if that is the case, it leaves a bitter taste.'

# 10 iconic World Cup moments

## 10 A knockout blow

The All Blacks were in the process of dismantling Wales in the 1987 World Cup semi-final when tempers began to flare. The Welsh could sense they were on the verge of being properly done over and were starting to panic. There was plenty of niggle which erupted when Welsh lock Huw Richards sought retribution after being clobbered in the head by a stray All Black elbow.

Richards landed a few major slugs on All Black lock Gary Whetton before being floored by New Zealand's No 8 Wayne 'Buck' Shelford. Richards – unable to defend himself against the blindside haymaker – was knocked unconscious.

That brought the scuffle to a close and Shelford, aware he was going to be in big trouble, tried to hide among his team-mates. Welsh physio Tudor Jones eventually managed to revive Richards and get the big man back on his feet, only for referee Kerry Fitzgerald to send the 26-year-old lock off. Shelford amazingly escaped any punishment, and with a man advantage the All Blacks went on to win 49–6.

'I don't regret what happened,' Richards told the *Daily Telegraph* in 2011 – the first time he had ever spoken of the incident. 'It was one of those things that goes on in rugby. I just happened to be the one who copped the punishment. I took a few elbows, but that seemed to go under the radar. The officials missed that. They saw me as the aggressor and decided to send me off.

'I played the game hard and saw no problem in sorting things out on the pitch. So, you can imagine how frustrated I was when I saw the ref pointing to the touchline. It wasn't far to go, but it felt like a very long walk.'

### 9  Campo's hour of genius

The Wallabies knew they had been lucky to win their quarter-final against the Irish at the 1991 World Cup. That late escape galvanised them and they were focused and confident when they lined up to play the semi-final against the All Blacks at Lansdowne Road. The Wallabies had also cleverly won the hearts of their Irish hosts by spending the week before the semi-final in Dublin visible and accessible.

All of this obviously inspired Australia's magical wing David Campese, who produced one of the great performances that included two flashes of match-winning genius. The first came when he broke free and tormented the All Black defence before firing the most astonishing no-look pass to Tim Horan. The second was his angled run across the All Black defence. He kept going and defenders didn't manage to get a hand on him before he slid in at the corner. Those two tries enabled the Wallabies to win 16–6 and then despatch England in the final.

### 8  Fire of the dragon

The Welsh were initially incensed they lost their captain Sam Warburton to a red card after 17 minutes in the 2011 semi-final against France. Coach Warren Gatland felt it was a horrendous call by referee Alain Rolland – he thought the official acted too quickly in brandishing the red card after Warburton had lifted and then dumped wing Vincent Clerc in a tackle. 'I feel hollow,' lamented the coach after his side were knocked out 9–8. 'We accept Sam has lifted him and it probably warrants a yellow card. But he lets him go, he doesn't drive him into the ground and the player is fine to carry on. What surprises me is that the reaction of the referee is instant.'

Rolland felt he had no choice and Wales felt the pain of history repeating. They had a man sent off in their only other World Cup semi-final appearance. Reduced to 14, the Welsh had little chance of salvaging the game despite fighting so gallantly to do so. 'That decision ruined the semi-final,' said Gatland. 'I felt our destiny for having a chance to make the final was taken away from us with the red card. In a fantastic tournament there have been one or two matches where the referee has not been consistent enough. No disrespect to France or their players, they didn't make the decision and they are in the final.'

Warburton was distraught but would later say he deserved the card.

## 7 Heaven sent

The South Africans have never worried much about where their points come from as long as they come. They took that philosophy to the extreme in their 1999 quarter-final against England in Paris when they scored a record five dropped goals. Fly-half Jannie de Beer – a limited and previously unspectacular player who was only playing due to an injury to the first choice Henry Honnibal – was the hero of the day, scoring a record 34 points with the Boks winning 44–21. No one had ever seen anything like it – de Beer landed all five in the space of 31 minutes during the second half. South Africa would win the ball, rumble into England's territory and then de Beer would pull the trigger from anywhere. He didn't miss a single shot and England could do nothing about it.

'I tell you, I have a strong belief that the Lord has got something to do with it,' said de Beer, a devout Christian, of his performance.

England were desolate – they had been booted off the park in those 31 minutes. Hooker Phil Greening, said: 'We tried to play but to be fair Jannie just kicked everything. He was superb today and we had no answer to that. They took their chances with five dropped goals.'

## 6 Pumas maul France

Everyone had the 2007 World Cup all worked out before the first game – the quarter-finalists were easy to predict except maybe there was a toss of the coin decision to be made whether Scotland or Italy would progress from Pool C. Obviously France and Ireland would emerge from Pool A – with the hosts warmly fancied to top the group.

France would begin with a regulation win against the Pumas in Paris to open the tournament – well, that was the theory. Except on the big night, the Pumas showed an amazing resilience and a previously unknown poise and composure on the ball. They were also fitter and more creative than anyone predicted and had France in trouble from the first quarter. The Paris crowd was stunned by the relentless control and confidence of the Pumas, who at the time were the bastard child of world rugby. They were the country neither the Six Nations nor the Tri Nations wanted to accommodate in their respective tournaments. The victory by Argentina made it impossible for them to be ignored – especially when they followed it up with a comprehensive defeat of Ireland to top the pool.

'Argentina should be proud. I think we do exist,' said Pumas skipper Agustín Pichot. 'We're not the best tactical players or the best technically, but our best resources are the passion and pride when we put on the jersey.'

France coach Bernard Laporte was shell-shocked: 'When you begin a World Cup and it is imperative to win the match and you lose, you can say only one thing, that the sky has fallen in on your head.'

## 5  Kirwan's solo flight

Thankfully John Kirwan's try against Italy at the 1987 World Cup was filmed and the imagery preserved, otherwise future generations might have doubted the brilliance of the All Black wing. What actually happened was that Italy kicked off deep and Grant Fox caught the ball on the touchline a few metres from the try-line. He threw a pass to Kirwan, who then proceeded to run through the entire Italian team and score. It was an incredible run from the big All Black, who was strong and agile. He swerved and stepped and blasted past the Italians as if they weren't there, and by the time he touched down at Eden Park everyone could see the All Blacks were really the only contenders at the inaugural World Cup.

'One of JK's great qualities was his ability to stand in a tackle and offload to someone else to score a try,' said John Hart, an assistant with the 1987 All Blacks and the man responsible for discovering Kirwan. 'But with that try he had to do a lot of work himself and beat a number of defenders, showing that he was also an outstanding finisher.'

Kirwan, a modest and selfless man, said of his heroics. 'It is turning out to be as famous as the try Gareth Edwards scored for the Barbarians against the All Blacks. I got the ball from Foxy and had a crack. What I really remember is how well Michael Jones played in that test. Wow.'

## 4 Cardiff feels Pacific thunder

If the truth be told, not many fans at the 1991 World Cup would have known where to find Western Samoa on a map. The Pacific Islanders were barely heard of and were expected to be cannon fodder for the big nations. When they opened their campaign against the Welsh in Cardiff, what chance was there of Western Samoa causing an upset? 1000 to 1? 10,000 to 1? More like 100,000 to 1 and even that would have been seen as generous. But what the established rugby world failed to realise was that the Samoans were an incredibly talented and well-organised side containing some extremely destructive and explosive tacklers.

The first 40 minutes saw Wales rattled to the bone. The likes of Apollo Pereleni and Frank Bunce wreaked havoc at the Arms Park, particularly the former who ended up dislocating the shoulder of Welsh lock Phil May in a colossal tackle. A fortunate decision by referee Patrick Robin to award a try early in the second half to To'o Vaega enabled the Samoans to win 16–13 and pull off the greatest upset in World Cup history. The victory was defining – it opened everyone's eyes to the quality of players in the Pacific and the potential of the tiny Island nations.

Samoa's captain Peter Fatiolofa said of the win: 'This game is all about physical confrontation. Tackling hard is second nature to us. They used to call the Samoans rugby's headhunters. Now we've gone from head to waist. Our tackling is legitimate, legal and has always been a crucial factor of our game. We commit ourselves immensely hard to tackling but there is no cheating about it.'

## 3  Springboks find sixteenth man

It was maybe only after the Hollywood movie *Invictus* was released that the full extent of South Africa's political landscape during the 1995 World Cup was realised. South Africa, having only been welcomed out of sporting isolation in 1992, were awarded the hosting rights for the third World Cup. President Nelson Mandela – elected in 1994 – saw the tournament and the Springboks as vehicles to unite the country. The Springboks had long been the team of choice for the white, right-wing population and hated by the blacks. Mandela felt there was a powerful statement to be made by supporting the Boks and showing the rest of the black population that forgiveness would be the most powerful tool in burying the shameful past of apartheid. His ultimate act was to come onto the field before the final at Ellis Park wearing a Springbok jersey. It was so unexpected and such a powerful gesture that the crowd were almost uncontrollable.

It was a gesture that also moved the players, particularly the only black Springbok Chester Williams, who was awestruck when Mandela greeted the team in the changing room before the game. 'When Nelson Mandela walked into the changing room wearing that Springbok rugby jersey, it was done. We had to win that game. Everybody expected him to wear a suit and tie. It changed the attitude and spirit of the team – and it changed the whole mindset of the nation.'

South Africa won the famously close final 15–12 in extra time, and after the game Mandela shook captain Francois Pienaar's hand and said: 'Francois, thank you very much for what you have done for our country.'

'No, Mr President,' Pienaar replied. 'Thank you for what you have done for our country.'

## 2 Jonny come lately

To describe the 2003 World Cup final as epic fails to do it justice. It was more than that. This was the game that was in danger of never ending. Neither side could get away on the scoreboard and the drama was endless.

When England thought they had won it in normal time, Australia levelled the scores with a penalty in the last minute. When they thought they had won it in extra time, Australia levelled the scores with another penalty. After 100 minutes they were tied at 17–all.

With just one minute of extra time left, Lewis Moody won a lineout for England. Mike Catt danced into the Wallaby midfield before captain Martin Johnson charged further to set up Jonny Wilkinson for the drop goal. The England fly-half switched to his weaker right foot but it didn't matter – he hit the ball beautifully and with 25 seconds remaining and under intense pressure, Wilkinson slotted the most amazing kick to win it for England.

'And then there was Wilkinson,' wrote Paul Ackford in the *Sunday Telegraph*. 'Is there no end to the story? Labelled a basket case earlier in the tournament, probed by a thousand putative media psychiatrists at dozens of press conferences, Wilkinson came through to win the World Cup for his country. It was his 24-point haul that destroyed France and his drop goal that brought the Webb Ellis Cup home to England for the first time.'

## 1 Lomu turns Catt into road-kill

If England had their time again they would surely refrain from talking themselves up the way they did ahead of their 1995 semi-final clash against the All Blacks. They exuded confidence in the days leading into the Cape Town encounter, which only served to rile the All Blacks.

'I can remember reading Tony Underwood talking in the press before the game,' said All Black coach Laurie Mains 16 years later. 'He said something along the lines that, yes, Jonah [Lomu] had been impressive but that he hadn't played anyone of note and it would be different when he did. I showed that to Jonah and something clicked in him. He became more focused than I'd ever seen.' It didn't help Underwood's cause that he winked at Lomu during the haka or that Frank Bunce and the other senior All Blacks had spent all week goading their wing about the cockiness of his opposite man. They wanted Lomu to be angry, as they all had seen what the 120 kg wing was capable of. No one really knew though until that game just what an incredible player Lomu was.

He delivered the iconic moment of the century with his first touch of the ball when he swatted away Underwood and Will Carling and then charged directly at fullback Mike Catt. There wasn't any space to exploit on the outside so Lomu simply ran over Catt, barely breaking stride and then stomping over his victim as if he was nothing but road-kill. It was an incredible moment, and Lomu would go on to score four tries in the most famous display of individual power running ever seen.

'When Jonah was in a mood like that, you just gave him the ball and gave him the ball,' said Bunce. 'Everything became about getting the ball into Jonah's hands and then supporting him.'

# PART 5

# Field Positions

---

## 10 best props

---

**10** **Rodrigo Roncero** (Argentina 1998–)

The Argentinean plays like a man who grew up scrummaging, which he pretty much did. All that red meat and love of the set-piece in Argentina means they are always going to produce high-quality props and Rodrigo Roncero is among the best to come off the conveyer belt.

**9** **Andrew Sheridan** (England 2004–2011)

The giant Andrew Sheridan, who was forced to retire prematurely, was a constant tale of hard-luck stories with injury, but when he was fit he was memorably good. Strong enough to think about weightlifting at the Olympics, Sheridan had a few tests in his career where he actually removed opponents, such was his destructive power.

## 8 Sylvain Marconnet (France 1998–)

Sylvain Marconnet looks like a prop – he's short and square and his nose has borne the brunt of many things it shouldn't have. He is a player who has done more for France than is fully appreciated – he is a rock-solid scrummager. A really good operator with all the tricks and just the right touch of nastiness. Strong and low to the ground, he's a tricky beast to tame.

## 7 Carl Hayman (New Zealand 2000–2007)

At 1.95 m and 120 kg, Carl Hayman was a big man with the raw strength that came from being a farmer. What made Hayman particularly special was his ability to contribute away from the scrums. He could hold his own there but also canter around and give and take a pass.

## 6 Patricio Noriega (Argentina 1991–1995/ Australia 1998–2003)

The giant frame of Patricio Noriega bashed scrums for the Pumas before switching allegiance to the Wallabies. It didn't matter what country he played for – the scrum he was in wasn't going to be moved. He has an almost square-shaped head and with 120 kg of carcass attached to it, everyone knew they had run into something solid when they were hit by Noriega.

## 5 Jason Leonard (England 1990–2004)

Jason Leonard is one of life's good guys and he was also a more than useful prop. He lasted 14 years in test football, which says volumes for his durability and consistency, and in that period he became one of the most respected scrummagers in the world game.

### 4 Olo Brown (New Zealand 1992–1998)

The All Blacks still hold Olo Brown today as the technically perfect tight-head. Brown's back was so straight coming into engagement that it was actually possible to eat dinner off it. He was quiet and unassuming and simply got on with the business of destroying every scrum he encountered.

### 3 Os du Randt (South Africa 1994–2007)

Os du Randt became as famous for his work in the loose as he did his scrummaging. Both were of the highest quality. At more than 125 kg it was never likely that du Randt would be pushed around in the set-piece, and when he got going with the ball in hand not many people wanted to be in the way.

### 2 Steve McDowell (New Zealand 1985–1992)

The All Black loose-head was technically immaculate. Deemed too small when he first made the provincial scene, Steve McDowell hit the weights hard and built himself into a wall of muscle. He was incredibly strong, and with a background in martial arts he was impossible to move. No one ever 'did' him, and he also managed to get around the field to good effect.

### 1 Jean-Pierre Garuet (France 1983–1990)

Even in France where quality scrummagers seemingly grow on trees, Jean-Pierre Garuet was considered supreme. Technically he was among the best ever seen, and while he was a genial and sporting type, he could handle himself.

# 10 best hookers

**10** **Marius Tincu** (Romania 2002–)

The combative Tincu is a legend in French club rugby and probably the best player ever produced by Romania. His core skills are all they need to be and he plays like an openside flanker in the loose. He's phenomenal over the tackled ball and one of the great organisers of the rolling maul.

**9** **Mario Ledesma** (Argentina 1996–2011)

The bald-headed Argentinean played for an age and never once looked like he was getting older. A ferocious competitor and a great scrummager, he played as though his life was on the line. A man willing to do whatever it took for his beloved Pumas to win.

**8** **Bobby Windsor** (Wales 1973–1979)

Known as 'The Iron Duke', Bobby Windsor was a class act. He had a naturally sharp wit which could often get him into trouble. But he never worried about that because he could handle himself. Tough and feisty, he was exactly the sort of bloke everyone wants with them in the trenches.

**7** **Keith Wood** (Ireland 1994–2003)

There was a time when it felt like there was nothing Keith Wood couldn't do on a rugby field. He was so energetic and driven that it was infectious. He could race around like he was a wing and yet tackle like he was a loose forward. An enigma if ever there was one.

### 6 Colin Deans (Scotland 1978–1984)

The Scotland captain was a quiet achiever – one of those blokes who was all too easy to underestimate because he wasn't a huge man, or much of a shouter. Colin Deans was supremely mobile before hookers were expected to be, and he was the master at timing his strike in the scrum.

### 5 Raphaël Ibanez (France 1995–2007)

Raphaël Ibanez was the man France couldn't get enough of. After he retired, they dragged him back because they missed his presence in the middle of the scrum and his accurate lineout throwing. He was also a natural and charismatic leader who led France in both of their historic World Cup victories against the All Blacks in 1999 and in 2007.

### 4 Keven Mealamu (New Zealand 2002–)

Keven Mealamu is the perfect size for a hooker, and with his low centre of gravity he has managed to drive the All Blacks over the gainline for the better part of a decade. His ability to hit low and hard is legendary, and he's one of the toughest men ever to have pulled on the black jersey.

### 3 Uli Schmidt (South Africa 1986–1994)

This barrel of a man was always hanging out on the wing looking to make his presence felt, and when he got going there was little anyone could do. While he might have liked the limelight, Schmidt could handle himself in the dark places, too.

### 2 Phil Kearns (Australia 1989–1999)

A bull of a man who lived for the tight exchanges, Phil Kearns would have loved it if there was nothing else in rugby but scrums. He was built for them, although he was surprisingly mobile and capable with the ball in hand.

## Sean Fitzpatrick (New Zealand 1986–1997)

Sean Fitzpatrick wasn't a natural hooker – he had to work hard to improve his throwing and scrummaging – but by the end of his career no one would ever have known. His hard work enabled him to become one of the most accurate in the game, while his work in the tight was without peer. He began to score tries later in his career and carry the ball to good effect.

# 10 best locks

**10** **Brad Thorn** (New Zealand 2003–2011)

The former Rugby League star was a thunderously good rugby player by the time he retired. He learned the technical subtleties of his craft and married them with his athleticism and natural love of carrying the ball. His time in the NRL helped him become a destructive tackler equipped with an incredible work-rate.

**9** **Fabien Pelous** (France 1995–2007)

The former French captain played an enormous amount of rugby, which is because Fabien Pelous was a seriously good player. He had bulk and aggression and used both to good effect. He moved around well for such a big man and had a good feel for the game, which is why he occasionally played at No 8.

**8** **Scott Murray** (Scotland 1997–2007)

The Scotsman was easily the best lineout forward in Europe for most of his career. A former basketball player, Scott Murray had timing and a natural spring that would enable him to steal opposition ball. He was also a bit wild when he played – oblivious to his own well-being.

**7** **Ian Jones** (New Zealand 1990–1999)

Built like a giant green bean, Ian Jones really had no business in test football. But he was massively resilient and deceptively strong. He operated in an era before lifting, so was a huge lineout presence and he put himself about, playing as if he was 15 kg heavier.

### 6 Ali Williams (New Zealand 2002–)

Once Ali Williams began to fill out physically he became a potent package – athletic and good in the air but also capable of hitting bodies out the way. He was probably the world's best lock in 2007 and 2008 until he was struck down by injury. But no one can survive 10 years in the All Blacks unless they are world-class.

### 5 Bakkies Botha (South Africa 2002–)

Obviously Bakkies Botha has had issues with his discipline, but in some ways that has just added to the package. He is built like a phone-box and no one gets the better of him. He does everything that is expected of a lock and does it to the highest standards. He would be welcome in any team.

### 4 Colin Meads (New Zealand 1957–1971)

The original enforcer, Colin Meads was way before his time. If he had been born 30 years later and exposed to modern training, he would have been a phenomenal player. He lived off his natural strength and ability to charge around the place like he owned it, which he usually did by the end of every test he played.

### 3 Victor Matfield (South Africa 2000–2011)

Victor Matfield can make an undisputed claim to being the best aerial forward to ever play. He studied the lineout in intimate detail, which is partly why he was so effective there. It also helped that he was a natural athlete with superb ball skills. A tough nut, too, who could get around the track.

### 2 Martin Johnson (England 1993–2004)

It took just one withering look from Martin Johnson for most grown men to be left a quivering mass. The England skipper was a man-mountain who commanded his territory with an iron fist. He smashed his way through a decade of rugby, but was also a ball player and natural athlete.

### 1　John Eales (Australia 1991–2001)

From kicking goals to winning lineouts to making try-saving tackles, John Eales could do everything. If he was merely assessed on his abilities to carry out the traditional skills of the locking role he'd be considered one of the best. The fact he could do so much more made him unquestionably the best.

# 10 best
# openside flankers

### 10  Josh Kronfeld (New Zealand 1995–2000)

At the 1995 World Cup everyone spotted the huge left wing straight away, and by the middle of the tournament Josh Kronfeld was also a household name. Wherever Jomah Lomu went, Kronfeld went. He was a supreme fetcher and support player, who had the engine to get around and be first man to the ball wherever it was.

### 9  Finlay Calder (Scotland 1986–1991)

Finlay Calder was a raw-boned presence who could hurt teams with his power in the tackle and his ability to carry the ball. He probably could have handled the blindside just as easily, because he had a love of the tight exchanges as well as a fondness for ranging freely out wide.

### 8  Neil Back (England 1994–2003)

Neil Back was initially told he was too small for test football. He quickly blew that theory out the water when the Lions picked him in 1997, and he showed the value of having an openside who could scorch across the turf and beat the big lugs to the ball. He was also able to hit well above his weight in the tackle.

### 7  Mamuka Gorgodze (Georgia 2003–)

Affectionately known as 'Godzilla', Mamuka Gorgodze is 120 kg of raw anger. No one can handle his power from close range, and when he's really angry he's super effective. He hits anything and everything and yet is surprisingly mobile. He has been a big star of French club rugby as a result.

### 6 Olivier Magne (France 1997–2007)

The memory of Olivier Magne roaming all over Twickenham during the 1999 World Cup semi-final is hard to shake. That was him at his best – rangy and electric, determined to have his hands on the ball. He was a quality athlete with the pace to damage teams.

### 5 Laurent Cabannes (France 1987–1997)

Laurent Cabannes never left anyone wondering what he was all about. He was energy and ferocity – yet level-headed and effective. He was a gazelle of a thing who left others gasping, the perfect man for a French team that was always a poetic mix of brutal forward play and glorious creativity from the backs.

### 4 Peter Winterbottom (England 1982–1993)

Peter Winterbottom was a hard man who never complained about anything, and even if he was bleeding or suffering, he'd get to the loose ball first. He played in an era where his key role was to terrorise fly-halves, and many still have nightmares about Winterbottom.

### 3 George Smith (Australia 2000–2009)

George Smith was a cussed operator with the ability to stay ridiculously strong over the ball. He was the ultimate ball-winner on the ground and capable of snatching possession he had no right to even be near. He not only pinched ball but he became expert at using it as well.

### 2 Michael Jones (New Zealand 1987–1998)

Michael Jones redefined expectations for opensides. No one had ever seen an athlete quite like him. A bone-crushing tackler and rangy runner who looked like a wing, Jones was the ultimate package. A deeply religious man, he actually played as if he was God.

## 1  Richie McCaw (New Zealand 2001–)

The All Black captain has played more than 100 tests and no one can remember him having a bad one. Most of his career he's been the main talking point before each test – such is his influence and ability to make an impact. McCaw is a supreme athlete who has been able to evolve from ball winner to ball carrier.

# 10 best
# blindside flankers

### 10 Mike Teague (England 1985–1993)

Mike Teague made a name for himself on the British & Irish Lions tour of Australia in 1989 when he showed he was a genuinely hard man. A member of the Gloucester club, Teague was a proper old-school type who thundered into things and never shirked. If he was ever hurt he would play on, and he was a quiet assassin on the side of the scrum.

### 9 Apollo Perelini (Samoa 1991–1993)

There has never been a more destructive tackler than Apollo '11' Perelini. The Samoan flanker scared the living daylights out of Wales at the 1991 World Cup when he dislocated lock Phil May's shoulder in an incredible hit. His stint in union was brief but unforgettable as, understandably with rugby still amateur at the time, league clubs pounced on a player with his phenomenal ability to tackle.

### 8 Jerome Kaino (New Zealand 2006–)

He was nominated as an IRB World Player of the Year in 2011 and was unlucky to miss out – to Thierry Dusautoir. Once Jerome Kaino got himself properly fit in 2010 he began to really hurt people. He is one of the biggest tacklers in the world game and a mobile player with good hands, one of the strongest ball carriers ever to play.

### 7 John Jeffrey (Scotland 1984–1991)

The 'Great White Shark' was instantly recognisable with his shock of white hair. John Jeffrey didn't need hair to make him stand out, though. He did that with the quality of his work – a tough farmer from the Borders, he put himself about and covered the ground. He was also an exceptionally good lineout option.

### 6 Simon Poidevin (Australia 1980–1991)

There are few Wallabies who did more for their country than Simon Poidevin. He was ever-present throughout the 1980s and probably didn't miss a tackle in that time. He was supremely quick and loved scrapping for the loose ball. One of the most consistent and durable forwards ever produced by Australia.

### 5 Ruben Kruger (South Africa 1993–1999)

Sadly the one opponent Ruben Kruger couldn't get the better of was cancer – the Springbok World Cup winner passed away in 2010. As a player he was respected the world over for the edge he brought and his ability to drive hard yards. He had enormous upper-body strength that left opponents wondering if they had been hit by a small truck.

### 4 Alan Whetton (New Zealand 1984–1991)

It was only after Alan Whetton retired that many New Zealanders came to appreciate just what they had in this bruising blindside. Whetton would be big even by today's standards, and he played with a lot of intelligence and guile. Could be an out-and-out nasty prick if that was required, as well.

### 3 Thierry Dusautoir (France 2006–)

It's always a bit confusing trying to work out whether the French see their No 6 as a blindside or an openside, but in the case of Thierry

Dusautoir there is no need to debate. His natural skill-set is perfectly suited to the blindside. Dusautoir shot to fame when he made 39 tackles against the All Blacks in the 2007 World Cup quarter-final and hasn't stopped knocking men down since. A deserved winner of the IRB Player of the Year in 2011.

## 2   Schalk Burger (South Africa 2003–)

The big South African would probably have to be killed before he'd give up. When he is on form he is more than a handful. His desire to keep coming and coming can be frightening: he never gives teams a break and he is such a big man to bring down. Some of his tackling is fearsome – real bone-shuddering stuff.

## 1   Richard Hill (England 1997–2008)

The great thing about Richard Hill was he could play across the back-row and not lose his effectiveness. He was a big man with incredible strength. He did all the thankless tasks and never wanted the limelight. Everyone who played against him ended up being hugely impressed.

# 10 best number 8s

### 10 Andy Ripley (England 1972–1976)

The slightly eccentric Andy Ripley was a marvel to behold at times. If he'd played in the professional era he would have been a global superstar. His engine was huge and his top-end pace was better than most wings. He loved to carry the ball into space and he played rugby precisely within the spirit it was intended.

### 9 Brian Lochore (New Zealand 1964–1971)

The man who would later coach the All Blacks to World Cup glory in 1987 was a rugged ball carrier and clever operator. Brian Lochore liked to play the ball out of the tackle and keep movements alive. He was a classic corner-flagger and big tackler.

### 8 Sergio Parisse (Italy 2002–)

The only pity is that Sergio Parisse has never been given the chance to shine in a dominant team. He has managed to produce world-class displays as part of a struggling team, which makes him more impressive. He can play with the ball, and in 2009 was rated by the All Blacks as the best No 8 in world rugby.

### 7 Juan Martín Fernández Lobbe (Argentina 2004–)

The bravery and work-rate of the Pumas captain are impossible not to admire. His appetite for contact is extreme and he loves nothing more than the close-quarters driving – his legs pumping and the Pumas going forward. He is also freakishly good in the air, an all-rounder with more yet to come.

### 6 Abdel Benazzi (France 1990–2001)

The Moroccan-born Frenchman was a thunderous big man on the hoof. He could blast holes by going through people but he was also surprisingly effective wider out. He was a long-striding athlete with a good range of skills that saw him use the ball well.

### 5 Iain Paxton (Scotland 1981–1988)

In 1985 Iain Paxton scored two tries at Murrayfield against Wales that other No8s could only have dreamed about. Paxton could cover the ground and play with the ball. He was also tough enough to occasionally play at lock, his athleticism allowing him to compensate for his lack of height in the lineout.

### 4 Morné du Plessis (South Africa 1971–1980)

The fact Morné du Plessis became such a revered figure in South Africa is testament to his ability to play with both brawn and brain. A deep-thinking, composed man, he exuded calm and confidence and continually did the right thing.

### 3 Lawrence Dallaglio (England 1995–2007)

Lawrence Dallaglio was a beefed-up, more athletic version of Buck Shelford. In his prime, Dallaglio could get over the advantage line no matter how many men were in his way. A crushing force who lived for the contact.

### 2 Buck Shelford (New Zealand 1986–1990)

Intense and ferocious, Buck Shelford was a mean figure on the rugby field. He drove straight and hard, would tackle anything and never left his post unmanned. He was the ultimate warrior – the perfect man to keep his team going forward.

## 1 Zinzan Brooke (New Zealand 1987–1997)

Zinzan Brooke could have been a world-class fly-half. The man was outrageous. He could drop goals, he could pass like a scrum-half and yet he never shirked the tough side of his craft. He was a bruiser to boot and, let's be honest, every No 8 since has been just a little bit of a disappointment.

# 10 best scrum-halves

**10** **Robert Howley** (Wales 1996–2002)

Robert Howley was one tough blighter who could bounce off the big boys in the close-quarter stuff, and who could really damage teams out in the open. He was a devastating broken field runner and capable of opening any defence.

**9** **Fabien Galthié** (France 1991–2003)

The enigmatic Fabien Galthié played with a combination of brain and brawn that made him tough to pin down. He was the man who set the tempo for the French and it pretty much went like this: if Galthié played well, France played well.

**8** **Roy Laidlaw** (Scotland 1980–1988)

The Borders in Scotland has produced an indecent number of classy scrum-halves – none more silky than Roy Laidlaw. He could scrap behind a retreating pack if needs be, but his best work was completed when his forwards were on top and he could sneak around the fringes and dart this way and that. Had a rocket pass.

**7** **Gary Armstrong** (Scotland 1988–1999)

Even the great Buck Shelford was a little wary of Gary Armstrong. Shelford says that Armstrong punched him in the chops in 1990 but, far from holding a grudge, the former All Black captain was hugely impressed at the courage and feistiness of Armstrong. That was him in a nutshell – a warrior who would throw himself about for 80 minutes and not care about the physical damage.

### 6 Sid Going (New Zealand 1967–1977)

Many New Zealanders feel they have never come remotely close to reproducing a scrum-half in the same league as Sid Going. He had the game to light up any field – speed and a good eye for detail as well as a long kicking game and an ability to see the field.

### 5 Agustín Pichot (Argentina 1995–2008)

Agustín Pichot was exactly the sort of scrum-half the Pumas needed. He was fiery and imposing – sniped around the fringes and played off the driving power of the pack. Was a masterful architect on the tactical front, the beating heart of the Pumas at the 2007 World Cup.

### 4 George Gregan (Australia 1994–2007)

There wasn't much of George Gregan, but he played way above his stature. He was a little piece of wire that could look after himself and put big men down in the tackle. He fired raking passes and clever little ones at all sorts of intriguing angles. A dogged customer – Gregan would rather die than lose.

### 3 Joost van der Westhuizen (South Africa 1993–2003)

Many teams were hurt by the running power of Joost van der Westhuizen, the bruising Springbok scrum-half who began his test career on the wing. When he ran, it was mostly well timed and deadly, and any loose forward not on his game would be embarrassed by the speed of van der Westhuizen. A rabid competitor as well, he never backed down from anything.

### 2 Nick Farr-Jones (Australia 1984–1993)

The Wallabies could have thrown Nick Farr-Jones the No 10 jersey and been confident they were going to get a special performance. Farr-Jones was that sort of player – composed, comfortable and always playing with his head up. He had the full range of ball skills and physical attributes to buzz about as if he was omnipresent.

### 1 Gareth Edwards (Wales 1967–1978)

Gareth Edwards was equipped to be a phenomenal player of any period. He had everything and more – the dive pass, the innate reading of the game, the bravery, the speed, the anticipation and the desire. Best of all, he was a good man who played the game in the right spirit.

# 10 best fly-halves

### 10 Andrew Mehrtens (New Zealand 1995–2004)

If Andrew Mehrtens had been defensively robust he'd have been one of the very best fly-halves. He had the kicking game and he was desperately quick across the turf. He could land goals and push the All Blacks into all the right places. He had the ideal temperament as well – a naturally engaging and intelligent man, he enjoyed playing under pressure.

### 9 John Rutherford (Scotland 1979–1987)

There was an elegance about John Rutherford that the Scots have never seen again in any of their other No 10s. Rutherford was composed and confident, capable of drifting past defenders and creating space for others. He always seemed to be thinking one move ahead, like the ultimate chess player.

### 8 Mark Ella (Australia 1980–1984)

Mark Ella was one of the first fly-halves to play on the advantage line. He could do that because his hands were so good and his movement so sharp and precise. He loved playing flat and bringing in runners on oblique angles, and through his exploits on the 1984 Grand Slam tour he inspired a generation into wanting to be just like him.

### 7 Jonny Wilkinson (England 1998–2011)

For a time Jonny Wilkinson was the best No 10 in the world game. He was the perfect player for the England team between 2000 and 2003. He was a pressure goal-kicker and the ideal man to use his boot to punish teams and keep his own side in the territory where they wanted to be. He wasn't a great passer or runner, but never really had to be.

### 6 Hugo Porta (Argentina 1971–1990)

Hugo Porta played test rugby for almost 20 years and hardly put a foot wrong. His core skills were immaculate. His right boot was cultured and ultra-reliable, while he was an astute tactician and game manager. The Pumas grafted for their points in Porta's day and he rarely let opportunities slip. It's unlikely the Pumas would be where they are now were it not for Porta.

### 5 Barry John (Wales 1966–1972)

There are plenty of people in Wales who will wonder why Barry John is only ranked fifth. It's only because of his premature retirement. Others did more because they played more, but few had the skills and vision of John. He could slip through the tightest defence and kicked the ball surprisingly well for a little man.

### 4 Phil Bennett (Wales 1969–1978)

For anyone that grew up with Barry John, it was scarcely believable that Phil Bennett was the next fly-half off the Welsh production line. Bennett was that bit more robust, with most of the attacking features carried by John. Bennett's other extra was his side-step – once he got going, there was no telling how many he might beat.

### 3 Carlos Spencer (New Zealand 1997–2004)

Carlos Spencer was not the complete player by any means, but he remains the most outrageously talented fly-half of any era. He invented the pass to himself and the banana kick. He was brilliant in the way he found holes and trusted his instincts to make things happen. The best running fly-half ever.

## 2 Stephen Larkham (Australia 1997–2007)

Stephen Larkham was unorthodox in the extreme. He was tall and gangly and not a great kicker. But he was a great player who hid his deficiencies with a supremely effective running game that saw him come from the strangest places and break any defence. He was a mystical player with a skill-set that is hard to believe will ever be seen again.

## 1 Daniel Carter (New Zealand 2003–)

There has never been a fly-half with the range of skills possessed by Daniel Carter. He is the everything man – a robust defender, a navigator, a runner and a supreme kicker. He can play any style and excel at them all. He is world rugby's highest points-scorer and may still be some way off his peak yet.

# 10 best wings

### 10 Joe Roff (Australia 1995–2004)

Joe Roff was a frightening size and a compelling unit when he was at full speed. A big man at 1.93 m and 105 kg, he ate up the ground and was one of the first modern wings to excel in the air. He scored tries at will when Australia enjoyed a boom period from 1999 to 2002.

### 9 Simon Geoghegan (Ireland 1991–1996)

What might Simon Geoghegan have achieved had he been born 10 years later and enjoyed being part of Ireland's golden generation of players? He could never be described as elegant on account of his 'wounded stag' running style but, however ungainly he appeared, he was not short of pace or instincts. The Lions kept a place open for him until the last minute in 1997 to see if he could recover from ongoing problems with his toe, which illustrates the standing in which he was held.

### 8 Philippe Saint-André (France 1990–1997)

It was all too easy to underestimate Philippe Saint-André and many opponents did. He could at times appear a little portly, but that never slowed him down or dulled his instincts. He has become coach of the French national team after successful club stints in England, and that has highlighted the depth of his rugby intelligence.

### 7 Ieuan Evans (Wales 1987–1998)

There was no stopping Ieuan Evans when he was in full flight. He was quick, strong and elusive – which is why he was a test starter in three Lions' series and won 72 caps for Wales. The man knew how to finish and where to be to get his hands on the ball.

### 6   Jeff Wilson (New Zealand 1993–2001)

Jeff Wilson scored a hat-trick on debut and never looked back. He was an all-rounder – happy at fullback and also on the cricket field, where he played several one-day internationals – which meant he could operate in any weather or on any surface. His trademark chip-and-chase was his best weapon and helped him score 44 tries in 60 tests.

### 5   Gerald Davies (Wales 1966–1978)

The little Welshman cut a dashing figure in the 1970s – always willing to take the outside channel and back his pace. He scored tries that were built purely on his top-end speed, and because he began his career as a centre, that gave him a wider range of skills. He scored 20 tries in 46 tests – a deadly strike-rate in a period when the game was not as open as it is now.

### 4   Bryan Habana (South Africa 2004–)

The great skill of Bryan Habana has been to continually evolve his game to keep himself valuable and relevant. When he started he was a deadly quick finisher. As he matured he became a great chaser and defender, and his bravery, positioning and anticipation have been remarkable.

### 3   David Campese (Australia 1982–1996)

He liked to mouth off a bit did 'Campo', but that was forgivable because he was extraordinarily gifted. His running was devastating; the subtle angles, the agility, the balance and the acceleration – he had it all. Campo was also a top-quality ball player and all-round footballer.

## 2 Rupeni Caucaunibuca (Fiji 2003–)

Before his lifestyle caught up with him, Rupeni Caucaunibuca was every bit as thrilling as Jonah Lomu. He could beat anyone for pace, and just like Lomu he could smash through if he had to. In 2003 and 2004 he scored tries that were ludicrously good. He made the game look phenomenally easy – coasting past world-class players for fun.

## 1 Jonah Lomu (New Zealand 1994–2002)

Who could ever forget Jonah Lomu in his prime? There has never been a player quite like him – 120 kg of ferocity capable of running like a man half his size. He destroyed everyone he played against. He could score tries no one else could and remains the only truly world-famous rugby player.

# 10 best centres

### 10 Will Carling (England 1988–1997)

England were reluctant to play expansive football in Will Carling's time, which never made sense given the ability of the skipper. He had raw pace and strength in the carry, which he demonstrated ably whenever he played Sevens. He was tougher than he was given credit for as well.

### 9 Tana Umaga (New Zealand 1997–2005)

Umaga started his career as a wing and moved to centre in 2001, where his defensive clout was enormous. No one ever got around Umaga or came through him, and as he matured he turned from finisher to creator. He had an incredible long passing game and was one of the best at getting his arms free for the offload out the back of the tackle.

### 8 Denis Charvet (France 1986–1991)

Impossibly good-looking and so very French, Denis Charvet played with a breathtaking elegance and style that made him compelling viewing. He was smooth across the turf and so aware of the space that anyone silly enough to give him a half-metre lived to regret it.

### 7 Scott Gibbs (Wales 1991–2001)

Scott Gibbs was a man who preferred to take the direct route. His power and acceleration were colossal, and he could knock even the biggest forwards out of his way when he dropped his shoulder and went for them. He was a battering ram with a brain and plenty of vision that allowed him to make holes, then exploit them.

### 6 Frank Bunce (New Zealand 1992–1997)

Frank Bunce won his first All Black cap at 30, and everyone had to wonder why on earth it took so long for New Zealand to realise what they had. Bunce was rugged and aggressive, yet he was also subtle and effective – an especially good distributor and organiser of the outside backs. And against all the odds, he actually seemed to become a better finisher in his later years when he was close to 36.

### 5 Mike Gibson (Ireland 1964–1979)

Footballers like Mike Gibson don't come along often. He was just as competent at fly-half, but it was in the midfield where he was able to find holes and drift through them. He was also able to make space for others further out from the heavy traffic and use his timing and accuracy of pass to hurt opponents.

### 4 Tim Horan (Australia 1989–2000)

There was never any chance of Tim Horan being caught behind the gainline or giving possession away cheaply. He was a direct and scorching influence who was at his best when he hit short passes close to the ruck. He picked tricky angles and had the power and agility to brush off tackles.

### 3 Danie Gerber (South Africa 1980–1992)

His dalliance with test football was all too brief because of South Africa's isolation, but the little that was seen of Danie Gerber left a big impression. He was a balanced runner who hit the ball at pace. He played with the ball out in front of him, which only the best have the confidence to do, and the hat-trick he scored against England in 1985 was a prime example of how much this man had to offer.

## 2 Philippe Sella (France 1982–1995)

There was just too much to admire about Philippe Sella. There was his strength. There was his speed, and he was a distributor who never wavered under pressure, and he crunched bones in the tackle. That made him a multiple threat and no one relished playing against a man who could dip into his bag of tricks and pull out anything he liked.

## 1 Brian O'Driscoll (Ireland 1999–)

Brian O'Driscoll has been a scarcely believable package of the best of everything. He has been provider and finisher; he has been tactician and battering ram; he has been strike runner and distributor. For 10 years he has been recognised as the best centre in the world and his standards have never slipped.

# 10 best fullbacks

### 10 Jean-Luc Sadourny (France 1991–2001)

A gliding, effortless player who drifted past defenders in the same way luxury cars coast in the outside lane of the motorway, Jean-Luc Sadourny had all the skills of Serge Blanco, just not the same profile on account of being a private, quiet man.

### 9 Matt Burke (Australia 1993–2004)

Capable at centre, Matt Burke always looked more at home when he played fullback. He had the raw pace to score spectacular tries, and the fact he was so disliked in New Zealand was the ultimate mark of respect – he was a player even the mighty All Blacks feared.

### 8 Tom Kiernan (Ireland 1960–1973)

Tom Kiernan was a superstar long before there were superstars. He could do everything, and when he retired he held just about every record in Ireland. A top class goal-kicker and reader of the game, Kiernan was the rock on which Ireland's game was built throughout the 1960s.

### 7 Gavin Hastings (Scotland 1986–1995)

'Big Gav' was a man for all occasions. He was a powerful beast on the hoof and could take the direct route, but was also a bit quicker than he looked. The key to his game was his immaculate core skills; he was brave under the high ball and had a booming right boot.

### 6 JPR Williams (Wales 1969–1981)

They don't make fullbacks like JPR any more. They don't really make players like him any more. The toughest fullback to ever play, he was a ferocious tackler and saved his nation and the Lions on many occasions. He was a direct and powerful attacking force as well.

### 5 André Joubert (South Africa 1989–1997)

Forget the dodgy moustache – Joubert was a class act. He was a Rolls-Royce sort of player in the way he purred majestically at the back, timing his intrusions to perfection. Would have made an even greater impact had South Africa not been in isolation during much of his career.

### 4 John Gallagher (New Zealand 1987–1991)

The international career of John Gallagher was brief but highly memorable. For four years he was the best fullback in the world. His main weapon was his timing and ability to hit the line at full tilt and coast past the defence. An elegant and cunning player, he was desperately missed by the All Blacks when he ran off to league.

### 3 Andy Irvine (Scotland 1972–1982)

Fullback had historically been the place for solid, defensive types until Andy Irvine transformed it into a position of adventure. Irvine opened minds to what could be achieved at fullback in an attacking sense. He was dashing and daring – brave enough to back himself and believe in the improbable.

### 2 Christian Cullen (New Zealand 1996–2002)

At full speed Christian Cullen could step and not slow down, which allowed him to leave defenders flapping at nothing cartoon-style. He had incredible instincts and popped up in all the right places. He was also immensely strong, which made him almost impossible to tackle.

## 1  Serge Blanco (France 1980–1991)

A magical player who made the heart race whenever the ball came near him. Capable of anything and everything, he made rugby a game everyone wanted to play.

# PART 6

# Heroes and Villains

---

## 10 great sporting/heroic acts

---

### 10 Dallaglio's selfless gestures

Having retired from international rugby in August 2004, Lawrence Dallaglio was one of the bigger surprises in the 2005 British & Irish Lions squad. The England No 8, though, had been in such good form for his club that coach Clive Woodward felt he'd be crazy to come to New Zealand without him.

It appeared to be an astute selection, as in the opening 25 minutes of the first game against Bay of Plenty in Rotorua, Dallaglio was the best player on the field. By some distance. But tragedy struck when he broke his ankle and his tour ended before it had really started.

Such disappointment would have been agonising for Dallaglio but despite that, and despite the physical pain of his ankle, he made sure that he gave his playing jersey to Bay of Plenty No 8 Colin Bourke. It was a nice touch that took class and selflessness, as did his decision to visit the injured Rudi Wulf. Dallaglio was due to fly home a few days after injuring his ankle, but he had read about the unfortunate Wulf, the promising New Zealand Under-21 player who had broken his neck diving into the shallow end of a swimming pool.

'He came and visited me when I was at home in my halo, when he was touring with the Lions and he gave me a lot of kind words and really put my spirits back up there,' Wulf said of his visit from Dallaglio. 'He just said to "hang in there and everything is going to be all right".'

### 9  Simon Taylor plays with a broken hand

Scotland were sure they had struck gold with 21-year-old Simon Taylor. The law student had been on the fringes of the Edinburgh team – balancing rugby with study – in 2000 when an injury crisis saw him picked to play at No 8 against Northampton in the Heineken Cup. He played a huge game, virtually won it on his own for the capital side, and did enough to impress not only the Scottish selectors but the watching British & Irish Lions manager Donal Lenihan.

It was apparent Taylor had the mobility and ball skills to be something special. After his performance against Australia later in the year – which was his second test – it was apparent he was also exceptionally tough. Taylor had broken his hand in two places just five minutes into the game. The swelling was extensive and the pain horrific, but he battled on for the full 80 minutes. 'He just shook his hand and got on with the game,' said Scotland manager Dougie Morgan after a visit to the hospital had revealed the extent of the damage. 'It was not until later that it was thought necessary to send him for an X-Ray.' Taylor was out for eight weeks but recovered in time to win a place on the Lions tour to Australia.

## 8 The one-legged All Black

All Black captain Richie McCaw was all set for the 2011 Super Rugby competition when just one week before the first game he was diagnosed with a broken bone in his foot. He required surgery and had a steel pin inserted in the bone of his little toe on his right foot.

He returned to action in mid-April, but was troubled by his foot and ended up having to miss several more games. By the time the test programme kicked off he was supposedly fine. He had no more problems. Except that he did – he just kept them in-house. Come the World Cup, McCaw was in serious pain. His foot was permanently swollen and the pin was grating on the bone. By the quarter-final he could no longer train and had to keep his weight off his foot. He played the quarter-final, semi-final and final in agony – X-rays would later show that the bone was still broken.

On the Friday before the final, Graham Henry and McCaw went fishing. 'I looked at his foot and said, "Hell, Rich, that bloody foot looks swollen mate, really swollen," ' Henry would later reveal.

'Yeah, Ted, it is,' was the reply.

'His ability to lead and be inspirational to that group of people was immense,' Henry continued. 'And because he couldn't even train, he got finer on the detail. Like he was outstanding, superb.'

## 7 The £250,000 kick

Stuart Tinner wouldn't be a name known to anyone but Saracens, and that's because he cost them a bit of cash. The unlikely Tinner was chosen to take part in a half-time promotion during the clash between Saracens and the Springboks at Wembley in 2009. It was a big night for the club, and they thought they would jazz up the break by selecting three people in the crowd to try to punt the ball from 30 metres out and hit the crossbar. The prize was a spectacular £250,000 ($650,000).

Life-changing money. But what were the chances? 1000 to 1? 10,000 to 1? Tinner was first up. He slipped off his shoes, booted it with his socks on, and slap – the ball thundered into the crossbar and he was a whole lot richer. He became a celebrity for a few days but didn't let it go to his head. Interviewed by Sky TV about what he would do with the money, he said: 'I think I will be keeping my feet well and truly on the ground and trying to get onto the property ladder.'

## 6 Colin Meads playing with a broken arm

Older and wiser, Sir Colin Meads has come to be a little embarrassed by the story of him playing for the All Blacks with a broken arm. That he did helped create the legend he became, but with a bit of clarity in his older age he's come to see it was not the best example to set.

The All Black lock broke his arm playing against Eastern Transvaal in a tour game in 1970. He played on, refusing to go off because back in those days no replacements were allowed. Talking to the *New Zealand Herald* about it in 2010, he said: 'I knew something was wrong. The doctor said I had a pinched nerve. And I said, "I'm not going off for a bloody pinched nerve!" He must have known it wasn't a bloody pinched nerve. It was hurting all right. I didn't know who did it so I couldn't get them back.'

The arm still hadn't healed by the time the first test with the Springboks rolled around. But Meads was going to play. No one argued with him.

## 5 Captain Courageous

The giant Scottish lock Mike Campbell-Lamerton was not only a formidable player and soldier, he was also a selfless and dedicated leader. Having been on tour with the British & Irish Lions in 1962, Campbell-Lamerton was made captain of the 1966 tour party that took on the longest and most ambitious schedule in the combined side's history.

Inevitably, with the team away from home for almost five months, the tour came off the rails. The Lions weren't much chop and they encountered not only an excellent All Blacks side, but one that was also the dirtiest. Campbell-Lamerton did his level best to keep the party together through the most difficult circumstances and even made the selfless decision to drop himself for the second and fourth tests. He decreed he didn't merit a place in the side and handed the captaincy to David Watkins for those games.

'Mike decided to stand down for the second and fourth tests and asked me to take on the captaincy,' said Watkins many years later. 'He only wanted what was best for the team and was someone whom I greatly admired.'

## 4  The early whistle

There was a ruthless streak a mile wide in Sean Fitzpatrick – that's what made him such a great player and an even better All Black captain. There was also, and this was probably less appreciated, an honourable and sporting side to the man who captained the All Blacks 51 times from hooker.

In 1997 the All Blacks opened their season with a home test against Argentina at Athletic Park in Wellington. It was a riot and the All Blacks were leading 93–8 with only a few minutes remaining. A Puma knock-on led to referee Brian Campsall signalling for a scrum, but Fitzpatrick had other ideas. He made eye contact with the referee, jerked his head in the direction of the main stand and said: 'That's enough, isn't it?'

Campsall thought about it and agreed, blowing for full-time. Fitzpatrick didn't feel there was any need for the Pumas to be humiliated by conceding 100 points which almost certainly would have happened. 'What point would it have served to have carried on?' he said a few years later. 'We'd won the game and scoring 100 points against Argentina – a team that had held us to a draw only six years before – wasn't going to do anyone any good. It seemed like a good time to end it.'

## 3  An All Black heart of gold

The front-row battle in the 2003 World Cup semi-final between Australia and New Zealand was as fierce as everyone had predicted.

The All Blacks were beginning to build a little domination in that area and managed one giant push early in the second half.

It sent the Wallabies reeling and they had no choice but to collapse. As they did, tight-head Ben Darwin was caught awkwardly and shouted, 'Neck, neck, neck!' Aware that Darwin was in trouble, All Black loose-head Kees Meeuws immediately stopped pushing and broke the engagement to ensure that neither he nor any of the All Black forwards could inflict any more damage. It was an act of sportsmanship that did at least save Darwin's life if not his sporting career. He was never able to play again after incurring a serious neck injury, but he was able to walk normally and make a full recovery thanks to Meeuws. The sportsmanship went even further, with Meeuws finding a phone number for Darwin and making contact a few days later.

'I wanted to get in touch with Ben to see how it was but I didn't want to make a big deal of it,' said Meeuws. 'I had a little chat with him and it was good to do so. You hate to see anyone injured when you play, even though you play hard. There's a time and a place for aggression and a time for compassion.

'Basically, Ben thanked me for what I did and I told him it wasn't a problem and I'd do it again. I hope that something good can come out of something as bad as this and that we can sit down and have a beer one day and talk about it and other things. If we become friends for life, that would be fine by me.'

## 2  Buck Shelford and his ripped testicles

Certain events are so horrific that they leave an indelible impression. The second test between France and the All Blacks in Nantes in 1986 was one of those games. The French came out snorting – angry to the extent that the All Blacks later wondered if their frenzy had been chemically induced. The violence throughout the game was off the scale and it rates as one of the dirtiest ever played.

The moment that encapsulated the mindset of both the French and the Kiwis came just before half-time when All Black No 8 Buck Shelford was left bleeding profusely at the bottom of a ruck. An errant stud had ripped his scrotum and his testicle was unravelling down his leg. Shelford walked to the touchline and with no hint of panic asked the doctor to stitch him up. It took a total of 40 stitches to stem the bleeding, but amazingly Shelford returned to play the second half.

'I was knocked out cold, lost a few teeth and had a few stitches down below,' Shelford would recall 14 years later. 'It's a game I still can't remember – I have no memory of it whatsoever. I don't even remember what the score was, I don't really want to either.'

## 1  Tana Umaga turns paramedic

Former All Black flanker Jerry Collins was one of the more destructive tacklers in test football when he played between 2000 and 2007. Not many people enjoyed being clobbered by Collins, who was the master at hitting in the chest with precision timing and explosive power.

In 2003 Wales No 8 Colin Charvis – himself a big man and a renowned heavy hitter – felt the full force of Collins in Hamilton. Charvis picked up from the base of a scrum and charged. Collins came off the back of the All Black scrum and hit the Welshman so hard he was unconscious before he hit the deck. Charvis was out cold – lying lifeless on the turf.

That was the cue for All Black centre Tana Umaga to run over while play continued, take out Charvis's mouth-guard and roll him into the recovery position. Umaga received the Pierre de Coubertin medal, becoming the first New Zealander to win the award. The Welsh Rugby Union also presented him with a figurine to honour his display of sportsmanship. 'When I got knocked out, Tana was brilliant – I was unconscious, but he rolled me over and ensured I didn't swallow my gum-shield,' Charvis said.

# 10 cult heroes

## 10 Dean Richards (England)

Dean Richards couldn't but help stand out as different when he played test rugby. The English No 8 was a bear of a man and didn't really do running around. He played at his own pace and was big enough and strong enough to do so.

When he had the ball, you could forget getting it back. He was brilliant at wrapping it up and rumbling forward with no urgency whatsoever.

His status as a cult hero was enhanced by playing at a time when the game was becoming increasingly faster and more explosive and players like Richards were polarising fans and coaches.

Supposedly not fast enough or fit enough to play test rugby, Richards won 46 test caps and played for the Lions. And he played them all with his socks down.

In 1996 when he was asked by the RFU to return a sponsored rowing machine, he joked: 'I suppose I'd better unpack it and put some oil on it. I don't want to create the wrong impression.'

Despite his athletic shortcomings he was respected the world over: Former England captain Will Carling once said of Richards: 'You only have to observe the squad when Dean talks, which isn't often. Everyone listens.'

## 9 Martin Castrogiovanni (Italy)

Argentinean-born, but a nationalised Italian, Martin Castrogiovanni became one of the best known and easily recognised figures in world rugby in the first decade of the twenty-first century.

By 2009 he was talked about as potentially being the best tight-head prop in the world. He was a regular in the vaunted Leicester

Tigers front-row and loved by all the Welford Road faithful. The Italians took enormous pride in him, too, for the way he gave their scrum a destructive edge. But there was more to him than a powerful set-piece. There was the straggly, never-brushed long hair that made him look like a bass player in a death metal band. His popularity was such that he and Tigers' team-mate Geordan Murphy opened a restaurant together in Leicester in 2010. The brutish, unkempt Italian prop and clean-cut Irish fullback were an unlikely partnership, but somehow it worked.

Ahead of the World Cup clash between Ireland and Italy in 2011 Murphy was asked about his strategy in playing against his great friend. 'I'm thinking of leaving some baskets of chips in the corners,' he said. 'That should do it. The amount he eats, it should distract him quite nicely.'

## 8  Graham Price (Wales)

The only failing in Graham Price's quest to be a cult hero is the weakness of his nickname – 'Pricey'. A player of his standing and ability deserved something better, but at least he was recognised for being in the 'Viet Gwent', the feared Pontypool front-row that featured Price, Bobby Windsor and Charlie Faulkner.

What gave Price cult status was his ability to mix legendary brutality with mobility. Not only could he crush a French scrum and indulge in the necessary off-the-ball antics required of that period, but he could also run around. He scored a stunning try in Paris in 1975 where the French lost the ball in the Welsh 22 and it was hacked downfield. Amazingly, as it bounced free near the French try-line, it was Price, all 115 kg of him, who gathered to score. Props didn't do that back then, so he was instantly welcomed into folklore.

That place was cemented when his jaw was broken playing against Australia. He was king-hit by bad-boy Steve Finnane but Price made a brave attempt to stay on. When former captain turned journalist Eddie Butler picked his greatest Welsh XV, he put Price in at tight-head and wrote this: 'Price was never quite the cold-hearted executioner that Bobby [Windsor] and Charlie [Faulkner] could be.

It wasn't Pricey that prompted the *Western Mail* to label Pontypool the Viet Gwent. He had instead a giant pair of lungs and a speed that no other prop could match, until the arrival of Gethin Jenkins. He also had hands made for catching any old rubbish slapped down to him as he peeled around the back of the lineout.'

### 7 Michael Jones (New Zealand)

A deeply religious and principled man, Michael Jones set new standards for rugby both on and off the field. The Samoan-born openside was a devout Christian, to the extent that he wouldn't play on Sundays.

It was a stance that cost him the chance to play at the 1995 World Cup where he was left at home due to the likelihood of the All Blacks playing on the Sabbath. It was his dedication and commitment to the game, his family and his God that made him an inspiration to thousands, but especially to the Pacific Islands community who saw him as a cult hero.

He had the requisite nickname – he was 'The Iceman' – and he played with such destructive force it was actually as if the wrath of God was within him.

Jones liked to adapt religious sayings to justify his aggressive tackling. 'You know the old saying – it's better to give than to receive.'

When he became coach of Samoa, he was in full lament mode at the 2007 World Cup. He was a touch fearful the game had become sanitised as referees seemed determined to penalise any tackles above the waist. 'If it carries on like this, I'll be telling my seven-year-old son to go play rugby league. We're walking on egg shells. We've had to try to conform, if that's the right word, to what the rules are now saying. It goes against the grain, against the essence of what we are. This is part of our DNA. The way we are wired is to tackle hard but you just can't afford to tackle too hard now. There's nothing like a good, hard, clean tackle. The big hit is part of the game, surely.'

## 6  Mick Skinner (England)

Mickey Skinner wasn't universally popular, but there was no question he had a cult following. There were significant numbers drawn to the Skinner brand, which was built on bad hair, big tackles and relentless abuse of anyone who didn't play in the forwards. He was a beer-drinking, pie-eating, loud shirt-wearing enigma in that he played for Harlequins – the chosen club of the city gent.

But that was Skinner – highly intelligent, yet keen to pretend he wasn't so he could pass himself off more easily as a man of the people.

He made a name for himself with one colossal hit on Marc Cécillon in the 1991 World Cup quarter-final against France. From there, he moved into the world of producing videos devoted to 'big hits', all sold under his name – which only a cult hero could actually get away with. He also had a nickname, obligatory for any aspiring cult hero – his was 'The Munch'.

His self-promotion was a little too much for some, and former Scotland captain David Sole was never sold on the England flanker as a genuine hard man. 'Skinner: The Big I Am. I wasn't a fan,' said Sole in the critically acclaimed book *The Grudge*.

## 5  Chris Latham (Australia)

The affection in which Chris Latham was held became apparent in 2003 when there were rumblings he was thinking of leaving the Queensland Reds. It felt like the entire state began trying to persuade him not to. Signs saying 'Latho Don't Go' appeared all over the Reds home ground and when he turned down Munster, the locals renamed the so-called Ballymore Hill, Latham Hill.

'When I looked at it again I knew I had a lot of unfinished business here,' Latham said when he re-signed. That decision endeared him further to the people of Brisbane and it was easy to see why. Latham was capable of the extraordinary – an ungainly looking creature, he was in fact lethally quick and inventive. He was brave and willing and pulled off the remarkable with ridiculous ease. He scored spectacular tries and loped around the field always looking for adventure. There was never any question that Latham was giving anything other than his soul to the cause.

## 4 Jean-Pierre Rives (France)

There may be a photograph somewhere in the world of Jean-Pierre Rives playing rugby and not bleeding. It would be a rare prize indeed, for the defining image of Five Nations rugby in the 1970s and early 1980s was of Rives, his shock of blond hair getting in his eyes, bleeding profusely from various head wounds. He rarely if ever didn't spill blood for his country, and the captain was revered for his Gallic passion and spiritual approach.

He was a little different. Not really big enough to cut it as a test loose forward, he compensated by playing with no regard for his personal well-being.

There was a touch of the psycho about him, and yet off the field he was all film-star good looks and one of the most cerebral and artistic men ever to play. He is now a world-renowned sculptor.

All this meant there was something deep and engaging about Rives – he was the thinking man's flanker. He had a super-cool nickname 'Casque d'or' [Golden Helmet] and such was his bravery he was often known as 'Asterix'.

He captained France in a record 34 tests, helped them win two Grand Slams in 1977 and 1981, and led his team to their first win on New Zealand soil. And he did it all while bleeding and being curiously profound.

'The whole point of rugby is that it is, first and foremost, a state of mind, a spirit,' he once said.

## 3 Sébastien Chabal (France)

There was a precise moment Sébastien Chabal earned his cult status – 23 minutes into a test against the All Blacks on 14 June 2007. That was when Chabal hit All Black No 8 Chris Masoe in a thunderous tackle. Masoe was just about knocked into the following week, and

Chabal secured his place in the 2007 World Cup squad. His legend grew from there.

He was a sitter for becoming a cult hero. He had the look – the flowing black hair, the beard, the piercing eyes and a nickname… 'Seabass'. He was a touch feral, as if he slept in a cave, but women the world over were keen. He played a bit like he was hungry for blood, too, and that made coaches the world over keen.

By the end of the World Cup he was the highest-paid player in the world, with endorsements from various French companies flooding in. 'So they [the French supporters] chant my name. So what? Let's not talk about it,' he told reporters during the tournament, who were keen to know how he felt about being a new hero.

There was nothing refined about Chabal. He was a staunch upholder of French culture and tradition, which only endeared him more to his people. Even when he effectively called referees corrupt in his autobiography, there was ample support – he was, after all, upholding the long-held French tradition of speaking his mind.

## 2  Peter Clohessy (Ireland)

The Irish prop was universally known as 'The Claw' and revered across Ireland. His reputation preceded him, which was kind of important in building the legend of The Claw.

Clohessy had numerous incidents in his career that saw him pick up lengthy bans – there was no suggestion he was ever innocent, and nor did he ever want to plead that he was. But no matter what he did, Clohessy always managed to pull it off with a touch of impish charm. He'd be available to talk about things over a few beers, smile whenever asked, allude to his nastiness and then move the subject on to matters of more importance. A lover of drink and good stories, Clohessy opened a bar in his hometown of Limerick, which was predictably massively successful.

Former Ireland captain Keith Wood, who played many years in the front-row with Clohessy, summed it all up the day before The Claw won his fiftieth cap.

'If he has occasionally gone over the top, it's out of sheer frustration and desire,' Wood told the *Daily Telegraph*. 'He wants it so badly. But I will argue all day and all night if necessary that Claw is not intrinsically a dirty player, not at all. The tragedy is that people often overlook what a fantastic rugby player he is.

'As a friend, he's the best. Fantastically loyal and always there to encourage you and lighten the mood with a joke. I've leant heavily on him during my time as captain and it distresses me I can't be alongside him as he wins his fiftieth cap.'

## 1 Colin Meads (New Zealand)

It has been 40 years since Colin Meads played a test, but even now he remains one of the most influential rugby figures in New Zealand. The legend of Meads has only grown stronger over the years.

He is the mythical man of the land – the classic farm boy from the sticks who never lost touch with his roots. Meads ticked every cult-hero box, then some more.

He had a great nickname, 'Pinetree', which enabled his eldest son Glynn to be dubbed 'Pinecone'. Then there were the stories about Meads – so many stories. He played with a broken arm. He was a thug yet he could run like a back. He punched his own coach once. He punched heaps of other people and became the first All Black to be sent off.

He was once photographed carrying a sheep under each arm – a picture which went around the world. This was training the Pinetree way. The fact he was picking up sick sheep whose throats would otherwise have been cut, and there was a photographer waiting when he got back, shouldn't spoil the story. He would tell the *New Zealand Herald* almost 50 years later: 'There are these photos of me carrying these bloody sheep. But you try and tell people!'

Fame has been his burden and it is something that puzzles him. He never went looking for it and hasn't courted it, but he's something of a national obsession. 'That's what I can't understand. I'm just an ordinary country boy. You know, not a well-educated person. This might sound too "gee, shucks, I'm just a boy from the sticks" to be true, but it really is.'

# 10 stupid acts

## 10 Riki Flutey's argy-bargy

A versatile utility back with a neat range of skills, Riki Flutey was expected to make big advances when he toured Argentina in 2001 with the Wellington Academy. But it became tough for Flutey to prove himself, as he spent most of the trip banged up in a police cell.

As is often the way, the Wellington boys headed out to explore shortly after arriving, and Flutey ended up in an altercation with local Rosario student Gabriel Capotosti. A powerful lad, Flutey went a bit nuts and broke Capotosti's nose and fractured his eye socket. The Argentinean police took a rather dim view of his activities and threw him in a cell for four days, where he genuinely feared he would never be released. 'I remember a couple of guards came in and stood over me for five minutes just staring,' Flutey would say nearly eight years later when the civil suit brought by Capotosti was finally dropped. 'That was the scariest point. I feared I was about to get a beating.'

He was placed under arrest until Wellington could come up with the bail of £24,500. He was allowed to return home – chastened and determined to refocus. 'It has been written up that I was a wild kid, the angriest kid in the world, and that was never the case. I'd had a fantastic upbringing, with strong values. What it came down to was a country boy moving to the big city ... and getting carried away.'

## 9 Punch-drunk

There has never been a more explosive or memorable test debut than the one made by Federico Méndez in 1990. He was already on track to stake a claim in the history books just by being selected; he was 18 and still at school and there he was asked to play hooker for the Pumas at Twickenham. The Pumas had one great weapon in those days – their scrum – and for someone so young to be able to command a place in such a critical setting was nothing short of phenomenal.

But Méndez made a much bigger impression with one act of madness. England were a good outfit at the time – full of hard lugs like Jeff Probyn, Peter Winterbottom, Brian Moore, Wade Dooley and Paul Ackford. The men in white were putting it about mid-way through the first half, just to give the Argentineans a distinct message about who was in charge. There was a bit of prolonged footwork at one ruck – one where Méndez happened to be lying prone on the wrong side. When the boots slipped from the torso to his head, a few Pumas piled in to sort things out. There was the usual skirmish – a few handbags drawn and dirty looks exchanged.

Meanwhile a volatile Méndez had regained his feet and decided to seek his revenge. Although it was Probyn who had inflicted the worst of the damage, Méndez just wanted to smack the first white shirt he saw. That happened to be the 2.02 m Ackford, who was pretty much minding his own business.

Méndez clocked him with a hammer-blow of a punch that saw the big lock drop like a sack of spuds. Ackford was out cold and Méndez was immediately sent off. Méndez blubbed all the way to the showers, knowing that his infamy would last a lifetime.

## ⑧ Pokere scams his way to the slammer

Steve Pokere had been a classy All Black in the 1980s – a lovely, balanced runner who was a joy to watch. He was also a devout Mormon and a hero to many. That status was revoked in 2004 when he was arrested on charges of defrauding investors of $3.9 million.

Pokere was given a two-and-a-half-year sentence for his role in setting up a financial trading company with members of his church and ripping off investors. The likeable and charming Pokere had little financial expertise but was assigned to the accounting department. His business partner Phyliss Mareroa would later tell the Serious Fraud Office that Pokere 'is not an accountant, he doesn't have a qualification ... but he gave our clients a level of comfort because he's ... got a nice way about him.'

That opinion was shared by Judge Roderick Joyce, who handed down Pokere's sentence: He said Pokere was 'humble, community-minded, a wonderful husband, father and provider and fundamentally a decent and honest man except for being involved in the fraud. He is yet another of the all-too-many people who fall foul of the awful temptations of greed.'

## 7 Fijian for life

As a former head boy of the prestigious Auckland Grammar School, Isa Nacewa really should have known the consequences of agreeing to play for Fiji at the 2003 World Cup. He says he didn't and tried for more than five years to force the IRB to annul the most damaging two minutes of his career.

Born in New Zealand with Fijian heritage, Nacewa played for Auckland as a 19-year-old during the early part of the 2003 National Provincial Championship and caught the eye. That piqued the interest of the Fijian selectors who were after a utility back to bolster their bench.

They asked Nacewa – who was eligible for both Fiji and the All Blacks – if he was interested. He was and he went to the tournament, making a two-minute appearance off the bench against Scotland in Sydney. He did nothing; he didn't touch the ball – it didn't even come near him – and he didn't make any tackles.

By 2005, Nacewa was a major star with the Blues and would have been close to All Black selection. But of course those two minutes for Fiji meant he was no longer eligible. As a non-eligible All Black his earnings were restricted in New Zealand. If he'd been an All Black he would have earned about five times as much in New Zealand and would also have had greater earning potential offshore.

He mounted a legal case to see if the IRB would allow him to play for New Zealand, but they refused and his dreams were shattered by those two minutes.

'I think this case shows how carefully players with dual eligibility have to think before they commit to one country,' said NZRU chief executive Steve Tew to the *Herald on Sunday*. 'We encourage players to take appropriate advice so that they can really understand any decision they make.'

Nacewa signed with Leinster in 2008.

## 6 Not so Smart

It's fair enough to ask why a normally sane, relatively intelligent man would glug down enough aftershave to send him to hospital. Old-school types might say it was because Colin Smart was a prop – which almost serves as an explanation.

Back in the day, all props prided themselves on their ability to drink – mainly volume, but if they could lay their hands on something vile that required a bit of courage to ingest, then all the better. England lock Maurice Colclough knew that Smart was a sucker for any challenge – particularly the ridiculous and dangerous. Which is why Colclough challenged Smart to a drinking contest after England had beaten France 27–15 in 1982. At the after-dinner function – a lavish affair – there were miniature bottles of aftershave at every place-setting.

Colclough pulled the top off a bottle and knocked it back in one. Not wanting to be outdone, Smart then followed suit, downing his bottle as his team-mates cheered him on. Unbeknown to Smart, Colclough had earlier sneaked out to empty his bottle and replace it with tap water.

A few minutes later, Smart could not stand up and was rushed to hospital to have his stomach pumped. Scrum-half Steve Smith would famously later say: 'He may have been unwell, but Colin had the nicest breath I've smelt.'

## 5 The double whammy

There were two acts guaranteed to get any Springbok coach of the mid to late 1990s into serious trouble. The first was to dump iconic captain Francois Pienaar – the man who had led the Boks to their

World Cup title in 1995; and the second was to be overtly racist at a time when South African rugby was trying to shed its abhorrent past culture of white supremacy.

Unfortunately Andre Markgraaff completed the double after he was appointed to the top coaching job in 1996. When the All Blacks beat the Springboks in Cape Town, Markgraaff amazingly accused his captain of feigning injury. Pienaar came off with a head knock which the coach disputed was real.

There was public outcry at the accusations and the way Pienaar was subsequently dropped and never picked again. Markgraaff was cast as the villain and under intense pressure for making such an unpopular decision. As would later be revealed, that pressure got to him: shortly after dropping Pienaar, Markgraaff held a conversation with an unidentified player. In this conversation he called black rugby officials and politicians 'fucking Kaffirs'. The conversation was taped and aired on national TV in early February 1997. Margraaff immediately resigned.

He said he was quitting in the interests of South African rugby and of national reconciliation. 'I'm not making any excuses,' he said. 'I was very emotional at the time. I apologise to the black people of this country and to the whites for causing them embarrassment.'

## 4 Dirty Rottnest scoundrels

Determined to improve in their third season of Super Rugby, the Western Force headed for a training camp on Rottnest Island off the Australian coast in late November 2007. It was one of those train-hard/play-hard affairs where they would batter themselves at training during the day and then get around the camp fire and bond as a team at night.

It was all going swimmingly until loose forwards Scott Fava and Richard Brown poured a little too much bonding fluid down their gullets. The former ended up being fined a whopping $11,000 for being drunk in public, for anti-social behaviour and most disturbingly, for harming a protected form of wildlife. Fava admitted to throwing a quokka – a native marsupial and national icon – to show off to his mates. Eye-witnesses said one quokka was tossed five metres by Fava. Brown was fined $5000 for his part in the affair.

'I interfered with quokkas in fascination of our icon, not to be cruel, not to show off in front of my teammates, and definitely not to hurt them,' Fava said. 'But whether sober or drunk, they should not be touched. I apologise profusely for being intoxicated and thus being clumsy in returning a quokka to the ground. I have a weakness, an alcohol binge-drinking problem. It's time it stopped and I have now started on the road to rehabilitation.'

## 3 Taxi for Scott Gibbs

The normally reserved and law-abiding Scott Gibbs was at a loss to explain why he endangered his opportunity to tour with the British & Irish Lions in 1993. Only a few weeks before the tour party was due to fly to New Zealand, Gibbs spent 12 hours in custody at a Bridgend police station.

The 22-year-old centre, who was one of the most promising midfielders in Europe, made the rather daft decision to jump in an empty taxi and drive it away. He was charged with drink-driving as well as stealing the taxi. He was found to be twice over the legal alcohol limit and had driven through the town centre at 60 miles per hour.

As well as having to face a court case, Gibbs also knew that the Lions wanted a full report to determine whether he could still make the tour. On hearing about the incident, Geoff Cooke, the Lions manager, said: 'It is not for me or the Lions management to take any moral stance. There is no reason for me to speak to Scott about this at the moment.'

Gibbs was fined £2160 and banned from driving for two years, but was able to tour with the Lions. Gibbs said: 'The fine was very high but I just wanted to clear the whole thing up and get on with my game.'

When Gibbs arrived in camp with the Lions, coach Ian McGeechan broke the ice by saying: 'How did you get here? By taxi?'

## 2  A lying Bastareaud

New Zealanders felt shame on a national scale when they heard that French midfielder Mathieu Bastareaud had been assaulted outside his Wellington hotel in a late-night attack. The outrage that a member of the French rugby team had been violently assaulted led to Prime Minister John Key publicly apologising to his French counterpart in June 2009.

According to the 21-year-old Bastareaud, he had been coming back to the team hotel at 4 am after a few drinks and was clobbered when he stepped out of his taxi. The French team left for Australia the following morning but laid a complaint with the police before they left. The police investigation struggled to find any CCTV footage or witnesses of the incident. As the week went by they began to become suspicious, suggesting they were no longer certain about the nature of the incident.

With the pressure mounting, a contrite Bastareaud came clean: he'd made the whole thing up. He admitted his injuries – a badly cut eye and damaged cheek – were picked up in his hotel room: 'I fell in my bedroom and scarred my cheekbone on the table in the room. I was ashamed and panicked and I thought I would be sent packing by the team management. I did not want my family to be ashamed. I panicked and I dug myself deeper into a hole.'

The saga ended with French Prime Minister François Fillon writing a letter of apology to Key.

## 1  A seal, A Hore and a stag

It was a classic case of something seeming like a good idea at the time – but it really wasn't. All Black hooker Andrew Hore was on a fishing trip off the coast of Otago in 2005 as part of a friend's stag celebrations. After a few drinks they spotted some seals on the shore and decided it would be a jolly good laugh to shoot at them.

As the party intended to do some hunting, there were firearms on board – semi-automatic at that. Hore and two other men began firing and their actions were videoed by a shocked tourist who was observing the seals. The men were arrested when they came to shore, and it was only then that the stupidity of their actions hit home. One of the seals had been killed and the men were accused of firing a total of 15 shots.

Hore – who would go on to win 50 All Black caps and a World Cup winner's medal – was fined $2500 and shamed by the exposure and subsequent damage to his reputation. His lawyer, Campbell Savage, spoke after the court case. 'There is simply no way he will ever do it again.' That was after Judge Rollo had humiliated Hore in his summing up. He described Hore's actions as a 'grossly irresponsible, spontaneous act of hooliganism'. Rollo said he believed the aggravating features of the offending were the number of shots fired, the close proximity to the public, and the fact that the area in which they were shooting was world-renowned for its wildlife.

# 10 thugs

## 10 Wade Dooley (England)

It was wishful thinking on the part of England lock Wade Dooley that he wasn't viewed as a thug. Throughout the late 1980s and early 1990s the giant policeman from Blackpool was almost guaranteed to be in the thick of any nonsense, of which there was plenty whenever he played for club or country.

He was a giant of a man and perhaps he saw it as his right to enforce the law both off the field and on it. After being hammered in the first test in 1989, the British & Irish Lions brought Dooley in for the second. The game was memorably dirty – the Wallabies full of accusations about what had been going on. It wasn't a coincidence that the filth arrived at the same time as Dooley.

His single worst atrocity, however, came in 1987 in a notoriously awful game between England and Wales in Cardiff. There was plenty of bloodshed and much of it on Dooley's fists after he broke the jaw of Welsh lock Phil Davis. 'I was never malicious but I used to stand up for myself,' was Dooley's assessment. 'But I'd like to point out that I was only ever sent off once, in a county match, for a toe-to-toe fight. Biting, gouging or kicking heads – I never did anything like that. I always did things up front and that was my downfall at times.'

## 9 Troy Flavell (New Zealand)

Troy Flavell had the potential to be an All Black great. He was a hulking great beast of a man yet nimble and aerobically gifted. At 1.98 m he was mobile enough to play at blindside and tall enough to be a lock, and when he scored a hat-trick on debut for the All Blacks in 2000 he looked like he had a long test career ahead of him.

What so many coaches admired about Flavell was that he had the aggression and passion to match his athleticism. Sadly, though, his career became more about the aggression than the athleticism. He had sprung to global notoriety when a picture of him playing for North Harbour in 1997 showed his thumb being pushed deep into the eye-socket of Wellington wing Steve Skinnon. The image looked worse than the incident in fact was, and his one-year suspension was reduced to four matches.

In 2003, desperate to recover his All Black place, which he had lost when new coach John Mitchell had taken over in 2001, Flavell was suspended for 14 weeks when he deliberately stomped on the head of Greg Smith. The Chiefs hooker needed more than 30 stitches and was still suffering headaches two years later.

If anyone was in any doubt about Flavell's propensity for thuggery, they would have been convinced he was a bad boy when he was fined $55,000 in 2004 for a bar brawl. Flavell had been carrying a tray of drinks and witnesses say he was deliberately pushed, causing the tray to smash. One witness account said the man who had pushed Flavell then asked: 'Are you as tough as they say? Let's step outside and see who is the toughest.' There was no need to go outside – Flavell punched his aggressor on the spot, sending a few teeth flying across the bar.

## 8 Vincent Moscato (France)

There was a touch of the loveable rogue about Vincent Moscato, the French prop who stomped about in the late 1980s and early 1990s. He was tough – so tough he decided to become a boxer and now wins regular film work playing thuggish types who don't say much but lurk in the background looking threatening.

It was Moscato who did much to establish Bordeaux-Bègles as an improving force in French rugby throughout the 1980s and he did so by playing close to the limits. When he won a call-up to the French national side in 1992 he showed how volatile he could be when he was sent off for head-butting against England.

It was after this that Moscato took to the ring – he'd earned a six-month suspension for his antics in the test arena. Mick Cleary of the *Observer* blogged in 2007 how he once phoned Moscato before one of his boxing bouts. After eventually getting through to Moscato at the bar he owned, and explaining who he was and that he wanted to write something, Cleary was met with a torrent of abuse. 'A British journalist, eh? You, who call me the beast of Bègles, call me an animal, a brute, an ogre, a thug, a savage…' Click. But Cleary covered the fight and he and Moscato would even become friends.

## 7 Jamie Cudmore (Canada)

To earn a reputation as a bit of a dirty bastard in French club rugby really does take some doing. The commitment to atrocities has to be total – and no one can doubt that Canadian lock Jamie Cudmore has always been devoted to the dark side of the game. Cudmore is a big man – 1.98 m and 115 kg – yet mobile and quick. It's that combination of size and agility and his profound desire to put himself about that has enabled him to become one of the most feared men in the Top 14 since he joined leading club Clermont in 2005.

His litany of crimes is impressive – multiple suspensions for punching and stamping. He has collected a serious number of red cards and has just about spent longer being suspended than he has being available. After a self-imposed exile from test football, he returned to national colours in 2011, earning this understated accolade from Canada coach Kieran Crowley: 'Jamie brings that physicality of the French style of game to the team and provides a bit of backbone to our team with that. You need it. You've got to have the physicality.'

## 6 Moaner van Heerden (South Africa)

Springbok lock Moaner van Heerden wouldn't have been able to fit in a phone-box. And if he had ever found himself in one, he'd probably have started a fight. Violence was in his blood.

New Zealanders know the name van Heerden all too well after he just about raked All Black lock Peter Whiting's ear clean off in 1976.

It was a nasty incident and one entirely typical of van Heerden, who had done his level best to frighten the British & Irish Lions in 1974.

'In the third test at Port Elizabeth, the Boks had brought in some heavies to try and sort us out, the main one being Moaner van Heerden,' Lions lock Gordon Brown told the *Scotsman* in 2003. 'Willie John [McBride] had singled him out and warned that he would have a go. The nearest Lion would then wade in and give van Heerden a doing. Sure enough, after 10 minutes, van Heerden belted Bobby Windsor and I was the nearest man; that's how I broke my thumb.'

### 5　Danny Grewcock (England)

Unfortunately for Danny Grewcock, he'll never be remembered for being the great player he so nearly was. Instead his legacy will be the number of red and yellow cards he received in a long and not quite glorious career. First capped in 1997, Grewcock made a total of 69 appearances and played five tests for the Lions.

This is impressive – yet nowhere near as thrilling as the list of suspensions he received. He was sent off playing for England against the All Blacks in 1998 and missed the 2007 World Cup because of a six-week suspension for fighting. He was also sent home from the 2005 Lions tour after being cited for biting All Black hooker Keven Mealamu. Grewcock was a Karate black-belt when he was younger, and his appetite for combat was relentless.

That he turned out to be a wild sort should have been obvious when he left a journalist quaking before a test against Italy in 2002. Grewcock had been selected ahead of captain Martin Johnson, and when the questioner asked whether Grewcock thought this could be a permanent move, the 1.98 m lock stood up and said: 'You want me to say I'm better than Johnson, is that it? Is that what you're after? Well, tough. I don't read what you blokes write anyway.'

### 4 Colin Meads (New Zealand)

New Zealanders have always happily stayed in denial, blissfully ignoring the fact that the man many consider to be the greatest All Black in history was just an incy-wincy bit of a thug. Colin Meads was a colossal talent, a rugby player who would have thrived in any era. Whenever public eulogies are made celebrating his 55-test career, the focus always falls on the memory of him romping across rugby fields with the ball in one hand. A player ahead of his time is the most common tribute paid.

But Meads himself prefers to remind everyone about his darker side. There are regrets in his career about some of the things he did, some of the players who felt the full force of his fury. He was sent off against Scotland in 1967– an era where no one was sent off unless they had committed the truly unforgivable – and globally he was feared for his desire to indulge in warfare.

His reputation in Australia was forever tainted for a vicious act in 1968 that ended the career of Wallabies captain Ken Catchpole. Rated one of Australia's greatest scrumhalves, Catchpole was lucky to walk again after Meads got hold of him. Pinned at the bottom of a ruck in a Bledisloe test in Sydney, Catchpole was grabbed by Meads.

The All Black lock wanted to 'clear him out', but he had Catchpole's leg like it was a chicken wishbone – the hamstring was almost pulled off the bone. 'I was driven into a splits position under enormous pressure,' Catchpole said. 'I could feel the muscles stretch like rubber bands, reaching the end of their elasticity and snapping.'

### 3 Martin Johnson (England)

Martin Johnson spent his formative years playing in New Zealand's King Country under the watchful eye of Colin Meads. Johnson arrived in New Zealand a bit skinny and a bit soft until Meads pulled him aside one day and said: 'It's okay to hurt people.' Those words seemingly became the Johnson mantra, and from that point he began building a fearsome reputation. He hurt people all right –

with his fists, with his boots, with whatever. Johnson was a law unto himself.

His worst act of thuggery was an assault on Robbie Russell during a club game between Leicester and Saracens in 2002. The Scottish hooker had annoyed Johnson at a breakdown and was grabbed by the collar, swung around and punched hard in the face for his troubles. His cheek needed numerous stitches. 'I shouldn't have done it. I overreacted to that situation. He [Russell] didn't really provoke me, I misread the situation,' Johnson would later admit.

A few months earlier Johnson had stood on the throat of Scotland's John Leslie in a test, leading to adverse media commentary about his violent nature. 'I am no thug,' he said to deflect the heat. 'I like to win and I am competitive. Of course I am concerned about my image and I've done everything possible to make it a good one.'

## 2  Bakkies Botha (South Africa)

Springbok lock Bakkies Botha is an unfathomable paradox: he's a devout Christian and family man off the field – all those who know him say he is kind, considerate and endearingly polite. On the field he's a demon, a snorting big box of a man who has rarely, if ever, been out of trouble in his long career.

He plays on the edge and usually beyond the edge of the law, and is rated as one of the nastiest thugs as a consequence. Listing all of his demeanours would take too long, but the two big highlights are: head-butting All Black scrum-half Jimmy Cowan in 2010; and biting, then punching, Wallaby hooker Brendan Cannon in 2003. 'He stuck his teeth into my shoulder and I was pretty struck by the impression his top and bottom teeth left on me,' Cannon said in 2009. 'I retaliated and the subsequent retaliation from him was to put his fingers in both my eyes.'

After Botha picked up a nine-week suspension for his attack on Cowan, Springbok captain John Smit was asked to comment on his lock: 'Only he himself can explain his actions,' Smit said. 'Only Bakkies could explain to you what goes on in there.'

# 1 Richard Loe (New Zealand)

All Black prop Richard Loe loved the fact he had a reputation. He felt he was already holding a significant advantage before the game kicked off if opponents were worried about him. 'The media gave me the perception of being an All Black enforcer. I was always quite happy for the opposition to be thinking about me and worrying about me before the game. I had to retire before my bluff ran out,' he said to *New Zealand Rugby World* in July 2011.

It wasn't strictly true, however, that the media 'gave' him that perception. He deserves plenty of credit for that himself. 1992 was his *annus horribilis* – the year he went a bit nuts. In a Bledisloe Cup test he infamously smashed Wallaby wing Paul Carozza's nose across his face. Carozza had dived in at the corner for a well-taken try when a few seconds later in dived Loe with his forearm and battered it hard into the much smaller man's face. There was an explosion of blood and outrage from the crowd, but no disciplinary action.

A few weeks later, Loe copped a six-month suspension for eye-gouging while playing for Waikato. TV cameras picked up appalling footage of Loe burying his fingers into Otago fullback Greg Cooper's eyes. Like, right into his eyes.

# 10 villainous acts

## 10 The hand of God

It would be understating things to say that Scotland and England didn't like each other throughout the late 1980s and 1990s. There was depth to the personal animosity many of the individuals felt, which meant there was always an edge when they clashed. While it was the Scots who had felt the hate more at first, the dislike was mutual after the Grand Slam decider of 1990. A culture of anything goes developed, with both sides prepared to do whatever it took to win. Breaking the rules was not a problem, which is precisely what England did in the last minute of the 1994 clash at Murrayfield.

Scotland were on the verge of another famous win, leading 14–12 with one minute remaining. England were scrambling to retrieve tackled ball in Scottish territory to set up one last attack. Suddenly the ball flew out of the ruck and Kiwi referee Lindsay McLachlan penalised the Scots for handling. England fullback Jon Callard slotted the kick to win the game 15–14. McLachlan had reacted to seeing a blue jersey handling the ball, but TV footage later showed the blue quite clearly to be the cuff of Rob Andrew's England jersey.

Such was the pain for the Scots and the sense of outrage that captain Gavin Hastings actually cried when he was interviewed after the game. More than 10 years later, Carling was interviewed about that incident. 'Was it Rob Andrew? Nah. Really? I can't believe that,' he said with a giant grin. 'But what I do know is that the Scots had been cheating throughout the game. Well, I certainly hope it was an England hand – because if it was Rob, then it was an even better day than I remember.'

## 9 The truth about Cullen

It had always been the expectation in New Zealand that long-term All Blacks would be treated with respect and, wherever possible, told in advance of the squad being made public that they were not going to be selected.

New All Black coach John Mitchell did not extend that courtesy to Christian Cullen in October 2001. One of the great attacking fullbacks the world had known, and with more than 50 caps to his credit, Cullen was one of three shock omissions from the squad named by Mitchell for the tour to Europe.

But Mitchell actually committed a more villainous act than simply not telling Cullen in advance – he misinformed the media as to why Cullen was not coming. The 26-year-old had damaged his knee the week before the squad was named and had met with All Black doctor John Mayhew. 'My advice to John Mitchell was that medically it was in the best interests of Christian Cullen not to be selected,' Mayhew told the *New Zealand Herald*. 'He has a chronic knee injury and needs some rest and rehabilitation.'

But Mitchell told the media Cullen had been dropped – which denied the fullback a major financial pay-out as well as the damage it did to his reputation. It was little wonder that Cullen fought for the truth to be revealed. 'The fact is, I tweaked my knee during the last game of the season for Wellington and I pulled out before the squad was announced – there's no doubt about that. John Mitchell was asked why I hadn't been selected on Sunday and he couldn't spit out an answer.'

## 8 Neil Back pushing over Neil Lander

England flanker Neil Back was internationally recognised as a tough, demanding but fair player. But that impression became hard to maintain when he underwent a moment of madness in the final of the 1996 Pilkington Cup final.

In the last minute referee Steve Lander awarded Leicester's arch-rival Bath a penalty try, which enabled the West Country club to win the title 16–15. Back, standing on the open side of the scrum when the award was made, shoved Lander to the ground, breaking rugby's oldest taboo – that the referee is sacred and to be respected at all times.

Back was banned for six months following a review of the incident, where his defence was built around a case of mistaken identity. 'I didn't realise the game had ended,' said Back. 'I ran in to join the other forwards and believed I was giving Robinson [Bath opposite Andy] – offside again – a push to clear the way. When Dean [Leicester coach Richards] told me I had pushed the referee I went into his room and apologised.'

Strangely, the judicial committee seemed to accept Back's claim but handed down the guilty verdict anyway.

## 7  Neil Back handling the ball

Actually, Neil Back may in fact have been a bit of a cheating bastard rather than an erstwhile legend. There was a minute to go in the 2002 Heineken Cup final with Leicester clinging to a 15–9 lead. They really were just clinging as Munster had a 5-metre scrum under the posts.

Scrum-half Peter Stringer had assessed where his backs were, had made up his mind what the play would be and was preparing to feed the ball into the scrum. As he crouched and presented, Back slapped the ball out his hand straight into the Tigers' side of the scrum. The referee was on the other side, missed the whole thing and the ball was booted into touch. Stringer was incensed but to no avail, the referee was never going to change his mind.

'I must be honest, I don't like people thinking I'm a cheat,' said Back a few weeks later. 'I don't think I'm a cheat, but this has undoubtedly tarnished my reputation and that is disappointing. I'd hope people would evaluate me over my career and not just label me for one incident.'

## 6  Changing-room haka

The All Blacks were wary of agreeing a change in pre-match protocol in 2005 because they feared the Welsh would use it as a precedent. And the All Blacks were right – when they returned to play in Cardiff a year later, the Welsh Rugby Union tried to force the All Blacks to do the haka before the singing of the Welsh national anthem. New Zealand had agreed in 2005 because it was 100 years, almost to the day, since the two countries had famously first clashed and that order of events would have replicated 1905.

But there was no way New Zealand would agree a second time, so they decided instead to do the haka in their changing room before the game and asked a TV cameraman to film it.

The anthems were sung on the field and then the game kicked off – leaving the crowd perplexed. They were then more confused why imagery of the All Blacks doing the haka inside was being shown on the big screens. There was bitterness that such great theatre had been missed and no one in the crowd knew who to blame, although the All Blacks were adamant they were not at fault.

All Blacks captain Richie McCaw said, 'The tradition needs to be honoured properly if we're going to do it. If the other team wants to mess around, we'll just do the haka in the shed. Traditionally fans can share the experience too, and it's sad that they couldn't see it today.'

## 5  Budge Poutney tied down

When Budge Poutney unexpectedly and dramatically quit international rugby in early 2003, he painted the most horrific picture of the Scottish Rugby Union. The meanness and pettiness of the organisation was villainous.

Poutney revealed that players' wives and girlfriends were left to pay their own way while the executives took their ladies everywhere on the SRU's tab; that after beating South Africa for the first time in 33 years in November 2002 there was a fax behind the team hotel bar from the union stating clearly there was to be no free drink for any of the players; and the one that really got him – being hounded to reimburse £7.50 for a Scotland tie he had kindly given to a broken-hearted supporter.

He told the *Scotsman*: 'I'm still getting regular demands from the SRU because I gave my Scotland tie to a young kid who was flying home to London with his dad after watching us lose to New Zealand. Him and his dad were both in kilts and a bit upset that we'd lost, and I just felt it might help cheer him up. It did, but the SRU just don't see that.'

## 4  The quick lineout

The Welsh were simply chancing their arm, but such a generous assessment can't be made of the match officials who failed to see the illegality of the quick lineout thrown to scrum-half Mike Phillips. The 2011 Six Nations encounter between Ireland and Wales in Cardiff was in the balance when the former's Jonny Sexton hoofed the ball into touch. Welsh hooker Matthew Rees gathered a ball on the touchline and threw it quickly to Phillips, who was able to charge over for a try from 40 metres.

What had sent the Irish into a fury was that Rees had not used the ball that was kicked out. One of the ball-boys had thrown Rees a different ball, which was totally against the rules, but when referee Jonathan Kaplan asked his Scottish touch judge Peter Allan whether the Welsh had used the same ball, the answer was yes.

Ireland lost 19–13 and captain Brian O'Driscoll was outraged. 'I didn't see it myself, but when half your team is saying it you take their word for it,' he said. 'I tried to relate that to Jonathan Kaplan and the touch judge and they were having none of it. I did mention it to him a few minutes later after I had seen it on TV and I told him that it was a massive momentum swinger and that it had had a huge bearing on the game, but he just shrugged that off. Games hang in the balance on decisions, everyone is human and wrong calls are made sometimes, but some are unforgivable.'

IRB referee boss Paddy O'Brien actually apologised to the Irish after the game, admitting that the try should never have been allowed.

### 3 National anthem being murdered

The French insist it was a genuine mistake, that they had no idea when they asked Durban-born reggae star Ras Dumisani to sing the South African national anthem ahead of their test in November 2009, that he would do such an appalling job.

The South Africans were so upset by how awful Dumisani had been that they wrote to the French Rugby Federation to complain. Dumisani was not only horribly out of tune – he seemed to forget most of the words to 'Nkosi Sikelel' iAfrika'.

Springbok wing Bryan Habana was in hysterics during the rendition, while other players were clearly not amused. 'As a union we were shocked and horrified by the rendition of the anthem and I contacted the French federation on Saturday morning to express our very grave concerns,' SARU president, Oregan Hoskins, said. 'Something went seriously awry in Toulouse and the upshot was that offence has been caused, not just to the Springboks and SARU but to South Africans in general.

'It was a joke,' raged lock Victor Matfield. 'The guys couldn't even sing [along] and even the crowd was starting to laugh. Every time you go out on the field and sing the national anthem, it's something that fires you up. It was a big disappointment.'

### 2 Rua Tipoki's weighty matters

Rua Tipoki's season was all over by September in 2001. North Harbour were in the midst of an impressive run in New Zealand's NPC, but would have to do without Tipoki, their talisman midfielder for the critical run into the play-offs. Tipoki had been ruled out with two broken wrists, an injury he incurred while lifting weights in the gym. It was freakishly unlucky.

And spectacularly untrue. Tipoki had really broken his wrists punching someone while playing in a festival game at Opotiki. As he didn't have permission from his employer to play in the game he decided not to tell the truth and fabricated a story that the damage had been caused by weights falling on him.

He begged team-mates Matua Parkinson and Rico Gear to help him with the cover-up. 'The real story will come out, bro,' was Parkinson's reply – as revealed to the *New Zealand Herald*. 'But how do I tell the boys?' Tipoki asked. 'I know the true story will come out, but I just can't tell anyone now.'

In Tipoki's exclusive interview with the *Herald* he told of the guilt and shame he felt for telling the lie. After two days of covering up, he decided to come clean. Gear and Parkinson, who, despite their reservations, had supported the lie, apologised to club officials.

The festival games were known by the Opotiki locals as the 'Pa Wars rugby series'. Tipoki was only meant to stay on the field for a few minutes so he could be filmed for part of a documentary about Maori lifestyle and sport. 'But once you get out there, everyone is after you and I did not want to run off the field,' he said.

Tipoki hit an opponent several times in the head after one skirmish and required several operations on his wrists to fix the damage.

## 1 The Cardiff dive

It's unlikely that Andy Haden or any of his family will ever be welcome in Wales. For Haden, the giant All Black lock, committed the ultimate act of villainy in 1978 when he made a conscious decision to cheat.

The All Blacks were chasing a Grand Slam and were in danger of falling at the second hurdle. The Welsh had outplayed them for most of the game and were leading 12–10 with two minutes left. Haden, never one to hide from controversy, decided he was going to take control.

'With Wales in front by 12–10, I knew there could only be a minute or so left,' Haden revealed in 1998. 'I went to Frank Oliver, my locking partner ... and told him the plan in four words: "I'm going to dive."'

And he did. He tumbled out of the lineout, and possibly could have won an Oscar in the process. Everyone in the western hemisphere would have been aware he had tumbled. And everyone except referee Roger Quittenton could see Haden had tumbled of his own volition.

There was no push, there was no infringement, but Haden was the type to get away with what he could. Wales had been done out of a legitimate victory despite the fact that Quittenton insisted the penalty was not for the supposed infringement committed against Haden, but for a barge by Welsh prop Geoff Wheel. 'Haden's perception is that his dive secured the penalty. That is a load of rubbish,' said Quittenton in response to Haden's confession.

H

# 10 nastiest acts

## 10 Duncan MacRae, Waratahs v British & Irish Lions, 2001

Having been liberal with the filth in 1989, the British & Irish Lions were actually remarkably restrained when they returned to Australia in 2001. Their tour was passing off without major incident until they encountered the Waratahs. It had seemed to the thousands at the ground and the millions watching on TV that this game, too, was playing out fairly.

But Waratahs fly-half Duncan MacRae had an entirely different impression. 'In the first half, I wore one in the gob from [Lions fly-half Ronan] O'Gara and in the second half, he gave me another one. Then, in a tackle, he kicked out at me.' McRae was using this as justification to explain why it was that a second after O'Gara allegedly kicked out, he had pinned him down and landed at least 10 savage punches. It was a grotesque sequence of blows that left O'Gara swollen, dazed and bleeding. McCrae was sent off and suspended for 13 weeks.

'I've been called a thug, a cheap-shot merchant and a psycho,' said McRae. 'I can wear it, even though it is very wrong, but for my parents and my girlfriend, well, that's not fair on them. I want to make it very clear that I am sorry for what happened. I regret it and I hope to catch up with him [O'Gara] and say so in person.'

He never did catch up in person, even when the two met again three years later in a Heineken Cup game between Munster and Gloucester. O'Gara told the *Independent* before that clash in 2004: 'I can't see how he will apologise to me at this stage, but if he comes up to me and wants to shake my hand, I'll have no problem.'

## 9 Schalk Burger eye-gouges Luke Fitzgerald, July 2009

It was both the casualness and needlessness of Schalk Burger's actions in the opening of the second test between the Springboks and British & Irish Lions in 2009 that surprised. Burger had a reputation for being abrasive and physical in the extreme, but he wasn't recognised as a dirty player. Hard but fair – that was the giant South African flanker.

But he was anything but fair when his first act of the test was to deliberately stick his fingers in the eyes of Lions wing Luke Fitzgerald. The Boks had taken the kick-off and cleared it – leaving behind the usual mêlée of bodies on the floor – one of whom was Fitzgerald. For some reason, Burger, without really looking, let his hand slide over the wing's face and then popped his fingers in the eye-socket.

Fitzgerald was left with blurred vision, but amazingly Burger was only yellow-carded – a decision that left the Lions angry and the South African unrepentant. 'Through my life and career I have always approached the game with the intention only of playing it hard and fair,' Burger said. 'I am not a rugby thug and will never intentionally engage in eye-gouging or similar illegal actions. This was also the case in the second test against the Lions. I will always play the game as hard as possible within the rules.'

## 8 Peter Clohessey stamps on Olivier Roumat, February 1996

There was a reason Peter Clohessey earned the nickname 'The Claw' – he wasn't always particularly nice when he played. The Irish and Munster prop sailed close to the wind, although he usually did his dirty business in the scrums to avoid detection. But in 1996 playing for Ireland against France in Paris, he committed the double offence of sinning – and doing so in full view of the TV cameras. Some, such as Clohessey himself, tried to claim it was reckless rather than malicious, but the footage of him stamping on French lock Olivier Roumat didn't support that contention.

The Frenchman was left bleeding from Clohessy's boot which appeared to have deliberately come down rather hard on the prone Frenchy's head. 'I don't know who kicked me,' said Roumat. 'I don't even know if it was a Frenchman or an Irishman. If it was intentional then, of course, whoever did it should be banned. It is strange that four French forwards were injured. In the past it has always been France who were accused of dirty play.'

There was nothing accidental about it – and that was the view reached by the judiciary, who handed Clohessy a 26-week ban.

## 7  Michael Brial assaults Frank Bunce, July 1996

The All Blacks were at the peak of their powers during the Tri Nations of 1996 and proving almost impossible to beat. They had hammered the Wallabies 43–6 in the opening clash in Wellington in a performance of sublime skill and power that left Australia shell-shocked.

The Wallabies were hungry for revenge when the two next met a few weeks later in Brisbane. But flanker Michael Brial was focused on settling an individual vendetta against All Black centre Frank Bunce. Brial reckoned Bunce had landed a cheap shot four years earlier during a provincial game and the flanker hadn't forgotten. So just six minutes into the Bledisloe test, Brial saw his chance for revenge, tangling with Bunce when the ball was nowhere in sight. In an astonishingly furious attack Brial landed 10 or 15 blows on the All Black, who chose not to retaliate. It was a brutal beating and left the All Blacks outraged that nothing was done about it.

'The referee saw what happened,' All Black coach John Hart said. 'Brial was punching Bunce uncontrollably. There was no possible excuse for what the player did, but the referee did nothing. That's unacceptable.'

Bunce, a man of honour who would later say that he deserved some kind of attention for the cheap shot he'd thrown four years earlier, said: 'I couldn't believe it. He went right over the top.'

## 6  The Murrayfield strangler, March 2007

The Irish reckon they know who did it, but the Scots were never able to find who it was that allegedly strangled Ronan O'Gara in the final minutes of their Six Nations match at Murrayfield in 2007. With the Irish leading 18–17, those last few minutes were desperate for both teams.

Irish fly-half Ronan O'Gara found himself at the bottom of a ruck, and while he was there a python-like arm crept round his throat and began to squeeze … and squeeze … and squeeze. 'Someone tried to choke O'Gara,' fumed an outraged Irish coach Eddie O'Sullivan. 'Someone had their arm around his neck, cut off his air supply and he went blue. I'd rather not say who it was. I believe it was deliberate. Putting your hand around someone's neck and trying to choke them is hard to do by accident. I didn't see it because I'm sat in the stands like everyone else and he was at the bottom of a ruck with people on top of him.'

## 5  Kevin Yates bites Simon Fenn, January 1998

There was mystery and intrigue in the strange case of the bitten ear in 1998. London Scottish flanker Simon Fenn arose from a collapsed scrum with blood spurting out of his ear and half of it missing. Officials had a classic 'whodunnit?' on their hands, which took the better part of a week to solve.

Fenn needed 25 stitches and the teeth marks in his ear were undeniable – clearly his injury was no accident. Eventually the finger of suspicion pointed to Bath prop Kevin Yates, who proclaimed his innocence. No one was buying it though, and the fact he refused to come clean only made the incident worse.

'In my experience as a referee, I've never experienced anything like it,' said match official Ashley Rowden. 'The player was clearly missing some part of his ear lobe. There was a lot of blood.' Yates was banned from playing for six months and later chose to sign for a spell in New Zealand in the hope he could leave behind the stigma he had gained for that awful incident.

## 4 Gavin Quinnell loses an eye, October 2010

The younger brother of Wales internationals Scott and Craig, Gavin Quinnell was gouged so viciously playing for Scarletts in 2010 that he lost the sight in his left eye. The tragedy led to a police investigation and an arrest was made of a 26-year-old man, but criminal charges couldn't be laid due to the incident occurring on the field. That was the advice of the Crown Prosecutor.

The incident took place in early October during a game between the Scarletts and Ebbw Vale. Quinnell was rushed to hospital immediately but surgeons couldn't save the eye. In a statement, Gwent police said: 'Following Crown Prosecution Service advice the 26-year-old man arrested on suspicion of assault has been released with no further action.'

A spokesperson for the Scarletts said: 'It is hugely disappointing that Gavin can no longer pursue his career as a professional rugby player as a result of the injury he sustained, but he has shown great spirit, dignity and bravery throughout and continues to look positively forward to the next stage of his life and what his options are.'

## 3 Johan le Roux bites Sean Fitzpatrick, July 1994

It's taken as a given that anyone selected to play for the Springboks in the front-row is going to be able to handle themselves physically. Historically, those in green jerseys numbered one to three have been special operatives – licensed to apply pressure in whatever means they deem appropriate.

In 1994 Johan le Roux went way outside the parameters of even this extreme code. In the second of the three test series against the All Blacks in New Zealand, he decided that he wasn't imposing himself enough – that he needed to do more to dominate the battle.

The All Black front-row of that period was one of the best in their illustrious history and captain Sean Fitzpatrick was particularly good at goading opponents with his legendary verbal assaults. Mid-way through the second half a scrum collapsed, and a few seconds later a highly agitated and combustible Fitzpatrick emerged with blood pouring from his ear. A good chunk of it was between le Roux's teeth – the Springbok having bitten the All Black skipper. It made for a vile scene – entirely feral and quite disturbing. Le Roux was suspended for 18 months, after which he said: 'For an 18-month suspension, I feel I probably should have torn it off. Then at least I could say, "Look, I've returned to South Africa with the guy's ear." '

## ② The Canterbury pack on Sandy Carmichael, Canterbury v British & Irish Lions, June 1971

The British & Irish Lions tour match against Canterbury in 1971 will be remembered as the dirtiest game ever played. Rugby supposedly broke out in patches but no one can remember – the memory can never get past the endless pitched battles.

This was one of rugby's blackest days – the sport at its worst as the Cantabrians took it upon themselves to wholeheartedly commit to the 'softening-up' process.

It was Scottish prop Sandy Carmichael who took the worst beating of the day. After a series of sickening attacks he was left with a shattered cheekbone that would end his tour. *Daily Telegraph* correspondent John Reason captured Carmichael immediately after the game on film – a photograph that left the blood of everyone who saw it running cold.

Reason described the state of Carmichael in print as well: 'His left eye was closed and a huge blue swelling of agonised flesh hung out from the cheekbone like a grotesque plumb. His right eye was slit between the puffed skin above and below it. His right eyelid was gashed and straggling with blood. Another gash snagged away from the corner of his eye. He was quivering with emotion and frustration. His hands shook as they tried to hold the ice packs on the swellings.'

##  John Ashworth, All Blacks v Bridgend, November 1978

The All Blacks arrived in the UK in 1978 totally focused to win a Grand Slam. That meant they were going to do what they felt they had to do – and it definitely meant if there was a chance to soften up likely test opponents in tour games, then that had to be taken.

That was clearly the thinking when the All Blacks played Bridgend and saw the legendary JPR Williams lining up at fullback. Williams was going to be one of the main threats in the Welsh backline so when he was spotted at the bottom of a ruck, All Black prop John Ashworth took the opportunity to make his mark.

Ashworth stamped on Williams so hard he put his studs through the Bridgend fullback's cheek. The bleeding was horrific – more than two pints of blood were lost and Williams needed 30 stitches.

'To be honest, what annoyed me most about that incident was that Ashworth never apologised,' Williams told the *Guardian* in 2005. 'I thought he might have caught me by accident at the time, but when I saw the replay there was no doubt it was deliberate and when my father – who was giving a speech at the post-match dinner – drew attention to it, 10 of the All Blacks got up and walked out.'

Despite his facial damage, Williams played on. 'I was the captain and felt I had a responsibility to my team,' he said.

# PART 7

# Can You Believe It?

## 10 strangest things

### 10 Slammed at the bar

Knowing that it was going to host World Cup games in 2011, Rotorua International Stadium would presumably have everything in best order during the 2010 ITM Cup – the New Zealand domestic championship providing the last chance to dry-run before the big event.

But everything was far from shipshape, as North Harbour's Mat Luamanu discovered in August that year. The big No 8 was warming up ahead of the clash with Bay of Plenty, and he ambled across to the posts while his team-mates ran through some drills. He was pushing on the upright to stretch when he was suddenly dazed and confused.

He was bleeding from the mouth, his tooth chipped. The crossbar had fallen on his head.

'I was leaning against the post warming my shoulders up and it went bang,' he said. 'Luckily I was just trying out headgear this week – if I wasn't wearing it, it probably would have cut my head right open. It was a real shock and I was bit dazed – it was like something hit me from the sky.'

The game had to be delayed by 10 minutes as officials scrambled for duct tape and rope to re-attach the cross bar. The cross-bar was welded on the following day.

## 9  Sweet potatoes

To no one's great surprise, alcohol was the inspiration for Erica Roe in 1982 when she performed what many consider to be the best streak at a sporting event. The 25-year-old Roe was a bookseller from Peterborough and was blessed or perhaps cursed with a 40-inch bust.

Britain was in the early years of Thatcherism and had endured the Falklands conflict that year, and the mood was restless at Twickenham where England were playing Australia in late November. At half-time Roe meandered onto the field, her hips swinging one way, her ample bare chest the other, and the crowd loved it. She became the figurehead for all streakers – this buxom brunette, cigarette in mouth and without a care in the world, holding centre stage at rugby's most hallowed ground.

This was the moment the rugby world stood still – a half-naked lady on the field of play ... what could be stranger? This had never been seen before. Even legendary commentator Bill McLaren was all of a fluster: 'I'm not sure who this young lady plays for,' he said.

The England players were in the midst of a huddle, listening to the inspiring words of captain Bill Beaumont, a man in possession of a notoriously large rump. He sensed he had lost the attention of his troops, so he inquired of scrum-half Steve Smith what he was staring at, and the reply was this: 'I'm not sure how to say this Bill, but some bird has just run on the field with your arse on her chest.'

Roe was escorted off the field by a police officer who famously placed his helmet across her chest. She now lives in Portugal and is an organic sweet potato farmer.

## 8 Keeping an eye out

British & Irish Lions lock Gordon Brown never tired of telling the story of the time he and his team-mates were on their hands and knees during the third test against South Africa in 1974 searching for a glass eye. The eye in question belonged to Springbok lock Johan de Bruyn and it was on the ground somewhere because Brown had punched it clean out of his opponent's socket.

The 1974 tour was one of the most violent and bloodiest in Lions history – and that is amongst a collection of seriously violent and bloody tours. The Lions had arrived in South Africa with their infamous '99' call, which was a code for everyone in the team to start a brawl.

The logic behind it was that the Lions thought it best to get their retaliation in first, and that the referee couldn't send them all off. Having won the first two tests, the Lions encountered an angry Boks side in the third, and De Bruyn had been brought in for the very purpose of sorting out Brown and his pals. Aware what was coming, Brown landed his king-hit first to send the glass eye flying.

'So there we are, 30 players, plus the ref, on our hands and knees scrabbling about in the mire looking for this glass eye,' recalled Brown, who died from non-Hodgkin lymphoma in 2001. 'Eventually, someone yells "Eureka!" whereupon De Bruyn grabs it and plonks it straight back in the gaping hole in his face.'

Brown said that at the next lineout, he looked across and there was de Bruyn with his eye back in, but a tuft of grass poking out from behind. It was a memory Brown would never forget and, shortly before his death, De Bruyn flew to London and presented the Scottish lock with the very eye that had been knocked out – it was mounted on a plinth.

## 7 Porn in a storm

Teenage boys across New Zealand were no doubt delighted by the programming error that saw hard-core pornography enjoy four minutes of air time during a popular Sunday afternoon rugby show. The Toyota-sponsored *Grassroots* programme features the best action from prominent amateur games in New Zealand. It is shown on the free-to-air Prime channel and usually attracts a demographically diverse audience, but particularly young men and families.

That was why there was considerable embarrassment on 6 July 2008 when the rugby disappeared to be replaced with adult entertainment. The pay-per-view Spice channel – which promotes itself as offering 'sexy, exotic women, fetish lifestyle, ethnic and gonzo for those who believe variety is the Spice of life' – enjoyed four minutes of air time

Sky subscriber Mike Steenson was watching the rugby show with his three-year-old son when the porn came on. He told the *New Zealand Herald*: 'At first I thought it was a prank. I'm not sure how many people were watching but it's not something you expect to come on, on a Sunday. You can't make mistakes like that.'

A profusely apologetic Tony O'Brien, head of communications for the Sky-owned Prime channel, told the same paper it was a technical fault. 'We apologise for any offence which may have been caused.'

## 6 What's the time, Mr Wolf?

Fiji were desperate to keep alive their chances of making the quarter-finals of the 2003 World Cup and knew they had to beat Japan in Townsville. Fiji coach Mac McCallion brought back veteran superstar Waisale Serevi for the game, believing his side needed some magic from the little maestro at fly-half.

Sadly they were denied that because Serevi dislocated his shoulder after just 10 minutes. But incredibly, as he was being helped off the field, the TV cameras closed in on him and around his gingerly held left wrist there were all sorts of strappings with biblical references written on them.

But unbelievably there was also a giant wristwatch – one of those G-Shock jobs that are about the size of Big Ben. How on earth could referee Nigel Williams have not seen it? And why on earth was Serevi wearing it in the first place? It was ridiculous, and maybe it was fortunate that he left after 10 minutes – before he was able to take someone's eye out with the ludicrous contraption on his wrist.

## 5 A kick up the backside

The Samoan team at the 2003 World Cup reached their final pool game with a slim chance of qualifying for the quarter-finals. They had to beat South Africa to progress – a daunting task, but not totally beyond their reach. Samoa had earlier pushed England close, so there was hope.

But that hope was all but gone by half-time. The Boks had come alive and a tired Samoan team were drifting out of the game and the tournament. They were actually taking a royal pounding and their misery was complete when in the final minute South Africa scored a memorable try to make the score 60–10.

One drunken Samoan supporter snapped at this point. He'd seen enough, and he jumped over the security barrier and made it onto the field where he set his sights on South African goal-kicker Louis Koen. Unfortunately for Mr Pitch Invader, he got the timing all wrong and ended up being booted squarely in the chops as Koen followed through with his goal-kick.

His one-man protest ended with a mouth full of leather and a night in the cells. The Australian Rugby Union issued an immediate statement: 'We are obviously very concerned about the incident, it is very serious and there will be a full review of all security arrangements first thing in the morning. We are advised by Queensland police that the alleged offender will be charged with an offence regarding a pitch invasion.'

## 4 Father of all fights

The closing stages of the Aviva Premiership reached a thrilling finale in 2010 when Worcester played Leeds in the final game of the season. The men from the West Country had to win to stay up – lose, and they would be relegated. So there was a bit riding on the game and some obvious tension being felt by the players and the crowd.

One man in the crowd feeling that tension was the father of Chris Cracknell. He was becoming increasingly agitated by comments being made by those around him about his son, who was playing flanker for Worcester. Unbeknown to him, the man most vociferous in his abuse happened to be the father of James Collins – the Worcester player who had replaced Cracknell junior on the field. Cracknell senior was so incensed he grabbed Collins senior by the collar and tried to land a few blows.

Worcester supporter Gary Dean, quoted in the *Worcester Evening News*, saw what happened next: 'We saw a fracas taking place between two guys 10 or 15 minutes after the final whistle. The one had the other guy by the shirt and the other was trying to punch him – people said it was the parents of Chris Cracknell and James Collins who were fighting. Cracknell then came over and started trying to hit the one man, but other players came along and held him back. Cracknell then dragged Collins' dad over the barriers and on to the pitch. There was a bit of aggro between Cracknell and Collins too. It was embarrassing to watch.'

Worcester lost 12–10.

## 3 The flour-bomb test

The Springbok tour to New Zealand in 1981 had split the host nation. The entire 56-day period South Africa were in New Zealand saw them subjected to protests of various size and intensity. It was perhaps fitting that the best should be left to last.

The series decider was at Auckland's Eden Park and the protesters were organised, resourced and more than ever determined to make their presence felt. They decided to hire light aircraft and drop flour bombs on the field. The danger would be too great for the officials to let the players carry on, so the game would be called off.

That was the theory. But the game was played with the incessant drone of aircraft buzzing overhead and spectacular explosions of white blasting off the ground. It made for an incredible sight – the players carrying on pretending they were blissfully unaware.

Yet one man most acutely aware of the flour bombs was All Black prop Gary Knight. He knew all about them as one landed on his head. Being a prop, and a renowned hard one even in that fraternity, he didn't fall to the deck when he was hit. He staggered around a bit, held his head, rubbed it and readied himself to carry on.

When the trainer came on to attend to him, Welsh referee Clive Norling cracked the immortal line: 'For God's sake don't pour water over him, he will end up battered.'

## 2 Who's your daddy?

When Bayonne play Biarritz, things can get spicy. This is a rivalry to last the ages – neighbours and passionate Basques, these two clubs define their entire season depending on how they go against each other.

In December 2011 they were locked in a typically ferocious battle that was threatening to boil over. Inevitably violence did break out, and in the thick of it was Biarritz No 8 Imanol Harinordoquy. A few punches were exchanged and there was all the usual pushing and shoving, but things turned decidedly odd when among the throng appeared Lucien Harinordoquy, father of the No 8.

Harinordoquy senior was incensed that his son had seemingly been targeted, so he came onto the field to try to invoke some kind of justice. He appeared to be trying to land a blow on Bayonne flanker Jean-Jo Marmouyet, but before he could get close enough Harinordoquy senior was hauled to the ground by Bayonne fly-half Benjamin Boyet. The Bayonne player later said of his actions: 'I tackled him because he was attacking one of my team-mates. I put him to the ground and Benoit August told me to stop, because it was Imanol's father.'

Understandably, Bayonne president Michel Cacoulaut was a little miffed: 'It is intolerable,' he fumed. 'The club will lodge a complaint against Mr Harinordoquy.'

All of which left Harinordoquy senior contrite and more than a little embarrassed by his actions. 'My apologies to the Aguilera crowd, Bayonne and Biarritz spectators, to both teams and their staff, to the French League and Federation as well as to the world of rugby in general. I was under pressure and for other reasons, I lost control. I regret my behaviour.'

For the record, Biarritz won 22–19.

## 1 The fat Bok invader

All Black flanker Richie McCaw couldn't be sure he was seeing what he thought he was seeing early in the second half of a Tri Nations clash against South Africa in Durban in 2002. The scores were locked at 17–all and the game had ebbed and flowed without much drama, yet one Bok fan, 46-year-old Pieter van Zyl, obviously didn't think so. When McCaw, who was packing down on the side of the scrum looked up, he saw the grotesquely fat van Zyl, crammed into his jeans and Bok shirt with his giant gut poking out the front, wrestle Irish referee Dave McHugh to the ground. McCaw was in the thick of it instantly, tackling van Zyl before players from both teams joined the mêlée and managed to land a few blows on the crazed fan.

'He was [a bit difficult to bring down], it was a bit of a bizarre thing to happen really. I didn't know what was going on,' said McCaw. McHugh was forced to leave the field on a golf cart having dislocated his shoulder and England's Chris White took over. As for van Zyl, he had a bleeding nose and a life ban for his troubles.

# 10 touring dramas

## 10 Motorway madness

It was 2003 – World Cup year – and the Welsh were heading to New Zealand and Australia for a June tour that would form a critical part of their tournament preparations. But in the weeks leading up to the tour the players were locked in talks with the administration about payment – they wanted more money for their efforts once they were in the Antipodes. The cash-strapped union wouldn't budge.

On the day the squad departed Cardiff for Heathrow, somewhere along the M4 the captain called to the driver to pull into a motorway service station. This was it – time for the ultimatum. The players either got what they wanted or they wouldn't get back on the bus.

The Welsh Rugby Union had no choice but to agree. 'It's one of those things we could have done without, but sanity has prevailed,' WRU chief executive David Moffett said afterwards. 'I was surprised and disappointed that we found ourselves in this position only minutes before the players were due to get on the bus.'

By the time the document was signed the team had missed their scheduled flight to Auckland. Fortunately for the WRU the business-class flights were flexible, meaning they only incurred a $10,000 administration fee rather than a $500,000 hit to buy new tickets. The players agreed to pay for their own overnight accommodation at Heathrow but lost a day of preparation and were hammered 55–3 by the All Blacks, hardly the sort of performance worthy of any payment at all.

## 9 How to win friends and influence people

The British & Irish Lions tour of Australia and New Zealand in 1966 was a disastrous business. The Lions won their two tests in

Australia – as they should have done, because the Wallabies were dire – but they lost the series to the All Blacks 4–0. It was a long, excruciating tour – 35 games over four and a half months. Things were so bad that future captain Willie John McBride would claim it as 'the most unhappy period of my rugby life'.

The Lions won 23 games, lost nine and drew three – a poor return that reflected how disjointed they were off the field. Their real problems began after the game against Canterbury, when captain for the day Jim Telfer said in his post-match speech. 'I would not describe today's game as dirty because all our games in New Zealand have been dirty.'

This sent the locals into a wild fury, and at one stage the tour was a ghost ship: the captain couldn't make the test team, while the coach John Robins was in hospital with a broken ankle and team manager Des O'Brien had disappeared to Fiji, supposedly on a reconnaissance mission but really to escape the hell in which he was trapped.

## 8   A pig of a campaign

It wasn't until the 2011 World Cup was over that any sense emerged of how much bitterness had been affecting the performance of the Samoan team. They arrived in New Zealand confident of progressing to the quarter-finals, having beaten Australia spectacularly a few months previously.

They easily beat Namibia and Fiji, but were squeezed out by Wales and the Springboks and were home after the first round.

It was at that point captain Mahonri Schwalger dropped a bombshell. In a report to the Samoan Prime Minister, Schwalger singled out union vice-chairman Lefau Harry Schuster, chief executive Su'a Peter Schuster, team manager Tuala Matthew Vaea and assistant manager Ryan Schuster for the team's failure.

'We as a team feel that our preparation was tainted by not having people in vital positions committed to their duties and responsibilities before every game,' said Schwalger. 'I feel that for our team to go forward we need to have committed people, or we will never go anywhere. From Harry, to board members that were there at the World Cup, they treated this as a massive holiday.'

The players had looked on, flabbergasted at the behaviour of the senior managers who they said had a string of old cronies coming through the team hotel for social engagements.

Vaea was fined 100 pigs on his return to Samoa.

## 7 Battle of Brive

The little town of Brive in the south-west of France is normally a great place to visit, especially when, as was the case when Pontypridd played there in September 1997, the Parc Municipal des Sports is bathed in glorious sunshine. The Welsh club had come for a Heineken Cup fixture that sickeningly turned into a ferocious brawl towards the end of the game. It was one of those old-fashioned fights where everyone was involved and proper punches were thrown. It was nasty, and the Welsh were left bitter that their No 8, Dale McIntosh, was sent off.

Worse was to come, though, when a second brawl erupted later that night in Le Bar Toulzac. Locals claimed several Pontypridd players fought with a group of Brive stars, including French internationalists Christophe Lamaison, David Venditti and Philippe Carbonneau, who all required hospital treatment.

Lamaison said: 'I had never been so scared in all my life – it was a nightmare. A few of our players and friends were in the bar, the atmosphere was good. The Welsh arrived at about half past ten. Two of them started it all off. They rushed at Philippe Carbonneau.'

McIntosh, Andre Barnard and Phil John were arrested and held in custody for 36 hours. Things got even trickier when the two sides then met in the quarter-final later that year; Pontypridd were unable to select the three men arrested as they were legally barred from entering the region while the investigation was ongoing.

It wasn't such a nice trip to Brive after all.

## 6   The tour from hell

Quite why England agreed to such a preposterous June schedule in 1998 remains a mystery only their administration can explain. They took a schedule that would see them play Australia in Brisbane, then the All Blacks twice in New Zealand, before a one-off test against the Boks in South Africa. To make matters worse, they would have to do it with a squad that was full of third-choice players.

Things started badly with a record 76–0 loss to the Wallabies. Then they were smashed twice by the All Blacks – 64–22 and 40–10 – and lock Danny Grewcock was sent off in the first test. This entirely miserable world tour ended with a respectable 18–0 loss to the Boks, but that game took a massive injury toll. Some, in fact most, of the tourists were mentally scarred for life. They conceded 198 points and scored just 32.

Some of their under-performance was due to the total lack of professionalism on display. Many players later admitted they lost the plot in terms of how much booze they drank. One of those was future England captain Lewis Moody, who said in his autobiography: 'A lot of the difficulty was down to the vast superiority of the opposition, but plenty of it was down to me, too, and it all started to go wrong on the very first night. I realise I was a moron. Just thinking about it makes me cringe. I was an embarrassment to myself, to my family and to my country, even if I was not the only one.'

## 5   Car park hijack

There is nothing quite like being held up and robbed at gunpoint to take the gloss off a tour. But England prop Graham Rowntree was grateful to be alive after he and team-mates Darren Garforth and Martin Corry were left lying face-down in a Kimberley car-park crying like babies.

In South Africa with England in 2000, the three amigos had played for the mid-week side against Nashua Griqas and such was their pride in their work that they felt they deserved a few beers.

So there they were – good front-row boys and a decent loose

forward – knocking them back late into the night. Aware they needed to get back to their hotel, they persuaded the bar staff to give them a lift. 'So we walked into the car park,' recalled Rowntree. 'We looked back and saw that the bar was being held up at gunpoint. We hid in the car park. Then the door of the bar opened and 10 or 12 blokes came out with guns. Everyone stood still but me, as my foot was in a carrier bag, and the robbers heard this. Next thing, we were on the floor at gunpoint throwing our wallets into the car park.'

All three were certain they were going to be executed, and despite being good front-rows boys and a decent loose forward, the tears poured out and they rocked in the foetal position.

After they made it back to their hotel, they vowed to keep the incident quiet until they were safely back in Blighty.

## 4 Coming in from the cold

The events of 9 December 1989 could have come straight from a John le Carré novel. Romania had played Scotland in Edinburgh earlier in the day and the two teams would later enjoy a convivial post-match function.

After sinking a few drinks, Romanian lock Christian Raducanu decided he was going to make a decision that would change his life. Romania was experiencing extreme political turbulence and the state had considered Raducanu and some of his other team-mates as defection risks, so had sent minders to keep a watchful eye on the team while they were in Scotland.

Raducanu headed out into Edinburgh's High Street and entered the nearest bar. The hired goons followed him, but unbeknown to them one of the Scotland players, Norrie Rowan, was able to smuggle the giant Romanian from inside the bar through one of the city's famed vaults and out to safety. The 2 m Raducanu accosted the nearest policeman and told him he wanted to defect.

'When I defected it was a spur-of-the-moment thing, because my family were still in Romania, but life was very tough there at the time,' Raducanu told the *Scotsman*. 'I had had quite a few drinks at the official banquet, and I just approached the first policeman I saw and asked for political asylum. He thought I was drunk. Two weeks later the communist regime in Romania collapsed, and all the barriers began to come down.'

## 3   A Royal mess

The World Cup in 2011 was not England's finest moment. It probably couldn't have gone any worse for them, either on or off the field. A tough victory against the Pumas in Dunedin was a good way to start – many of the team certainly thought so as they decided to celebrate rather hard.

Management took the squad to Queenstown for a few light days – light on training, hard on drinking, as it turned out – where scandal erupted as footage of occasional captain Mike Tindall leaked, showing him in an embrace with a woman who wasn't his wife. The big deal of course was that only six weeks earlier Tindall had married Zara Phillips, grand-daughter of the Queen. The tabloid scandal was huge.

Then three other players were accused of making lewd and inappropriate remarks to a female worker in Dunedin – she wanted $15,000 compensation.

In their second game against Romania they were accused of swapping the match balls to help kicker Jonny Wilkinson, and after they were dumped out of the quarter-final by France, it was revealed they had been speeding while on a day out with tournament sponsor Land Rover in West Auckland. To finish off, star player Manu Tuilagi was fined for jumping off a passenger ferry as it came into dock in Auckland and skipper Lewis Moody was fined for wearing a branded mouth-guard even though he was told not to wear it.

Coach Martin Johnson resigned once back in England, and a supposedly confidential review into the campaign was leaked. RFU director of élite rugby Rob Andrew was quoted in the report saying: 'Some of the senior players were more focused on money rather than getting the rugby right.' Players claimed the coaching team were years out of date and were even borrowing back moves that Romania had tried against them. 'To go into World Cup games not having a game-plan, any structure or clear idea of what we were going to do in attack was astonishing,' was the most damning comment.

## 2 A nation divided

It is unlikely that anyone – Kiwi or South African – derived any enjoyment from the Springbok tour of New Zealand in 1981. It remains one of the great landmarks of New Zealand history – a tour that split a nation and saw protesters take to the streets and to the skies to try to prevent games from going ahead.

South Africa's abhorrent apartheid policy had seen them frozen out of world sport, but New Zealand's Prime Minister Robert Muldoon refused to allow sport to be politicised and the Springboks were invited to take on the All Blacks in a four-test series.

The country was incensed – or at least half of it was – and New Zealand was subjected to 56 days of unprecedented civil unrest. More than 150,000 people marched in 200 demonstrations across 28 centres; there were acts of virtual terrorism that included dropping flour bombs onto Eden Park during the final test, and one woman even tried to crash her car into a group of Springbok players as they walked down the street.

For the South Africans though, the hardest thing was seeing their hosts at war with each other. 'When we arrived in Gisborne and we saw the protesters and when they dropped glass and other things on the playing field, we realised it was going to be quite tough,' Springbok captain Wynand Claasen told the *New Zealand Herald* in 2006.

'We were totally unprepared and I don't think even the New Zealanders knew it would be that intense.'

## 1 Lost in translation

At least everyone ended up being able to laugh about it – that's the key to this hilarious tale that saw a strictly social team from Dorset somehow facing a fired-up professional outfit on a trip to Romania.

The Dorchester Gladiator 3rd XV was full of elderly gents – well-heeled types who still liked to get out of a Saturday afternoon and chug around even if their ailing bodies paid for it the next day. Best of all, they could use rugby as a ticket to escape the wife and kids for a few days, which is why the Dorchester crew headed to Romania in 2000. They had arranged to play a similar team of veterans from the lower ranks of the Steaua Bucharest club.

But the language barrier had obviously not been cleared; when the Gladiators arrived at the ground, they were met by TV cameras and thousands of spectators. When they looked over at the team they were about to face, they didn't see similar portly types. What they saw was the Romanian club's top team – a Steaua First XV crammed with full internationals. Gladiators' vice-captain, Rod Thomas, a 37-year-old surveyor from Dorchester, would later say: 'We had been out for a few beers on the Friday night after arriving in the country, so one or two of the lads were feeling a bit fragile.' While the Romanian team started warming up like the real professionals they were, he said most of the Dorset team stood about smoking cigarettes. 'We tried to convince them we weren't any good but they thought we were just trying to wind them up and refused to believe us,' he said.

Most of the Dorchester side were dead on their feet after just 50 minutes, which was hardly surprising given that many of them were over 40. To their eternal credit, the visitors were able to keep things semi-respectable with a 61–17 defeat, and recorded highlights of the game were shown on Romania's six o'clock news.

# 10 unlikely call-ups

## 10 Brian Lochore leaves his wife a note

The All Blacks were desperate to save the series against the British & Irish Lions in 1971. The Lions had been magical all tour and had captured the imagination of the New Zealand public.

The series may have been tied at 1–all but the momentum was with the visitors and there was a sense that the All Blacks were clinging on, almost powerless to prevent the inevitable. When regular lock Peter Whiting was ruled out the day before the third test, the selectors took the unusual decision to ring former captain Brian Lochore, who had actually retired 12 months previously.

An incredibly loyal man, Lochore felt he couldn't say no. He would famously leave a note on the kitchen table of his farmhouse for his wife Pam that said: 'Gone to Wellington. Playing test tomorrow.'

Asked to play in the unfamiliar position of lock – he was a No 8 – Lochore wasn't able to have the influence he wanted. The Lions won 13–3 and Lochore arrived home on Sunday, never to play another test.

## 9 Brewer sneaks into All Blacks

The injury-prone but highly talented Mike Brewer was not selected for the All Blacks tour of England and Scotland in 1993. Brewer was a favourite of then-All Black coach Laurie Mains – both men cutting their respective playing and coaching teeth in Otago.

Brewer hadn't played enough during the year, however, and was not match-fit when the squad was picked. He did still travel to the UK as a sponsor's representative. By this stage he was fully recovered, and the man who had effectively been picked ahead of him, Liam Barry, had failed to impress Mains.

Strangely, the All Blacks had been given a weird itinerary whereby after playing England in their final test they stayed on to play the Combined Services and then the Barbarians in Cardiff.

Mains called in Brewer to sit on the bench for the Barbarians test, snubbing Barry and upsetting many of the senior players who felt it was the wrong call. Worse still, Brewer was given 15 minutes of game time and set a precedent of playing for the All Blacks while not actually being an official member of the squad.

## 8 Martin Corry becomes Wizard of Oz

Martin Corry was initially surprised, then hurt that he had not been selected for the British & Irish Lions tour of Australia in 2001. The England No 8 had been strongly tipped to make the squad and back up the hugely experienced Lawrence Dallaglio. But it was Scotland's Simon Taylor who the Lions were eyeing as their man to put pressure on Dallaglio.

The young Scot had little test experience but was an exceptional talent who had impressed. But after one strong performance where he scored a try, Taylor was on the plane home with a knee injury.

Corry was sent for – he'd been in Canada with the England team – and arrived late on a Sunday night before having to play on the Tuesday.

'When I got there, it was literally a case of "here's your playbook. You need to learn this because you're playing tomorrow." It was all a massive rush,' said Corry a few years later. 'With jet lag and everything, I didn't really know where I was. I then played the Saturday as well so it was all about trying to focus on the games rather than thinking, I'm on a Lions tour.'

Dallaglio never recovered from a knee injury he picked up, and Corry nailed the test spot and was one of the stars of the tour and indeed the test series.

## 7 Lachie Munro cabs it to Eden Park

Having just returned from a punishing three-game stint in South Africa, the Blues had numerous injury issues as they prepared to face the Sharks in round four of the 2009 Super 14.

Those problems intensified when starting fullback Paul Williams damaged his leg in the warm-up and had to pull out 10 minutes before kick-off. Winston Stanley came into the starting team, but that left the Aucklanders a man short on the bench.

Coach Pat Lam had no fit bodies available at the ground so he rang Lachie Munro, a member of the wider training squad. Munro was a 15-minute cab drive from Eden Park, enjoying a day out at the races.

'The only person I could think to call was Lachie,' said Lam after the game. 'He told me he'd only had one beer, so I told him to get here as quickly as he could.'

Munro arrived 20 minutes after kick-off and was forced into action for the final 15 minutes as several Blues players felt the effects of their travel schedule. The Blues lost 35–31, but Munro was surprisingly composed and involved.

## 6 Jamie Salmon plays for and against the All Blacks

Educated at the world-renowned Wellington College in Berkshire, Jamie Salmon would no doubt have been ridiculed mercilessly if he had said to his school chums that within three years he'd be playing for the All Blacks.

First, he was English, and second, only the very best of the very best ever cracked the All Blacks – and they just weren't in the habit of selecting 20-year-old Englishmen.

Except in the case of Salmon they did. He headed to New Zealand after he left school, cracked the Wellington provincial team, and shortly before his twenty-first birthday lined up for the All Blacks at centre to play against Fiji in a non-cap international. A year later in 1981 he made his test debut against Romania in Bucharest, winning three caps before deciding to head home to England in 1983.

Amazingly, he came out to New Zealand in 1985, this time as a member of the England touring squad. He won 12 caps for the country of his birth, and is to this day the only man to have played both for and against the All Blacks in test matches.

## 5 Adam Ashley–Cooper denied his pie

There was surprise when the virtually unknown Adam Ashley-Cooper was selected in the Wallabies Tri Nations squad in 2005. He had barely even played Super Rugby, and the 21-year-old utility back was a little shell-shocked to find himself in such esteemed company.

He hadn't made the match-day 22 for the clash against South Africa in Perth, so was sitting in the stands alongside the other squad members not required for duty. A little peckish, he was about to fetch himself a meat pie when his phone rang. It was Wallaby coach Eddie Jones telling him to get down to the changing rooms as starting second-five Elton Flatley was pulling out due to blurred vision. This was 10 minutes before kick-off.

Ashley-Cooper made his debut off the bench in the final few minutes. 'For me it was chaos trying to get everything together and everyone's having a little word trying to calm me down, but I had to just take it all in and just relax and get out there and warm up,' Ashley-Cooper said afterwards.

'A lot of things were running through my head last night. I was actually thinking, I've only played three Super 12 matches, and here I am on the bench for the Wallabies.'

His foray was brief but it was enough to impress Jones, who acknowledged the exceptional circumstances. 'Seriously, he was going to start tucking into his pie and he gets a phone call that he is on the bench for Australia. He's a good young player ... he's got the potential to be a very strong running outside centre cum winger.'

## 4 Troy Flavell's long day

Even within the élite environment of the All Blacks, Troy Flavell was recognised as one of the most durable and aerobically fit athletes in the squad. That was tested to the extreme in June 2007 when, having not been picked in the 22, Flavell completed a heavy weights session on the morning of the second test between the All Blacks and France in Wellington.

In the late afternoon he and a few other non-playing squad members were sent to a CBD hotel to carry out a social engagement, before making his way to the ground an hour before kick-off. He quickly changed into his training kit and helped the team warm up before making his way into the stands to watch the game.

No sooner had he sat down than he was asked to kit-up as starting lock Keith Robinson had damaged his back. Flavell didn't have time to get properly strapped or change into his 'proper' underpants, and instead had to sit on the bench with his boxers under his shorts.

He then had to play almost 60 minutes when Ali Williams was forced off with a broken jaw. 'Initially I was unsettled by it all,' said Flavell, who had in fact played pretty well in what was a record victory for the All Blacks. 'But once I was out there for a little bit you got into the groove of the game. The prep was not as good as it could have been but it could have been a good thing, getting it dumped on me.

'I felt like I went all right, so all these years of being so pedantic about my prep went out the window. I am a real creature of habit. My week has to be exactly the same and I really worry about that.'

### 3  Brian McKechnie clears his head

Legend has it that Brian McKechnie played his heroic hand against the Welsh in 1978 while nursing a moderate hangover. Back in those days, All Blacks not required for test duty were let loose on a Friday night. Known as the 'dirty-dirties', the non-playing members of an All Black tour party made sure they enjoyed the touring experience.

Southlander McKechnie awoke on the morning of 11 November that year with no greater ambition than to finish the day in a better state than he was starting it. Events went well off-course when fullback Bevan Wilson was forced to pull out of the test team. McKechnie would have to sit on the bench – which should still be okay as back then replacements were only allowed for injuries, and what chance was there of another fullback being struck down?

Every chance as it turned out. Canterbury's Clive Currie's jaw suffered the misfortune of becoming acquainted with Steve Fenwick's head and the latter inflicted serious damage.

McKechnie was on and much needed as the All Blacks trailed 12–4. He would soon slot two penalties and then find himself lining up another from 37 metres in the dying minutes after All Black lock Andy Haden had infamously 'fallen' out of a lineout. McKechnie nailed the kick to win the game. Two years later he would be part of more sporting scandal – he was the New Zealand batsman who had to face the infamous underarm ball in the game against Australia.

## 2 Andy Nicol the ultimate tour guide

At first, Scotland scrum-half Andy Nicol assumed it was a joke. He was in Sydney as a tour guide to a group of British & Irish Lions rugby fans. He was getting ready for a walk across the Harbour Bridge at 11 pm the night before the third test in the series. His phone rang showing a number he didn't recognise.

'I was convinced it was a wind-up by someone with a comedy Irish accent. And then I realised it really was Donal Lenihan [Lions manager] and he was being deadly serious!'

Serious about telling Nicol he was required on the bench for the deciding test. Having not been in the initial 67-man wider squad chosen earlier in the year, Nicol was a wild card but the Lions had no choice: Austin Healey's back had suddenly gone into spasm and there wasn't time to fly someone over from the UK.

The 30-year-old Nicol hadn't played for two months and reckoned he'd maybe been 'for a few runs in that time'. But he would later admit: 'I wasn't in great shape to be honest. I'd been leading a tour group around Australia, and we all know what goes on with tours.'

Matt Dawson was tackled heavily in the opening minute and for the next four looked like he was going to have to come off. 'I was so worried about getting on in the first minute. I hadn't played since May 1 and hadn't even seen a rugby ball since then. I threw about three passes to Jonny Wilkinson and saw about half-a-dozen lineouts on the Saturday and that was it.'

Thankfully Dawson stayed on and Nicol wasn't required.

## 1  Stephen Donald lands a whopper

Stephen Donald became the unlikeliest hero at the 2011 World Cup, his story almost the stuff of Hollywood. The Waikato fly-half had won 22 All Black caps since 2008, but was dumped by the national team at the end of 2010 when he suffered a horrible tour of the UK. After being part of a poor Chiefs campaign in 2011 and spending much of the season injured, he was nowhere near making the All Black World Cup squad.

When Dan Carter was forced out of the tournament before the final pool game, the selectors called up Aaron Cruden. Had they thought about calling for Donald instead? 'No,' was the one-word emphatic reply from coach Graham Henry. But when Colin Slade was also forced out the tournament in the quarter-final, Donald was summoned. He hadn't played for five weeks and was on a whitebaiting trip in the Waikato when the call came to get himself to Auckland.

'He was whitebaiting when I talked to him today,' said Henry the day Donald arrived in camp. 'He's been running up and down the side of a river. One of the criteria of selection was two pound of whitebait. So there's always some benefits.'

Clearly unfit and overweight, Donald was on the bench and not required to play in the semi-final. But 30 minutes into the final Cruden incurred a serious knee injury. On came Donald for his first run in six weeks wearing a jersey that didn't fit him as a result of his increased girth. But he played brilliantly, making several breaks, some good tackles and then kicking the winning penalty.

'He is a tremendous team person. He's very popular in the group, a good professional,' said Henry of Donald after the final. 'I had a long talk to him after the game and he had a huge smile on his face to be part of this because you people [media] have given him a bit of stick at times – and perhaps he deserved it occasionally – but he has got great character.'

# 10 psychos

## 10 Trevor Brennan (Ireland)

Long before Irish loose forward Trevor Brennan properly flipped and earned himself a life ban, it was easy to tell that he was someone to be given a wide berth. Maybe it was his mad eyes, or his fiery thatch of ginger hair, or his missing teeth – there was always a hint of the crazies about Brennan who, despite or possibly even because he was a bit mental, had won 13 Irish caps

He wouldn't win another after a mad day in January in 2007 when he ended up punching, repeatedly, an opposition fan in the crowd. The chap who felt the fury of Brennan was called Patrick Bamford, an Ulster fan who was allegedly leading some abusive chanting during a Heineken Cup match against Toulouse. Brennan, who was on the bench for Toulouse and warming up at the time he was the subject of this abuse, decided to deal with things his own way – by grabbing Bamford by the throat and smacking him in the chops.

Such acts of madness are not such a big deal in France; the security staff at Stade Ernest Wallon barely flinched, and Brennan was able to take the field in what was a critical Heineken Cup game. Just for good measure he picked up a yellow card in case anyone was in any doubt about him being a total psycho.

The organisers of the European Cup were not so relaxed about Brennan's actions and fined him £20,000 and banned him for life. 'It was the view of the committee that Mr Brennan's behaviour was completely unjustified and that he caused serious harm to an innocent spectator and significant damage to the image of Rugby Union,' a released statement said.

## 9 Joseph Ntshongwana (South Africa)

Life is a little different in South Africa, where there appears to be a greater acceptance of violence. Even allowing for that, there was still considerable shock when former Springbok Under-21 and Blue Bulls player Joseph Ntshongwana was charged with three counts of murder and one of attempted murder in 2010.

The 33-year-old, a committed Christian, went on a murderous rampage to allegedly avenge the rape of his teenage daughter. His daughter was allegedly infected with HIV during her ordeal. He hacked to death, with an axe, four men in townships outside Durban whom he thought were responsible.

According to police one man was decapitated, and Ntshongwana stalked the area at least four times prior to the attack. One witness statement said: 'He didn't seem to make any effort to try and conceal himself. He was just driving around the townships in a car, then he would get out and attack someone. It was almost like he wanted to wipe out all the men from one particular area of the township.'

And another 37-year-old man, who managed to escape said: 'He drove slowly past me, before pulling up. He then jumped out of the car with an orange bag. I thought it was a gun. He said: "Did you know we would ever meet? Why did you rape my daughter and give her HIV? You destroyed her future." I was puzzled. I told him I didn't know what he was talking about, but he lunged at me with the axe, aiming at my torso. I ducked and ran away as quickly as I could.'

## 8 Michel Palmié (France)

The Béziers team of the 1970s would have to be one of the most terrifying to have ever taken the field. There were psychos throughout the pack – proper ones who would do anything on the field and much worse off it. Michel Palmié was one of the crew to enjoy a reputation as a total head-case.

The giant lock had little concept of what the rules of the game actually were. He was seemingly there to inflict pain on anyone who wasn't wearing the same jersey as him. Armand Clerc discovered that in 1978 when the Racing Club hooker was blinded in one eye after being punched by Palmié. It was a punch that would earn Palmié a life ban – and it was easy to suspect the ban wasn't so much for that one punch, but for the thousands of others he had thrown in a career infamous for its brutality.

Bobbie Windsor, the Welsh hooker of the 1970s who was a little liberal with his fists himself, said of Palmié in his autobiography: 'Once the ball went out of the scrum, nearly everyone else, especially the referee, would be watching the ball. That's when Palmié and his henchmen did their dirty best. He'd see you trapped at the bottom of the pile, he'd give a quick look round to make sure the ref wasn't looking and then, bang …'

 **7 Laurent Siegne (France)**

French prop Laurent Siegne played in the 1980s when some of the filth of the 1970s had been cleaned up. It wasn't so easy to be a psycho by then – there was tolerance of thugs but the full-scale nut-job routine was a little harder to get away with. But Siegne got as close as it was possible to get to being a fully-fledged psycho.

The All Blacks knew that every time they encountered him there would be trouble – the sort of trouble that could quickly get out of hand. It was, though, as a coach that Siegne could get a better handle on being a psycho. When Scotland fly-half Gregor Townsend joined Brive in 1998, he encountered some astonishing scenes in the changing room: 'When I signed for Brive, Laurent Siegne was coach. He would be fighting his own forwards in the dressing room before matches. My warm-up routine usually consisted of a couple of hamstring stretches, so I just hid in the corner.'

Siegne had been in charge in 1997 when Brive and Welsh side Pontypridd waged a war on the pitch during a Heineken Cup match that continued into a bar in town and never really ended.

## 6 Alain Estève – 'The Beast of Béziers' (France)

It is easy to see why men of a certain age have lost interest in the modern game. To them there is no soul or character in the highly sterilised environment of today. There are certainly not men like Alain Estève around any more, a man so ludicrously scary he was dubbed the 'Beast of Béziers'. And at 2.05 m and 125 kg he was indeed a beast, roaming the fields of France and beyond throughout the 1970s.

His ferocity was built on, but not exclusively confined to, his size. He thought it best to belt the living daylights out of every player he encountered just to remind them he was a touch mental – the sort of bloke who might indeed eat a live frog or stick his head in a fire for fun. A quiet night in for Estève would probably have been sinking 30 lagers and then eating his television.

The enormous beard he grew made him plain terrifying, and no one in the world enjoyed playing against him, particularly as he was never one to allow the rugby to get in the way of his chosen sport of violence.

Bobby Windsor, the Wales hooker, frequently came up against him. 'When we packed down, I'd hear him say, "Bob-bee, Bob-bee" and then this big fist would come through and smack you in the chops. To get my own back I booted him in the mush as hard as I could. He got up and gave me a wink. It takes a lot to scare me but I thought, Bloody hell!'

## 5 Steve Finnane (Australia)

The Wallaby teams of the 1990s and 2000s would dearly have loved a character with the reputation of Steve Finnane. The highly successful barrister won six caps for Australia between 1975 and 1978, and despite his relatively short international career, managed to establish himself as one of the more volatile and explosive to wear the gold jersey.

There is a fine line between being a thug and a psycho, and what pushed Finnane on the wrong side was his intelligence and career off the field. He was a highly successful barrister, which made him scary – a Jekyll and Hyde type who could flick the switch and become someone else once he crossed the white line.

The big prop earned immediate notoriety in New Zealand when he and young Auckland lock Alan Craig were ambling away from a lineout exchanging the usual pleasantries expected from tight forwards. Without much warning, Finnane landed a massive punch on Craig.

It was for a similar but more potent punch in 1978 that Finnane penned his name into the history books. In a test against Wales he clobbered an unsuspecting Graham Price, breaking the Welsh tighthead's jaw. 'I still get asked about that incident so often, especially every time Wales play Australia,' said Price in 2011. 'It was very early in the game, before we'd really got warmed up, and I got caught by the shot. I don't think that he set out to do the damage he did, he was just trying to intimidate me.

'But he caught me coming out of a scrum with my jaw at its most vulnerable – open and gasping for air – and the photos obviously went around the world.'

### 4  Gérard Cholley (France)

Mention the name Gérard Cholley to any player who encountered him in the 1970s and they smile now. They didn't back then, as Cholley was off-the-scale nuts. He had been a paratrooper, and the French military special forces aren't particularly keen on rational types. Their recruit of choice is hard-wired to prevent them from weighing up the pros and cons of most situations. They simply act on instinct, which usually ends in blood flowing followed by death.

That training stayed with Cholley throughout his career. With hands the size of plates, he left a trail of carnage wherever he went, and in one game against Scotland the 130 kg prop put four men away – one after the other, bang, bang, bang, bang, down they went. That was the way Cholley did things; he was a prop who saw his role not so much as an enforcer but as an eliminator.

Long before Sonny Bill Williams, Cholley mixed rugby with

boxing and enjoyed a legitimate career as a recognised pugilist before he retired in 1979 bringing relief around the globe. He hasn't retained much interest in rugby, claiming it has lost its way – that it has gone soft: 'There is no fear in rugby any more,' he lamented.

## 3 Bees Roux (South Africa)

Bees Roux was an aggressive and at times sparky prop with the Cheetahs and then the Bulls, whom he joined in 2009. Naturally he was expected to be aggressive and feisty as part of his role, but he certainly wasn't expected to be pleading guilty to murder charges in October 2011.

He was able to avoid going to jail on the condition he paid the widow of Metro police officer Sergeant Ntshimane Johannes Mogale, whom he killed, R750,000 and that he was not convicted again of a violent crime.

The fact he avoided jail or that there were extenuating circumstances behind the murder should not really hide the fact that Roux was an out-and-out psycho. He had been driving home – under the influence of alcohol – when he was pulled over by Mogale. Roux alleged in court that Mogale then demanded the PIN number to his bank card and asked to be driven to a location the Bulls prop didn't know.

Aware things were not as they should be, Roux decided to launch himself at the police officer. 'I realise that I should have stopped any further assault on the deceased when he landed on the road outside the car,' said Roux. 'I was in a state of agitation and turmoil as a result of the incident, the likes of which I'd never experienced before. I proceeded to assault the deceased where he was prone on the ground by hitting him with clenched fists.'

## 2 Armand Vaquerin (France)

Armand Vaquerin is the most decorated player in French history, having won 10 Top 14 titles in the 1970s. He is, however, more famous for being psychotic on the rugby field and for ending his own life at just 42 in a game of Russian roulette. He played for the once mighty Béziers club in the Languedoc region of France, a club with a reputation for breeding hard men – real nutters who didn't hold back. He won his first title in 1970, and amassed 26 French caps before retiring in 1984.

At that stage he probably didn't qualify as a bona fide psycho; he was a touch unhinged and violent, but in comparison with some of his team-mates he was only in the middle range. It was post-playing when his loose wiring became a problem. Without that release every weekend he was perpetually looking for ways to encounter danger, which partially explains why in 1993 he walked into a bar in Béziers – le Cardiff – that he partially owned, carrying a pistol.

Vaquerin was keen to play Russian roulette, and to drum up interest offered to start. Sadly, the one bullet in the gun happened to be in the relevant chamber and he blew his own brain across the bar.

### 1 Marc Cécillon (France)

To be considered the biggest psycho in all of France really does take effort and some spectacularly bad judgement. Marc Cécillon can rest easy. His title as King of the Crazies is likely to be his for life.

The strange thing about Cécillon was that no one really picked him as a total head-case. A hulking loose forward in his day, he won 46 caps (was even captain five times) between 1988 and 1995. He was aggressive but never dirty or wild. But once he retired, his life spiralled out of control.

Alcohol was the root cause of his inexorable descent towards a 14-year jail sentence for murdering his wife. 'I fell into alcoholism whilst being totally wrapped up in my own little bubble,' he told the court during his wife's murder trial. 'I exploded without knowing why.'

Like a few others, he had nothing to fill the void once he retired, which is why he turned to booze. And it was through consuming enormous amounts of it that he ended up being woken by the police on the morning of 8 August 2004 to be arrested. He had no recollection of the preceding evening, but the court was told that

Cécillon shot his wife five times at point-blank range during a garden party in the town of Saint-Savin on 7 August 2004.

He was reported to have arrived at the party drunk and slapped the hostess for no apparent reason before being asked to leave. Mrs Cécillon refused to leave with him. He went home and returned shortly afterwards, pulled out a Magnum handgun and shot her in the presence of about 60 witnesses.

'I wanted my wife to come back with me. I wanted the two of us to leave together,' he said in court. 'Why did I shoot? It is a question I shall ask myself all my life. I didn't plan anything. I wish I could understand.'

# PART 8

# Highs and Lows

---

## 10 iconic moments

---

### 10 Paul Thorburn's monster penalty 1986

Scotland were threatening to record a rare away win against Wales in 1986. The Scots, full of new faces, had scored three tries and were playing a high-tempo game that the Welsh were struggling to contain.

It was the boot of fullback Peter Thorburn that was keeping Wales in the game. He landed his fourth penalty to push Wales 16–15 ahead with 10 minutes remaining. From the kick-off, Scotland flanker Finlay Calder caught Welsh fly-half Jonathan Davies late, and a penalty was awarded on the 10-metre line.

The BBC's legendary commentator Bill McLaren was flabbergasted. 'You won't believe this but that is the Welsh 10-metre line and Paul

Thorburn is going to attempt a goal,' he said. 'It is miles to those goal-posts. He is of course a big goal-kicker. He scored 438 points last season for Neath, but this would be a monster.'

It was in fact measured at 62 metres – the longest kick ever recorded. 'I had told [captain] David Pickering I would have a go and knew that if I missed it would still leave play in the Scotland half,' Thorburn said a few years later. 'I probably kicked more important goals, but that was my longest. There was an element of hit and hope about it, but I remember I gave it a real hoof.'

That led McLaren to commentate thus: 'What a belt he's given it ... that is amazing. I have seen all the great goal-kickers in the world in the last decade but I have never seen anything like this.'

The ball had scraped over, breaking Scottish hearts. They knew then it was not going to be their day and Wales won 22–15.

## 9 Cyril Brownlie sent off, 1925

Cyril Brownlie was the eldest of three Hawke's Bay brothers who played for the All Blacks. While younger brother Maurice was recognised as much the better player, it is Cyril who made the greater historic footprint on account of being the first man to ever be sent off in a test match.

Brownlie was at lock for the All Blacks in their 1925 encounter with England at Twickenham, and received his marching orders early in the game after a skirmish that didn't seem by all accounts to be overly dramatic. But Welsh referee Albert Freethy saw it differently and ordered Brownlie off. The disgrace was enormous – so bad that Prince Edward (later to become Edward VIII) tried to intervene to have the New Zealander returned to the field.

The royal intervention was in vain, and Brownlie trudging off the field has become one of the iconic photos of New Zealand rugby.

## 8 Jeremy Guscott's winning drop goal, 1997

The British & Irish Lions surprised everyone with the style of rugby they played throughout their tour of South Africa in 1997. They were all about ball in hand, trying to run the bigger South Africans off their feet.

It was a major twist to the plot, especially when a small but mobile Lions pack was able to dominate the first test of the series and put the Lions 1–0 up. The second test in Durban was proving an altogether tougher game for the visitors. They were clinging on thanks to the boot of Neil Jenkins, whose five penalties cancelled out the Springboks' three tries. The game would have been all over if the Boks had not missed an incredible nine kicks at goal.

They knew they had ridden their luck to be sitting at 15–all, but they mustered one last huge effort to turn over the ball deep inside their territory and hack it downfield. From the ensuing lineout on the Boks' 22, fly-half Gregor Townsend crashed another five metres to leave the Lions eight metres short. Scrum-half Matt Dawson fired the ball back to Jeremy Guscott, who struck the sweetest drop goal to win the test and the series.

'It is used in some of the advertising for this current Lions tour, but every time I see it [the drop goal], I can't remember myself being there and slotting it over,' Guscott said when the Lions returned to South Africa in 2009. 'After the final whistle, even though I was jumping up and down and giving it the 2–0 victory sign, back in the dressing room all I could think about was, What if I had missed?'

## 7 Peter Jones says buggered, 1956

The All Blacks had travelled to South Africa in 1949 and suffered the humiliation of losing the test series 4–0. It was a black year in the All Black annals, so when the Boks came to New Zealand in 1956 there was massive desire for revenge. The country was hooked by a tour against the old enemy and it lived up to the hype.

The All Blacks won the first test 10–6 at Carisbrook but were then defeated 8–3 in Wellington in what is deemed to be one of the most brutal encounters ever played.

National interest in the tour was at unprecedented levels, particularly given the physical pounding meted out to All Black prop Tiny White in that second test.

The famously tough Kevin Skinner was recalled from retirement to deal to the Boks in the third – which he did – in a game that also saw Don Clarke make his debut and go on to become one of the great All Blacks.

That third test was secured 17–10, and the fourth was a lung-bursting epic that saw the All Backs prevail 11–5 in a classic contest. The defining try was scored by All Black No 8 Peter Jones, who created a lifetime of controversy when he was interviewed by radio straight after the game and famously said: 'I am absolutely buggered.'

New Zealand had a landmark quote – one that would eventually lead to the world's largest car manufacturer arguing in court that the word 'bugger' was acceptable to use in advertising.

## 6 Italy's flying start, 2000

Italy had campaigned for a decade to be included in the Five Nations. It was a battle for the Italians to persuade the notoriously risk-averse Home Unions and France to make any changes to their beloved tournament, especially one as bold as allowing a new entrant.

When Italy joined in 2000 they needed to make a dramatic statement, which they did when they opened their campaign with a 34–20 victory against the Scots. A masterful performance by Italy's Argentinean-born fly-half Diego Domínguez, who scored all 34 points, kept the doubters quiet.

The 250-to-one rank outsiders had made an indelible impression, and the scenes of euphoria in Rome were classic. 'I feel sorry for the Scots that they had to face us first,' said an elated Italian coach Brad Johnstone. 'We'd worked on our basics: the scrum, second-phase rucking and mauling and defence. It's like putting down the foundation for a house before you build the walls.'

## 5 All Blacks win a series in South Africa, 1996

The mighty All Blacks had achieved almost everything by the end of 1995. There was one thing, however, that they had never been able to do: they had never won a test series in South Africa.

Great players and great teams had all travelled in hope, won single tests over the years, but never a series. It was a source of great pain for the world's best rugby nation. The transition to professionalism in 1996 saw an oddity in the scheduling, where the All Blacks had a long-arranged three-test tour of the Republic. They also had to play a pre-test in South Africa as part of the newly created Tri Nations.

The All Blacks won the Tri Nations encounter in Cape Town 29–18 and then went to Durban where they won the first official test of the series 23–19. The second test in Pretoria was an epic.

The Boks came out roaring and ferocious. The All Blacks were under siege for the first half-hour before they were able to grind their way back on top and open the game up. They began to play flowing and enterprising rugby to lead 33–26 with five minutes remaining. The Boks came at them hard but the All Blacks held on, and when the final whistle blew, hard men like captain Sean Fitzpatrick collapsed to their knees and openly wept.

'We felt the sheer intensity of it,' Fitzpatrick told the *New Zealand Herald*. 'That game in Pretoria was the most unbelievable game. In the last two minutes we had a lineout. We went running across one side of the field to the other and I ran past [All Black prop] Olo Brown who was heaving with his throat burning. I said, "Come on mate we've got a minute to go, let's do it." Don Clarke was standing in the tunnel and he put his arm around me with tears running down his face. He said, "Sean, thank you so much for doing something so many All Black teams tried to do in the past." '

## 4  Ireland win the Grand Slam, 2009

Ireland had their golden generation of players throughout the first decade of the new millennium, but for all their talent, they were still light on actual achievement. There had been three Triple Crowns, but a Grand Slam – the true sign of greatness – proved elusive.

Not since 1948 had the Irish enjoyed a Grand Slam, and they thought the opportunity had been blown again in Cardiff in 2009 when Welsh fly-half Stephen Jones dropped a goal with four minutes remaining. Wales led 15–14 – surely that was it? That was until the composed Irish played their way deep into Welsh territory and fly-half Ronan O'Gara, as if he was under no pressure, slotted an equally impressive field goal.

The drama didn't end there, though. Ireland transgressed at a breakdown to concede a penalty just inside their half. It would be the last act of the game, but Jones didn't have the distance to land the goal and the Irish had their moment.

'It's fantastic,' said an ecstatic Ireland captain Brian O'Driscoll. 'It feels like reward for a lot of hard work over a lot of years. We have had some good times and some not so good times. This is a great time.'

## 3  Scott Gibbs' Wembley try, 1999

Wales' Cardiff Arms Park was being rebuilt for the World Cup, which is why they had to play their Five Nations games at Wembley in London throughout the 1999 Five Nations. As fate would have it, they would play England on the final day with the English knowing victory would secure a Grand Slam.

It was unprecedented – Wales playing a home game against England in the English capital. Unfortunately the Welsh players didn't respond well to the occasion. They leaked three tries and were trailing 31–25 with eight minutes remaining. It was all but over, especially when England had a kickable penalty. But they chose to go for the try, lost the ball at the lineout and were then penalised. Wales cleared, and from a lineout inside England's territory won it clean off the top. The ball was moved to inside centre Scott Gibbs, who smashed through a gaping hole in the midfield.

'I can remember busting through and thinking what the hell do I do now?' he would later recall. What he did was skip past the next three defenders and score the most incredible try that brought the Welsh to one point behind. 'I crossed the line and for a split second I thought I am sure we have won this game,' Gibbs continued. 'The hard work for me had been done, but all the pressure was now on Neil Jenkins.'

The Welsh fly-half banged over the conversion and the crowd

were delirious. Wales had won 32–31 with the best last-ditch play in modern rugby.

## 2 Errol Tobias selected for the Springboks, 1981

The notion that a black man would one day play for the Springboks was too hard for many to comprehend. The Boks were the very symbol of South Africa's apartheid system – rugby was the chosen game of the white man, which is why it was largely hated by the black community. There was also the problem of the apartheid system making it impossible for blacks to play with whites.

But in 1981 Springbok coach Nellie Schmidt decided he was going to take the revolutionary step of picking Errol Tobias, a classy fly-half who had a vast range of skills. Tobias made his debut on 30 May 1981 and then toured New Zealand later in the year. It was an incredible sight – a black man in the Springboks at a time when political turmoil was at its peak.

'Of course there were people who thought that a black man should not be playing for the Springboks,' Tobias said to the BBC in 2003. 'I knew there were people who were saying that, but I decided that I was going to show South African people that all men are born equal. I wanted to show them that colour doesn't matter – if you have got the skills, then you should play for your country.'

There were just as many in his township who were angry that he was representing the Springboks at a time when the oppression of the regime was getting worse. 'Some people reacted furiously to my selection,' he said. 'They felt that the apartheid laws should be removed before I played for South Africa, but from a sports point of view – I was no politician. We had no say in politics, we didn't even have a vote, so all I knew at that stage was to play rugby.'

## 1 Gareth Edwards' try against the All Blacks, 1973

Even now the try by Gareth Edwards playing for the Barbarians against the All Blacks in 1973 is regularly judged the best scored. There are two generations who can spout, almost verbatim, the commentary by Cliff Morgan, and countless hours have been spent re-enacting events which began with a promising attack for the All Blacks.

'Kirkpatrick to Williams,' began Morgan. 'This is great stuff. Phil Bennett covering, chased by Alistair Scown. Brilliant! Oh, that's brilliant! John Williams, Bryan Williams, Pullin, John Dawes. Great dummy! David, Tom David, the half-way line. Brilliant by Quinnell.'

As everyone knows, at this point the Welsh scrum-half storms into play – taking the last pass to blast over in the corner of Cardiff Arms Park. 'This is Gareth Edwards,' screams Morgan. 'A dramatic start. What a score! Oh that fellow Edwards.'

The Barbarians won the game 23–11, and Edwards has recounted that moment almost as many times as everyone else. 'I have never run so fast on a rugby pitch,' Edwards told the BBC. 'Earlier in the movement I had been tracking back and then suddenly play came sweeping past me so I had to start sprinting flat-out just to offer some support. I was absolutely at full pelt when I called to Derek. The All Blacks were expecting a pass to John Bevan, which was another thing which worked in our favour.'

# 10 tragedies

Rugby has had its fair share of tragedies. Here are just a few of them – in no particular order, for obvious reasons.

## 1 Nicky Allen (New Zealand)

However little consolation it may be, there was at least one good thing to stem from the premature death of Nicky Allen – head injuries incurred on the field were at least taken more seriously. Allen was a gifted fly-half who was good enough to play for the All Blacks as a 21-year-old. He had two tests under his belt, having broken into the side in 1980.

He was exactly the sort of player the All Blacks were after: talented but brave; instinctive yet capable of following patterns. He had everything to be a great No 10, but it all ended when he was just 26. The period after his debut was marred by a run of nasty injuries. In 1984, just as it looked like he was finally maturing into the world-class talent many thought he'd be, he died after incurring a serious head injury in a Sydney club game.

The rigorous checks and drills that players now have to endure after suffering head-knocks are partly attributable to Allen. His brother Rob has been an occasionally vociferous advocate for better procedures. In 2004 he wrote to the New Zealand and Australian Rugby Unions to try to raise awareness about the dangers of head injuries in the sport. 'There's no vendetta here to rugby, but we feel like the problem is too often swept under the carpet and players are not really being looked after properly,' Allen said. 'This isn't us causing trouble, but obviously we are sensitised to concussion since Nick's death'

## 2 Matt Hampson (England)

No one has been able to deal with adversity quite like Matt Hampson. He has become one of rugby's most inspirational figures despite being paralysed in March 2005.

Well on his way to an England jersey, Hampson was a beast of a tight-head prop with the physique and attitude to make it in the test arena. He was training with the England Under-21 team when a scrum collapsed. He took the entire weight of the collapse on his neck, and it's likely he would have died there and then were it not for the fact that test referee Tony Spreadbury was helping the squad with their technical engagement and he happened to be a trained paramedic.

Hampson was classed as C4/5 tetraplegic, meaning he could not feel or move below the level of his injury. He requires a team of 10 people to look after him, and someone has to be alert all night as he is connected to a ventilator to sleep. His daily life is a 24-hour battle. Even brushing his teeth is an ordeal of epic proportions, yet he hasn't wallowed in the self-pity that could have arisen thinking about the life that was his until that tragic day in 2005.

He told the *Daily Telegraph* in 2011 that despite the seriousness of the accident, he never fully comprehended just what state he was in. 'Nobody ever tells you. Nobody says you're never going to walk again, or you're going to be paralysed, or you'll be on a ventilator. But if I'd been told, that would have stunted my progress.'

## 3 Aaron Hopa (New Zealand)

A late convert to rugby – only taking it up in secondary school – Aaron Hopa was a touch freakish in how far he managed to progress. Rugby wasn't his game until his late teens, yet he played with a natural athleticism and aggression. By 1995 he was beginning to make his mark with the Waikato side but wouldn't actually command a regular place with them or the Chiefs until 1997. It says much about his quality that at the end of what could be fairly described as his first full season as a professional, he made the All Blacks.

Coach John Hart saw Hopa as a versatile offering – capable of playing both at loose forward and at lock – with the ability to get around the field and make his presence felt at the set-piece and collision. While he played only a minor role on that tour, there was a sense of Hopa being on the track towards fulfilling his potential when his life was cruelly ended.

Hopa drowned in a diving accident in December 1998. He was with many of his Waikato team-mates when the tragedy occurred, and the grief was felt throughout the region. He was just 27.

'We were not aware of how many lives Aaron touched,' a spokesperson for the family told the *New Zealand Herald*. 'To the family, Aaron was always a wonderful person, son and brother, but the support has truly shown that Aaron was far more than that. He was a sportsman, a mentor, an idol, a role model, a friend.'

## 4 Prince Obolensky (England)

There haven't been many Russians who have represented England, and certainly none as memorable as Prince Alexander Sergeevich Obolensky. A member of the Rurik dynasty, born in St Petersburg in 1916, the young prince was educated in England. He had earned two Oxford Blues for rugby and had joined the Leicester club, but his selection for England in 1936 still caused a major controversy.

Citizenship would be granted later that year, but by then no one cared that he wasn't English. He scored two brilliant individual tries on debut to help England beat the All Blacks 13–0.

His performance was sublime and had the reporter for the *Morning Post* in a lather: 'Runners we have seen before but never such a runner with such an innate idea of where to go and how to get there. His [Obolensky's] double swerve to gain his first try was remarkable enough, but the extraordinary turn-in and diagonal right to left run which won him his second and which drew forth that great Twickenham rarity, a double roar of applause, will never be forgotten by anybody who saw it.'

Obolensky joined the RAF at the outbreak of World War II and on 29 March 1940 – the day after he was named in the England squad to play Wales – he was killed when his Hurricane Mark 1 crashed on landing during a training drill. He was 24.

## 5 Yves Frantz Loys Marie Le Pelley du Manoir (France)

Yves Frantz Loys Marie Le Pelley du Manoir, who was thankfully prepared to be known as Yves du Manoir, may have been born into an aristocratic family but he played rugby like he was a man of the people.

He was only 20 when he won his first cap for France on the wing in 1925 against Ireland. Although the French lost, the crowd at Colombes instantly fell in love with du Manoir's swashbuckling style of play and began chanting his name (the shortened version, obviously). He was man of the match and would play seven more tests, even being named as captain for the game against Scotland in 1927.

He was due to play the Scots again in 1928 but declined as he had to sit an exam that would enable him to qualify as a military pilot. But the plane taking him to his exam crashed shortly after take-off and he was killed. His Paris club – Racing Métro – named their stadium after him and it still takes his name.

## 6 Dan James (England)

No one will ever be able to fully comprehend the pain and misery Dan James must have felt, or the agony of his parents who took him to Switzerland when he was just 23 so he could undergo an assisted suicide. James was a former England schoolboy international who was left paralysed from the chest down after a scrum collapsed during a training session with the Nuneaton Club in Warwickshire.

His decision to take his own life sparked fierce public debate – while he was severely paralysed by the incident, James wasn't terminally ill. His parents were questioned by the police on their role in assisting him to travel to the clinic.

Long-serving secretary of the Nuneaton club, Maggie Mander, spoke to the *Daily Telegraph* in October 2008 a few days after James' death. 'I think it is possibly one of the worst things that has ever happened to our club and it is still very raw for a lot of us,' she said. 'It was such a terribly tragic accident and my heart goes out to his family. Dan was an amazing character and a typical student with long blond hair, always wearing his flip-flops whatever the weather. He was always one of the first to get up on the coach after a game and get everyone singing.'

## 7  Solly Tyibilika (South Africa)

As a Springbok flanker, Solly Tyibilika had been in some tough places. That did little to prepare him for the events of 13 November 2011. The 32-year-old Tyibilika, who had played for the Boks and Sharks, and was still playing amateur club football in 2011, was in a Cape Town bar on the day in question. He was shot several times at close range in a gangland-style execution that afternoon. A witness told the *Daily Voice* newspaper that his killers walked calmly up behind the flanker and ordered other patrons to move out of the way before blasting him with a hail of bullets.

The man, who did not give his name, said: 'One of them came to me and told me to move to the side. He said he wasn't here to shoot me, but Solly who was sitting behind me. I ran and went under the table and then I heard them shooting too many rounds to count. This was not a robbery because they left all the other patrons alive and killed him. And Solly clearly didn't expect it because he didn't show any sign of fear while sitting there.'

Tyibilika won eight caps between 2004 and 2006 and played for the Sharks against the British & Irish Lions in 2009. South African Rugby Union president Oregan Hoskins said: 'Solly was a trailblazer among black African Springboks and to lose him so suddenly and in this brutal manner is very distressing. His emergence was a demonstration of what can be achieved when talent is combined with opportunity in what is always a very competitive position in Springbok rugby.'

## 8 Shawn MacKay (Australia)

The Brumbies squad were shattered by the death of team-mate Shawn MacKay in April 2009. The Australian side had played the Sharks in Durban and some of the team, including the 26-year-old MacKay who was recognised as a talent at both XVs and Sevens where he had been a regular on the international circuit since 2004, had headed out for a few drinks.

MacKay was walking back to the team hotel at 4.30 am when he was hit by a vehicle that was a privately contracted emergency response unit. He suffered a cervical spinal fracture and dislocation, a fractured skull as well as a broken leg and multiple facial fractures. He was placed in a coma and, despite the seriousness of his condition, had responded favourably to the extent there was some hope he might recover.

But shortly before the Brumbies played the Cheetahs in Bloemfontein six days after he was injured, MacKay died. 'After his surgery, Shawn contracted an infection in his bloodstream,' said Brumbies chief executive Andrew Fagan. 'He deteriorated rapidly and suffered a cardiac arrest from which he didn't recover. It's devastating news for his family and for all of the Brumbies community. Our thoughts and those of the players are with his family at this most difficult time.'

## 9 Max Brito (Ivory Coast)

The Ivory Coast were the surprise package at the 1995 World Cup, having qualified for the first and, as it has turned out, only time in their history. While they predictably suffered major defeats to France and Scotland, they battled hard to only lose 29–11 to Tonga in their final game.

But that test was marred by the serious neck injury Ivory Coast wing Max Brito endured after just three minutes. He was hit hard in a tackle by Inoke Afeaki and then pinned awkwardly when players from both sides piled on top of him scrambling for the ball. Two of his vertebrae were shattered and the 24-year-old was left quadriplegic.

If that wasn't tragedy enough, he would reveal to *Le Monde* newspaper 12 years later that his life was virtually without hope. His wife had left him and his teenage sons barely spoke to him and he was largely bed-ridden. 'It is now 12 years since I have been in this state,' he said. 'I have come to the end of my tether. If one day I fall seriously ill, and if I have the strength and courage to take my own life, then I will do it. This bloody handicap. It's my curse. It kills me and I will never accept it. I can't live with it and it's going to be with me for the rest of my life.'

## 10 Nick Duncombe (England)

The randomness and suddenness of Nick Duncombe's death was heartbreaking for all those who knew him. The 21-year-old was one of the most promising scrum-halves England had produced in years, and having won two caps in 2002 after just three games of professional rugby, he was expected to win many more.

Relatively small even for a halfback, Duncombe made up for a lack of stature with his speed, agility and bullet pass. He had been struggling with a hamstring injury in the early part of 2003, so he and fellow injured Harlequin, fullback Nathan Williams, headed to Lanzarote for a mid-season break. Assuming his hamstring came right, Duncombe was in line for a Six Nations recall on his return. But he came home in a coffin.

He complained of a sore throat mid-morning on 13 February. Later that night he woke Williams up to tell him he was feeling really unwell and his friend took him to hospital. Duncombe died mid-afternoon on 14 February from a virus.

'Nick was one of our brightest and most talented players in the game,' said England coach at the time Clive Woodward. 'The two caps he gained with England last year would have been, I believe, the beginning of a long international career, which had already started so well with some superb performances for the England Under-19 and Sevens teams.

'Nick was hugely popular with the squad and at Harlequins, and his attitude to the game was outstanding. I'm sure that all supporters and players will share the loss of one of rugby's brightest stars.'

# 10 major surprises

## 10 Teddy bear's picnic

In 2006 the New South Wales Waratahs loved nothing better than playing practical jokes on one another. Stephen Hoiles managed to persuade inside back Shaun Berne to pose for what he thought was a photo shoot for a men's health magazine. The photographers were not, however, from a magazine; they were just mates of Hoiles and they could barely keep straight faces as they persuaded Berne to pose with no top cuddling his favourite teddy bear.

After a particularly poor training session in Dunedin, Waratahs coach Ewen McKenzie ordered the squad into the team room to watch a video about how real men trained. The video was actually of Berne's photo shoot with the soundtrack 'I'm too Sexy' overlaid. Berne is said to have nearly died from the shock, but got his revenge by placing a paddling pool with goldfish into Hoiles' apartment.

'We managed to get him to pose for about 120 photos in a few different outfits – in a tight vest, with his shirt unbuttoned, modelling ties and so on,' revealed Hoiles a year later. 'We got it all on video, put a few songs in the background and showed it to the team. He wanted revenge, but I said if he went too far I'd release the photos to the media.'

## 9 London's lady boy

Since cracking the Wasps' first team as a precociously talented teenager, Danny Cipriani has been a favourite subject of the British tabloid media. He brought much of that upon himself with his love of late nights and celebrity bedroom conquests. In 2007 he made the front page of the nation's favourite red-top, the *News of the World*, when it was revealed he had been dating one of the so-called Cheeky

Girls – a minor pop sensation from Romania topping the charts at the time.

Cipriani earned the immediate respect of his senior team-mates, who were intrigued and a little envious of the young playboy in their midst. They were just as intrigued and more than a little surprised to read the following week in the same organ that he had been unfaithful to the lovely Monica Irimia of the Cheeky Girls with the equally lovely Larissa Summers, a model of some repute.

Their surprise was tiny in comparison with Cipriani's as the paper revealed that Summers had actually started life as Darren Pratt.

Wasps team-mate Simon Shaw wrote in his column for the *Daily Mail*: 'This has been a very unusual week for London Wasps. It started on Sunday morning when texts started arriving on my mobile urging me to buy a certain tabloid newspaper. I have to admit that I was intending to buy that paper anyway following the previous Sunday's story about my team-mate Danny Cipriani and a "liaison" he was reported to have had with Miss Larissa Summers. As a result of the latest revelations, Danny – or to give him his new name, Danny Cipriani Who Slept With A Man – was responsible for the biggest turnout ever for a Wasps recovery session on a Sunday after a match.'

## 8 Brotherly love

Scotland and British & Irish Lion lock Gordon Brown idolised his big brother Peter and longed to play a test with him. Gordon would stand in the crowd at Murrayfield and dream that one day he'd be out there, playing in the same team as the man he said was his hero.

Peter was first capped in 1964, and by the time Gordon was piquing the interest of the national selectors, Peter was on the outer. Gordon played the Five Nations in 1970 while Peter remained out of favour. A few days before Scotland played Wales in Cardiff in 1970, Gordon received a phone call. 'I usually got a phone call from a press guy before a match who would tell me the team and, sure enough, before the match against Wales in Cardiff the phone rang,' Gordon told *The Scotsman* shortly before he died.

'It wasn't the journalist, it was Peter. "Great news," he said, "I'm back in the team."

' "Who's out?"

' "You are," replied Peter.

'It was the only time in my life I doubted his parentage,' continued Gordon. 'But then he tore a calf muscle just before half-time and the physio, who happened to be our dad, waved the towel as a sign to the selectors for a replacement and I ran on as sub for my big brother.'

## 7 The only gay in the village

Gareth Thomas was one of the most celebrated figures in Welsh rugby, having won 100 caps and having captained his country and also the British & Irish Lions. He was a tough player, capable at wing, centre and fullback and had earned a reputation as a bloke who could look after himself. An assault charge from his time with Toulouse was testament to that.

Universally known as 'Alfie', Thomas had married his teenage sweetheart in 2001. They divorced in 2007, their marriage stretched by their failure to have a child. It was, as it would be revealed two years later, also stretched by the fact that Thomas was a homosexual. Having kept his sexuality a secret for his entire career, the pain of doing so was tearing Thomas apart, so in December 2009 he decided to tell the truth.

'It is the toughest, most macho of male sports, and with that comes an image,' Thomas said. 'In many ways, it is barbaric, and I could never have come out without first establishing myself and earning respect as a player. Rugby was my passion, my whole life, and I wasn't prepared to risk losing everything I loved. I just happen to be gay. It's irrelevant. What I choose to do when I close the door at home has nothing to do with what I have achieved in rugby.'

## 6 Bulldogs bitten

In July 2008 Sonny Bill Williams was locked into a five-year contract with the NRL club the Canterbury Bulldogs. He signed the contract in 2007, pushing his salary to $500,000 a year, and declaring at the time that he wanted 'to be a Bulldog for life'.

So it was a surprise in the extreme to his club that he was spotted at Sydney Airport leaving the country in 2008 just a couple of days before a critical game. There had been no prior warning – Williams just took off without a word, clearly in breach of his contract.

Bulldogs chief executive Todd Greenberg said: 'I've had QCs look at his contract and there is absolutely no get-out clause. I'm shocked that he's left because I saw him at 7.30 this morning.'

But Williams was unrepentant. He was off to France to play rugby for Toulon and to hell with the consequences. It was a massive defection and no one saw it coming. Williams was banned from the NRL for five years, but was free to play rugby. He would later justify it by saying: 'If a lawyer, if a teacher, if a bus driver, if they're on $40,000, and they get offered a lot more to go somewhere else, what do you think they're going to do?' Williams told the *Footy Show*.

'Are they going to change bus companies? Or are they going to sit there and say, "All these people want me to stay here because I'm the best bus driver in the jurisdiction." It's just common sense. What I've done, it's shown it's just not about me, it's about the boys getting a fair go, you know what I mean?'

## 5   Is this seat taken?

Welsh captain Sam Warburton made headlines for all the wrong reasons at the 2011 World Cup when he was sent off after 17 minutes for what was deemed to be a dangerous tackle on French wing Vincent Clerc. It was an act that pretty much ruined his side's chances of making the final.

He stayed on in Auckland to do media work and to attend the IRB annual awards. He was booked on a flight out of Auckland that would take him first to Brisbane, then to London. He was the last man on the plane, threw his bag in the overhead locker and flopped in his seat. When he turned to the passenger next to him he got the fright of his life – it was Clerc.

'It was unbelievable,' Warburton told the *Independent*. 'There must have been 10 flights out of Auckland that day but not only was I on the same plane as the French boys, but I was next to him.

'Vincent and I just looked at each other for a second and I thought, This could be really awkward. But we shook hands and he asked me for a massage, which really broke the ice. That was the only time we mentioned the tackle. We just chatted about stuff in general, he's a good guy.'

## 4 The agony of choice

Former Northampton fly-half John Steele was appointed chief executive of the Rugby Football Union in the latter half of 2010. His first task was to review the organisation and restructure the senior management posts.

He gained board approval to create the new post of performance director. When the role was originally advertised, the description was clear – the new appointment would be head of the playing structure; even the England national coach would have to report to the performance director. Three candidates were on the shortlist and due to be interviewed when Steele decided to change the job description and cancel the scheduled interviews. The performance director would no longer have any jurisdiction over the national team.

The change was agreed at a board meeting on 27 April 2011, only for the board to then call an emergency meeting the next day and change it back to the original description. When it no longer offered the national team component, the lead candidate – former England coach Sir Clive Woodward – withdrew his application. Even when it was changed back, Woodward wouldn't change his mind. There was enormous media surprise at such indecision, but Steele remained confident in late May that he would survive the scandal.

'It has been a challenging couple of weeks, but what is pleasing is that we have got a board who are united behind a way forward,' Steele told the *Daily Telegraph* on 31 May.

Steele was sacked on 10 June when another emergency board meeting decided they had lost confidence in him.

## 3 Don't wait up

The All Blacks were in turmoil in 1998. They lost an unprecedented five tests in a row and the country was in shock. The All Blacks had been awful and the public mood was volatile. Incumbent coach John Hart was under pressure to stand down or be sacked.

The New Zealand Rugby Union decided to put the job up for tender and interviewed both Hart and Blues coach Graham Henry. The latter had an impeccable record having coached Auckland to several provincial titles and the Blues to the first two Super 12 titles and to the final in 1998.

But while Henry was the favourite, the board retained Hart. A few days later, Henry called a press conference in Auckland and famously said: 'I am going to Wales and I am going tonight.'

He'd agreed in the wake of his rejection to take over as the head coach of the Welsh national team, and the NZRU board were so thrown by this surprise announcement that they instigated what became known as the 'Henry Clause': no one in future who coached a foreign national team would be eligible to coach the All Blacks.

The clause was revoked a few years later, leading Henry to say: 'They [NZRU] have learned over time. They did not make the right decision when they introduced the Henry Clause, but they are looking at things differently now with hindsight.'

## 2 Hammer time

Mark Hammett was appointed coach of the Hurricanes for the 2011 season. He arrived from the Crusaders where he had been assistant for five years and was determined to change the culture at his new franchise.

The Hurricanes had been New Zealand's most consistent underachiever – they had played in a final and four semi-finals, but it was considered a poor return. Hammett was convinced that the Hurricanes needed stronger leadership.

He failed to connect with his new players and the Hurricanes started the season poorly and got worse. They were a rabble and struggling near the foot of the table when Hammett dropped a bombshell. He had decided to sack star player Ma'a Nonu and captain Andrew Hore. Both men were senior All Blacks and had played more than 100 games for the Hurricanes. But Hammett had decided he didn't want them around in 2012 and shocked the country when he told them to move on.

Hurricanes chief executive James Te Puni tried to justify the decision to the *Dominion Post*. 'He's [Nonu] clearly a fantastic player and, ironically, it's been noted he's playing very, very well in the last couple of weeks. Our view though is we've got a bunch of other midfielders who are coming through.'

It seemed like a crazy decision at the time – and even crazier when Nonu played a key role in helping the All Blacks win the World Cup and was deservedly shortlisted as an IRB Player of the Year.

## 1 The big coke bust

Matt Stevens was a promising international prop in the English team, having made his debut in 2003. Born in South Africa, he was not your typical front-row forward obsessed with beer and violence. He delivered his first major surprise in 2006 when he showed extraordinary ability as a singer. The near 120 kg lug could carry a tune and made the final of the TV show *X-Factor: Battle of the Stars*.

However, a much bigger surprise would follow in 2009 when Stevens tested positive for cocaine and was subsequently banned for two years. He was seen as the long-term successor to incumbent tight-head Phil Vickery and the rugby world was at Stevens' feet. He had fame, celebrity and so much potential – and he'd just about thrown it all away. 'I was tested for a prohibited substance but it's not performance-enhancing, so you can take what you want from that,' he said on the day news broke of his failed test.

'It's pretty distressing talking about this. When you think about how much time people have put into my career and I have thrown it away. Like any drug problem you don't know it's happening, and then it mounts up and before you know it you have a problem and an illness.'

# 10 scandals

## 10 Sneaky broadcast deal

When the game turned professional at the end of 1995 it was apparent there were suddenly new commercial opportunities. The Rugby Football Union could see that as the biggest fish in the Home Unions, they had more financial clout than their Celtic brothers, and decided to secretly test the broadcast market.

The Home Unions had historically sold the TV rights for the Five Nations (France did their own thing) collectively and split the total pie equally. But England decided, against the express wishes of the Celts, to accept an £87.5m five-year deal from BSkyB to broadcast all their home games.

The Celtic nations were livid and the decision was made to kick England out of the Five Nations, but despite such a threat the RFU were unrepentant and refused to compromise. The English could see that a tournament without them would hold little broadcast appeal. Tony Hallett, the RFU secretary, insisted: 'The RFU is fully committed to the Five Nations. We will continue to speak to the other unions. We are keen to resolve the differences we have. The RFU has no wish to be kicked out of the Five Nations.'

England knew they would always win and be richer in the process, and compromise was eventually reached when they agreed to unscramble the contract so that BSkyB renegotiated a fee for the home games excluding the Five Nations. That allowed England to be part of a collective bid for future tournament rights and they were reinstated in early September.

## 9  World Cup wally

Mike Tindall's flirtatious escapades with a lady who wasn't his wife were actually only the tip of the iceberg, but came to be the epicentre of a disastrous and catastrophic period for England rugby.

The occasional skipper and several team-mates had a night out in New Zealand's Queenstown after England had beaten Argentina at the 2011 World Cup. Video footage was made public of the recently married Tindall cavorting with another woman and the media beat it up. Things escalated when Tindall was economical with the truth to coach Martin Johnson about how much he had drunk and where he had really been. Tindall didn't reveal that he had headed to another bar with the woman, where they were accused by the *Mail on Sunday* of carrying on like canoodling teenagers. Johnson had initially played down the events, but had to admit that Tindall had lied: 'His [Tindall's] recollection on his whereabouts that night was inaccurate and he has issued a statement apologising. He did not mean to mislead anybody,' Johnson said.

England endured a miserable campaign, and Tindall was fined £25,000 when he got home and kicked out of the Elite Player Squad. He was reinstated and the fine reduced by half on appeal, but Johnson decided to resign and the Tindall scandal came to epitomise all that was wrong with the national team.

## 8  Bring back Buck

Even to this day, there is usually someone at an All Black test with a banner that says 'Bring back Buck'. The nation has not made peace with the way the iconic Wayne 'Buck' Shelford was dropped as captain in 1990.

The thunderous No 8 was the perfect leader for the All Blacks. He was popular and committed to an extent no one had ever seen before. Shelford famously played on after having his testicles ripped in a test against France. That kind of commitment won the nation's heart, as did his record – he led the All Blacks to 13 victories and a draw.

It was a glorious period and the nation was dumbstruck when after a 2–0 series defeat of Scotland in 1990, Shelford was dropped. Suspicion remains that some of the senior Auckland players wanted him out to make way for the rising talents of Zinzan Brooke. There was also some talk that the Auckland contingent didn't like the ferocity and intensity Shelford brought to training and life away from the field.

But the mystery has never been solved. The closest Shelford has ever come to offering any insight was in 2010 when he spoke to the *New Zealand Herald* and said it was down to politics – he found out some players were having closed-door meetings about getting rid of him. 'I'm not scared of bloody enforcing my opinion to people,' he told the paper.

## 7　57 old farts

There were only two weeks until the start of the 1995 World Cup and England took the rather serious step of firing long-term captain Will Carling. For such drastic action to be taken, surely Carling must have gone nuts.

What he had actually done was dare to criticise the administration of English rugby. This was the time when the players were professional in every sense except being paid. The sport was on the cusp of revolution – a revolution that would begin in the final weeks of the tournament.

The craggy old boys clinging to power were outraged when Carling was interviewed on TV and said: 'If the game is run properly as a professional game, you do not need 57 old farts running rugby.' His comments referred to the bloated bureaucracy at the RFU and their refusal to move with the times. After seeing the programme, the RFU, led by president Dennis Easby, called an emergency meeting and decided to sack Carling. 'We have decided with regret that Will Carling's captaincy of the England team be terminated forthwith,' they said.

'For an England captain to say that is totally unjustified,' Easby went on to tell the *Daily Mail*. 'It has brought the game into disrepute.

This was a totally unsolicited comment, an insult to people who have done an awful lot of voluntary work.'

The RFU were ridiculed by the English media for their pompous and precious stance, and after Carling issued a grovelling and presumably insincere apology, he was reinstated as captain four days later.

## 6 No angel in Cardiff

Almost 40 years on, and the name Keith Murdoch is still well known in New Zealand. This is a scandal that remains alive and present and will always leave a sense of guilt and distaste among Murdoch's All Black team-mates.

The fearsome prop, who was reputed to have towed his car up the steepest street in Dunedin with his teeth, was on a tour of the UK with the All Blacks in 1972–73. He had scored a try in the 19–16 victory against Wales in Cardiff and was enjoying a few drinks in the Angel Hotel later that night when he assaulted the doorman, punching him in the face.

There were fears within the All Black management that the incident was going to blow up in the media. There was also pressure applied by the Home Unions, who wanted Murdoch sent home – a decision that was then made by All Black team manager Ernie Todd without consultation with the players. The incident had been bad but not catastrophic, and it was a massive over-reaction to send Murdoch home, knowing that he would be humiliated and would probably never play for the All Blacks again.

But when Murdoch's plane bound for Auckland stopped in Darwin, he got off and disappeared into the Australian outback. He's been there ever since, his side of the story untold.

His All Black team-mates bitterly regretted not standing up to management, and in 2002 they made video presentations that they hoped would persuade Murdoch to come back for the tour's thirtieth anniversary celebrations. He never did, prompting lock Andy Haden to say: 'He was let down by the rugby union and they should admit that. If he feels comfortable coming back, then an official union acknowledgement should be made.'

## 5 The non-spear tackle

In the first minute of the first test between the All Blacks and British & Irish Lions in 2005, there appeared to be a rather obvious instance of foul play. All Black captain Tana Umaga and hooker Keven Mealamu cleaned out Lions skipper Brian O'Driscoll long after the ball was gone. It wasn't so much of a cleanout, either – O'Driscoll was lifted and then tipped, driven into the turf hard enough for his shoulder to dislocate and for his tour to end just 41 seconds into the series.

It looked suspect and yet, while the incident was cited, commissioner Willem Venter dismissed it. That incensed the Lions and, to make the scandal bigger, Venter had managed to find footage of Danny Grewcock at the bottom of a ruck biting Mealamu's finger. The Lions lock was suspended for six weeks and the two All Black aggressors were let off scot-free. The ill-feeling between Umaga and O'Driscoll became legendary, and the Irish skipper was still harbouring resentment six months later. 'I still do stand by the fact that I was a bit surprised that nothing ever did come of it [the tackle],' he told *The Times*.

Umaga toured with the All Blacks later that same year but was rested for the test against Ireland. He and the coaches all agreed it wouldn't be a good idea for him to play.

## 4 The big boast

Lawrence Dallaglio appeared destined to enjoy a long and successful stint as England's rugby captain after he was appointed to the role in 1997. He was only 25 when given the job. But in 1999 Dallaglio was sensationally dumped as captain when he was the lead story in the now defunct *News of the World* on 30 May.

Dallaglio had told the paper that he had smoked cannabis and taken ecstasy during celebrations after the British Lions victory over South Africa in 1997. He also claimed he had made 'big, big' money from dealing in drugs while a student. What Dallaglio didn't know when he had made these claims was that he was speaking to an undercover reporter. Once the scandal broke he quickly went into defensive mode – claiming at first his drink had been spiked, then issuing a statement. 'I have not taken drugs during my rugby career,' he said. 'I have admitted experimenting with drugs in my youth, which I bitterly regret. However, I vigorously refute the suggestion that I have ever dealt in drugs.'

The *News of the World* responded through then editor Phil Hall by saying: 'We stand by our story. Lawrence Dallaglio is damned in his own words and frankly, we are amazed at his denial.' Dallaglio was stood down as captain, but he recovered to be one of the best loose forwards in England's history.

## 3 Bath and the drug tests

The summer of 2009 was a bad one for English rugby. Just as the ramifications of the Bloodgate saga were beginning to become clear, four senior players at Bath had their contracts terminated.

The team had travelled to London for an end-of-season party where senior player Justin Harrison admitted taking cocaine in the toilets of one pub. The whole evening fell under an internal investigation after some players were involved in a fist-fight with members of the Harlequins first team. The review found that on boarding the coach home, former Wallaby lock Harrison grabbed the microphone and shouted: 'Class A, it's OK, everyone's doing it'. Academy youngsters were among those on board and some later complained to club officials.

Two days after the party Harrison was asked to attend a meeting with club officials, and when he was asked to supply a urine sample for a drug test, he resigned with immediate effect. He was subsequently banned for a year, with team-mates Michael Lipman, Alex Crockett and Andrew Higgins also banned for refusing to take drugs tests.

'I wish to express my acceptance of my suspension by the RFU,' read a statement issued by Harrison. 'I deeply regret the incidents of Sunday, May 10, 2009 and the subsequent damage to Bath and the game itself.'

## 2 Grannygate

Prior to 2000, players didn't actually need to provide any documentary evidence they were qualified to play for a particular country. That's why Shane Howarth and Brett Sinkinson were both able to play for Wales and David Hilton for Scotland.

The former two were New Zealand-born, and Howarth even won four All Black caps in 1994 before he shifted to play for Newport in Wales. Howarth's form was so good that then national coach Graham Henry wanted to pick him. Howarth believed his grandfather was Welsh, and that was enough. Sinkinson was in on the same basis, and Hilton won 50 caps for Scotland on the grounds that he too had a Scottish grandparent.

But Howarth's grandfather was English, Sinkinson's grandparent in question was born in Oldham and Hilton's was also English. All three were subsequently ruled ineligible and the scandal was huge. The IRB was forced to immediately tighten eligibility rules and demand documentation be produced for those claiming grandparent links.

'It [nationality of grandparents] only really came to light in 1997 when it had to come up for me to get into Britain,' said Howarth after the scandal broke. 'I asked Mum about it and she said my grandfather is from Wales. I said I needed documentation – she said she couldn't supply any.'

## 1 Bloodgate

The most staggering thing about what became known as 'Bloodgate' was that none of it was made up.

The saga began when Harlequins were trailing 6–5 in the quarter-final of the 2009 Heineken Cup with five minutes remaining. The English club were searching for a drop goal to win it, and to that end were determined to get former All Black fly-half Nick Evans, who had limped off earlier with a knee injury, back on.

That could happen only if he was being used as a temporary blood replacement and, lo and behold, wing Tom Williams miraculously came to the sideline with blood coming out of his mouth. Except it was fake blood, as it would later transpire. He'd been sent on the field with a fake blood capsule in his sock. Leinster were suspicious and, as would later be found out, their team doctor had followed Williams off and down to the changing room. Afraid they were going to be sprung, Harlequins doctor Wendy Chapman shut the door and actually did cut Williams' mouth.

In a TV interview after the game, Harlequins director of rugby Dean Richards was asked whether, hand on heart, Williams was bleeding when he came off. 'He came off with a cut in his mouth and you have a right to bring someone off if they are cut, which is what we decided to do.' Asked then if his conscience was clear, he said, 'Yeah, very much so.'

It actually got worse. After an initial investigation by tournament officials, Williams was banned for a year, the club fined £215,000, and Richards, Chapman and Harlequins physio Steph Brennan were all acquitted. But then Williams decided he wanted to come clean, revealing he had been bribed by the club to lie.

In the end Richards was banned for three years and sacked, Chapman lost her job as an A&E consultant and Brennan was banned for two years.

'I took full responsibility for it,' said Richards after being handed his ban. 'It was a farcical situation, it really was. It didn't pan out particularly well on the day. Everybody looked at it and thought, That's unreal, which is what I thought on the touchline as well. But I had to hold my hands up.'

And the worst thing of all? Evans pushed the drop goal wide and Harlequins lost.

# 10 memorable quotes

**10** If we have to play against New Zealand, I'll explain it like this. To win, their 15 players have to have diarrhoea and we will have to put snipers around the field shooting at them and then we have to play the best match of our lives.

Argentina's lock Juan Martín Fernández Lobbe tried to explain optimum conditions required for the Pumas to beat the All Blacks at the 2007 World Cup should they meet.

**9** At the end of the day we can sit down and criticise the players, but they tried as hard as they could. The problem was all that effort wasn't rewarded because we made some poor decisions at times and we didn't show good execution of our skills at times. That is what rugby is about. Some of that should be credited to Italy and some of it was our own doing. So for my mind we just take the win – be happy about that because test wins are to be valued, be positive about the fact we didn't get any more big injuries and then flush the dunny and move on.

All Black assistant coach Steve Hansen had allegedly been using the 'flush the dunny' analogy for 12 months in private. After an appalling All Black performance in June 2009 when they were lucky to beat Italy in Christchurch, he used it in public.

**8** The same people who threw their robes on the ground when Jesus rode on a donkey were the same people who crowned him and hit him with sticks, and were the same people who said afterwards how we shouldn't have done that, he's the son of God. So that's exactly what we do. You have to look at history as repeating itself. And I'm not saying that I'm God.

Springbok coach Peter de Villiers provides the most bizarre justification of why he emptied his bench so early in the first test against the British & Irish Lions in 2009. The Boks had been leading 26–9 with half an hour remaining and were nervously holding on at the end, scraping home 26–21.

**7** What are they going to do? Ban me from coaching? What difference will that make to Namibian rugby? Fine me? I haven't been paid. Zero minus whatever the amount is effectively amounts to zero. And if they really, really want to put me in the dock [after the World Cup] they will find me somewhere between the Monets and the Manets in the St Petersburg museum, where my wife and I are headed to put some salve on our souls after this unfortunate experience.

Namibian coach Dave Waterston had a blast at the IRB after they decided to investigate earlier comments he had made about having to borrow tackle bags and other equipment before their pool clash with the Wallabies at the 2003 World Cup. Namibia lost 142–0.

**6** I'm not going to go to him as a dentist if he gives an exhibition like that as a referee. The tragedy is if you're a ref – and I feel sorry for the refs too – and you want the big appointments you've got to lick the backsides of some of the top nations. Unfortunately, that's the way it's done. I presume it's the same in soccer.

Waterston again at the 2003 tournament. This time he was unhappy at referee Andy Cole – who also a dentist – for not sending off Irish lock Paul O'Connell for a stamping incident.

**5** The only memories I have of England and the English are unpleasant ones. I have decided to adopt the same attitude as them: I despise them as much as they despise everybody else! And as long as we beat England I wouldn't mind if we lost every other game in the Six Nations.

French No 8 Imanol Harinordoquy ahead of the 2003 Six Nations clash with England at Twickenham. The English were to gain their revenge – not only did they beat the French in London, they beat them again in the semi-final of the World Cup later in the year. They also came up with a neat riposte for Harinordoquy – dubbing him 'Harry Ordinary'.

**4** Sky: Brendan, how disappointed are you?

BV: Ah disappointed, disappointed, very disappointed.

Sky: What went wrong? Because you got off to such a wonderful start.

BV: Eh yes, interesting ... I wonder what went wrong? Will have to think about it. Will definitely have to think about it.

Sky: What did go wrong?

BV: Will have to look ... think about it, think about it deeply, very deeply.

Sky: Did it hinge on the end on a bit of genius from Sireli Bobo [wing]?

BV: Bit of genius. Bit of magic ... Sireli Bobo, very interesting. Three cheers for Sireli Bobo. Very good. Very good.

Sky: What were you happy with about your side?

BV: Happy..? Happy ... everything. Everything. Very good. Very happy with my team.

Sky: But you didn't win though, did you, Brendan?

BV: Yah, well, we didn't win ... that's true.

Sky: Why didn't you win?

BV: Ah, good question that. Very good question. It is important to win. It is important. We must try harder. Absolutely, yeah.

Sky: So you think it was a lack of effort?

BV: Lack of effort ... lack of effort ... I don't think it's a lack of effort.

Sky: So what is it, Brendan?

BV: Ah what would it be? Let me think. I'm not sure. Let me think about that one. I'll think about it deeply.

Sky: Thank you, Brendan.

BV: Thank you very much.

Saracens coach Brendan Venter gives the most surreal post-match interview to Sky Sports in the UK. Venter was talking after his side had lost a crucial Heineken Cup game 24–21 to Racing Métro. The defeat all but eliminated the London club, but Venter's bizarre behaviour stemmed from the anger he was feeling at the fine of £21,850 he was hit with following Saracens' game against Leinster earlier in the year. He was fined for 'being inappropriately critical of ERC, the tournament, match officials and the sport of rugby union'. As a result Venter was deliberately obstructive, choosing to offer no opinions or answers in a minute-long interview that became a YouTube sensation.

**3** There were no true world champions in the 1987 and 1991 World Cups because South Africa were not there. We have proved our point. The difference between being winners and being a sorrowful lot is fragile. We were not there in 1987 or 1991, and I have my personal doubts about us being able to do anything in terms of winning the World Cup in those years.

South Africa Rugby Union president Louis Luyt gave the most extraordinary speech at the closing dinner of the 1995 World Cup. His comments led to the All Blacks walking out, with several other teams not far behind. Springbok team manager Morné du Plessis was mortified and, when asked to comment on the speech, said: 'Tired and emotional are the words that come to mind, though I am not sure that I followed the theme at that part of Mr Luyt's speech.'

**2** I've got my own observations about the last two tests, and maybe I can't say it in public, but we do have a World Cup in New Zealand next year and maybe it was the right thing for them to win the games so they can attract more people to the games next year.

Peter de Villiers again, this time speaking a few days after the Boks had lost consecutive tests to the All Blacks in New Zealand in 2010. The Boks had a man yellow-carded harshly in each test.

**1** I can understand the hate!! Haha good luck u racist biased prick. Get s.a. into next round. The plan was obvious. Can't wait 2 meet irb members in public. Wasn't about world cup today. RWC has been invalidated when they give us half the rest as the rich. It was about us v world champs. I'm proud to be Samoan! Irb, my bum, kiss it!

Samoa's controversial centre Sapolu Fuimaono fired off this Tweet after his side were defeated 13–5 by South Africa in their final pool game at the 2011 World Cup. The 'racist prick' to whom he was referring was Welsh referee Nigel Owens. Samoa felt – and they were supported by video evidence – that they had scored a legitimate try with 10 minutes remaining. Owens didn't give it and then sent off Samoa's fullback Paul Williams for an innocuous scuffle. Fuimaono was handed a six-month suspended ban for his outburst. He admitted he had been drinking before he filed it.